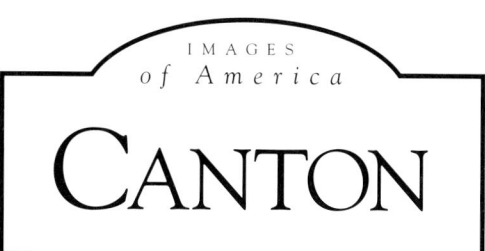

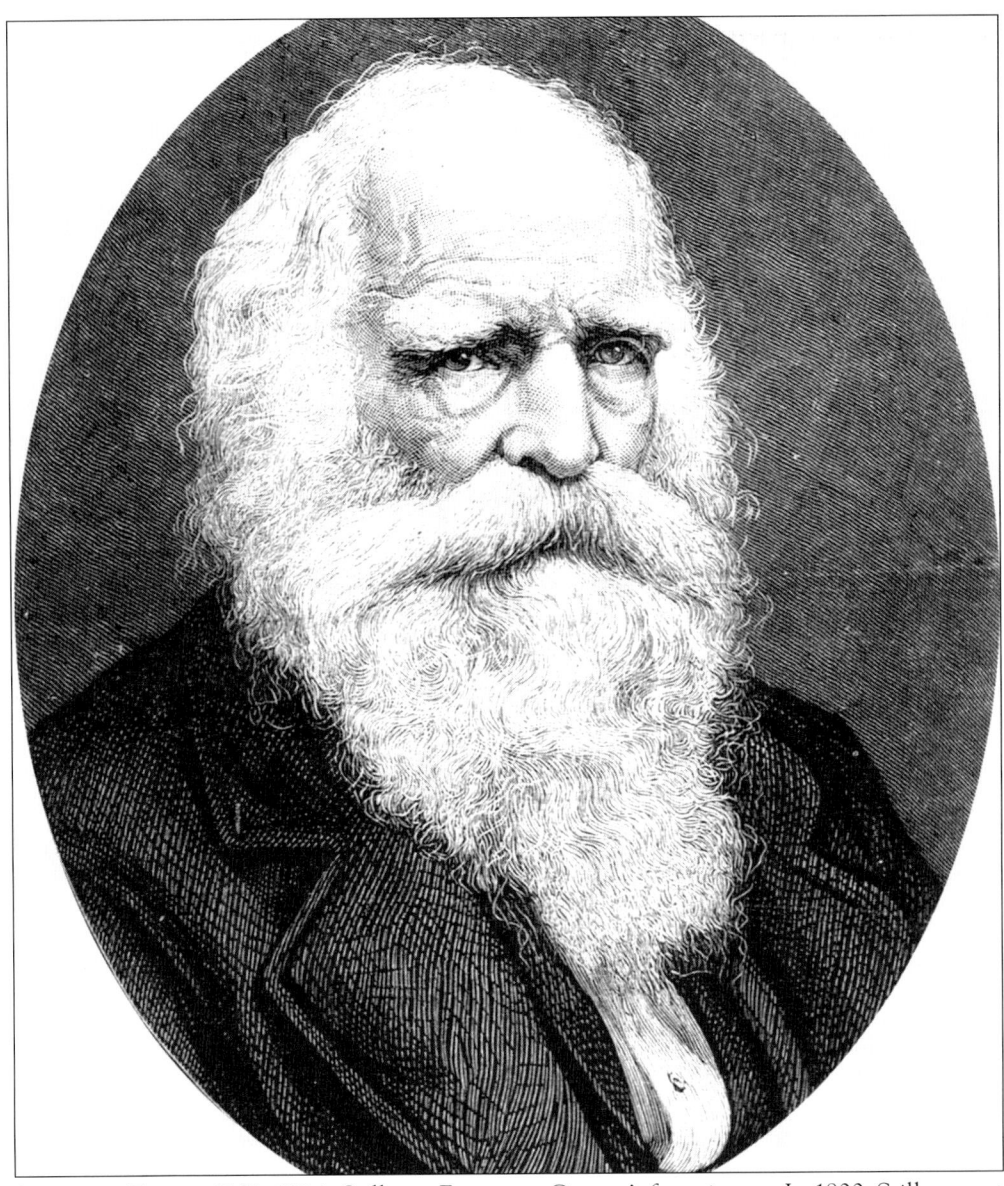

STILLMAN FOOTE 1763–1834. Stillman Foote was Canton's first pioneer. In 1800, Stillman set off for new lands in northern New York from Middlebury, Vermont, with his father, Daniel, and millwright Daniel Church. As a result of his trip, he became owner of the mile square on which Canton village now stands. Foote purchased a wheat crop from Daniel Harrington in exchange for a horse and saddle and bridle. Foote and Church built a sawmill on the west bank of the Grasse River where the Cascade Inn now stands. After his father died in 1801 from smallpox, Foote returned the following spring with his wife Louisa Donahy Foote and their three children, Chauncey, Henry, and Louisa. Recognized as a leader by his contemporaries, Stillman was elected first town supervisor on 1806. Stillman operated a marble factory using rock from Crary Mills and operated a bloom-forge on the east side of the river. Following the death of his wife in 1811, he married Mary Pember of Connecticut and they had three children, Delia, Stillman Jr., and Mary. Foote, the founder of Canton was held in high regard as a pioneer who made great contributions to the town and village of Canton.

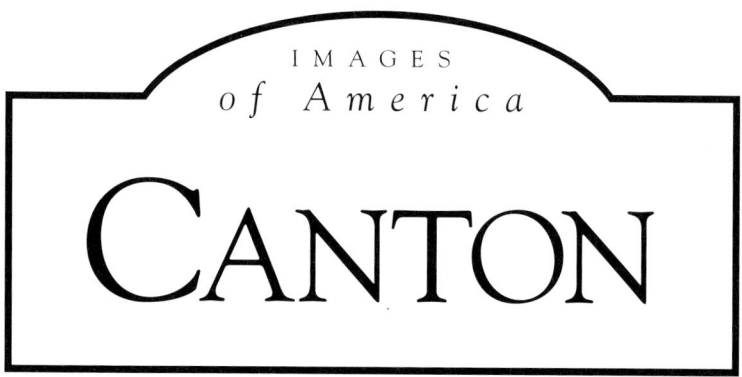

Linda A. Casserly, Julie Sherman Grayson, and Judith C. Liscum

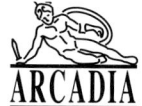

Copyright © 2005 by Linda A. Casserly, Julie Sherman Grayson, and Judith C. Liscum
ISBN 0-7385-3877-9

Published by Arcadia Publishing
Charleston SC, Chicago IL, Portsmouth NH, San Francisco CA

Printed in Great Britain

Library of Congress Catalog Card Number: 2005926841

For all general information contact Arcadia Publishing at:
Telephone 843-853-2070
Fax 843-853-0044
E-mail sales@arcadiapublishing.com
For customer service and orders:
Toll-Free 1-888-313-2665

Visit us on the internet at http://www.arcadiapublishing.com

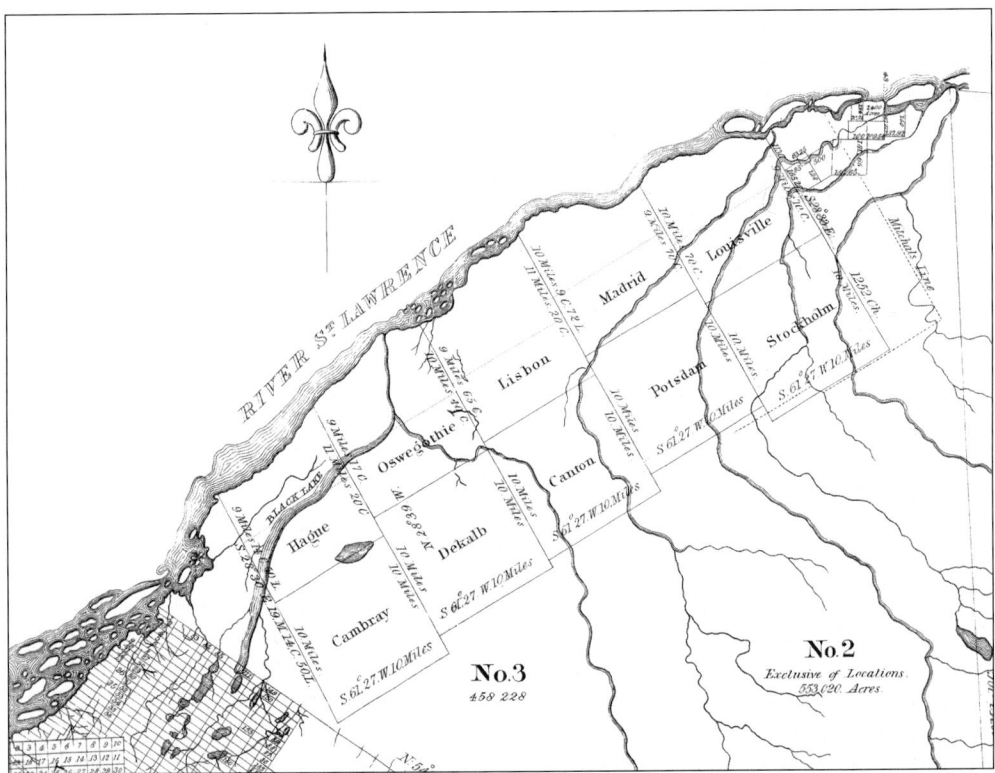

ORIGINAL TEN TOWNS. In 1787, the State of New York sold "The Tens Towns" of northern New York at the Old Coffee House in New York City. A wealthy fur trader, Alexander Macomb, was the principal purchaser. Richard Harison and Stephen Van Rensselaer acquired the town of Canton just before the beginning of the 19th century.

Contents

Acknowledgments		6
Introduction		7
1.	Rivers, Mills, and Factories	9
2.	Family Farms	17
3.	From One-Room Schools to Campuses	25
4.	Main Street and Side Street Businesses	37
5.	Houses of Worship	57
6.	Public Buildings	61
7.	Stately Mansions	71
8.	Personalities	83
9.	Villages and Hamlets	95
10.	Recreation and Historic Interest	111

ACKNOWLEDGMENTS

Most of the photos and information used in this publication came from the extensive collection of the Canton town and village historian. First, it is important to thank the source of this historical compilation—the generations of individuals and families who contributed to the collection, and to earlier historians for preserving Canton's wonderful history. We also must recognize Canton's very skillful photographers of the past: Benjamin Kip, Harry Copeland, Dwight P. Church, Roy Bassett, and Ray Jubinville. Factual information was gathered from Dr. James Payson's Commercial Advertiser column "History of a North Country Town" and from Carl M. Witherbee's book, *Reminiscences of the Village of Canton*.

In addition, we are grateful to all of the organizations and individuals who loaned photos and information for this project: St. Lawrence County Historical Association (SLCHA), St. Lawrence University (SLU) Archives, the Rensselaer Falls Historical Association, Christopher Angus, Marion Barr, Janet and Pete Bullis, Ian Burnham, Gary Bushaw, Connie Ellen, Eileen Elmer, Janet Favro, Beverly Gauthier, Lora and David Gibson, Kebbyn and Melanie Giffin, Ruth Glascock, Judy Lawrence Gray, Sally and Kyle Hartman, Ann Huntley, Carol Johnson, Karl Keller, James Kelly, Jacqueline Lane, Darlene Leonard, Geraldine Liscum, Hope Mayhew, Phil McCarthy, Marilyn and Brad Mintener, Jack Newman, William Olin, Marie Rocca, Marilyn and Bill Rodee, Lance Rudiger, David Thompson, James Todd, Otis Van Horn, Jessie Wainwright, Doug Welch, Frank and Beulah White.

We recognize Varick Chittenden, retired professor of English at the State University of New York at Canton, for his willingness to contribute to *Canton* by writing the introduction. We offer special thanks to David Martin for his knowledge, guidance, and patience assisting us in the scanning and layout process.

Lastly, we offer our appreciation to the Bicentennial Committee of the Town of Canton for their encouragement and financial assistance with this project. It takes a whole town to publish an Arcadia book!

Introduction

Just imagine how much better we would all understand and appreciate the trials and triumphs of our early ancestors if we had photographs of American rebels at the Boston Tea Party, of immigrant laborers digging the Erie Canal, and of crowded slave ships arriving in Southern ports. Closer to home, think how incredible it would be to see snapshots of Stillman Foote crossing the Grasse River on horseback, of Silas Wright pulling weeds in his garden, and of a young Irish family building a log home on Irish Settlement Road with only a few neighbors to help.

The age of photography for most Americans began, however, around the mid-1800s. For the last three quarters of Canton's 200 years, photographers have recorded the passing scene of life in this vibrant rural community in the St. Lawrence River Valley. Some were professionals like Harry Copeland, Benjamin Kip, Dwight Church, and Ray Jubinville, who collectively captured an invaluable array of images of our public life for scores of years. But it was snapshots in particular—mass-marketed still photography made available to many people by the late 1800s—that have given us lasting insight into the daily existence of Canton people at work and play, at home and school and church, in moments both serious and amusing.

Canton, a volume of selected images, reveals a great deal about the rich history of the community. In viewing this wonderful collection as the town observes its bicentennial, it is most striking to see how much is different, yet how much is still the same. For example, on page 23 is the Drury-Blount-Favro farm and home at Brick Chapel:

> Just before reaching Brick Chapel from Canton and, turning right onto the Barnes Road finds a traveler at this seventh generation homestead. Jan Favro is the great-great-great-great granddaughter of one of Brick Chapel's founders, John Richardson. He was the settler who donated the land for the church and the cemetery. Mrs. Favro operates the 240-acres as a hobby farm and still operates the sugar bush, as did generations of her ancestors. The remodeled farmhouse has been updated, but in case of "emergency," the privy is still attached to the back of the house.

In a few words, this description—which implies the arrival of one major improvement, indoor plumbing, points out continuity and change in one family and one farm that have been here since the very early years of the town. Think of how much more has occurred in that time in America: the Civil War, the Industrial Revolution, two world wars and other foreign conflicts, the Depression, and the age of space exploration, to name a few.

But for the Favro farm, the small Brick Chapel neighborhood, and most of the town of Canton, life has been more personal. In the many generations since they were founded, there have been countless christenings and weddings and funerals; birthday parties, Christmas mornings, family reunions, sugaring-off parties, and church socials too numerous to mention. Then there were the firsts—the electric light, milking machine, telephone, radio, family car, tractor, television set, and computer. If only we all had taken pictures of such events in our families and saved them for the future, what insights that would give us. It is fortunate that at least some people did capture pictures of people, places, and events and that those images survive. That is how books like *Canton* are possible.

For many generations of Cantonians, some things have remained the same, or nearly so. The village green on Main Street, Trinity Chapel in Morley, the Pyrites fire department, the Crary Mills Grange hall, the Wainwright store building in Rensselaer Falls are still a few of the landmark places in the communities. Taylor Park is still the place to go on hot summer days; Appleton Arena has been the winter home for hockey players and figure skaters for a very long time; *The Plaindealer* still publishes the official news; and the Cascade or McCarthy's and, yes, McDonald's (where the Canton Diner used to be) is where we get the rest. Some old families live on. The names of Patterson, Coakley, Tupper, Huntley, Whalen, Palmer, Locy, Rodee, Sanderson, Lawrence, Judd, Bullis, Lawrence, Aldous, Todd, Sheridan, Ellsworth, Foote, and Tracy are just a few that still fill the Canton phone book after all these years.

But other things have come and gone, as they are apt to do. The St. Lawrence County Fair left years ago, and the fairgrounds buildings as well, the Rushton canoe factory, the sawmills and gristmills on the downtown islands, the American House and the Hotel Harrington, the Morley school, the Pyrites paper mill, and the county almshouse were just a few of the vital parts of Canton life that fell to fire or demolition over time.

It is tempting to define our history with the stories of people who have been successful in the world, and Canton surely has some of those: statesman Silas Wright, artist Frederic Remington, canoe builder J. Henry Rushton, financier A. Barton Hepburn, and author Irving Bacheller are among them. But it is the people of everyday circumstances whose experiences make up the narrative arc of daily existence for most of us, and that is what this book is about. There is, for example, Ed Lincoln in his meat market in Morley; Phil Van Horne, one of Rushton's skilled carpenters, in front of Healey's Lunch Spot on Main Street; W. E. Church feeding his prized Rhode Island red hens at his hennery; Nona Kennedy and her students in the Knox Schoolhouse; colorful Commercial Advertiser editor John Finnegan; Jake Tompkins, the barber, whose father lived in slavery and later moved north to work in logging camps; and Dr. James Payson, distinguished minister, professor, and founding teacher at the School of Agriculture, now SUNY Canton College of Technology.

There were the also the big events—big, at least, for a town like ours: the building of the county courthouse, commencements and other college activities at both St. Lawrence University and "the Aggie School," women's suffrage marches and prohibition protests, the arrival of visitors such as Madame Curie at the Harrington and President Taft at the Riverside Hotel in the Falls, the war maneuvers in 1940, the burning of the town hall in 1962, and the great ice storm of 1998. Sometimes a photographer was present, sometimes not.

These selected images, from both public and private collections, help to give us glimpses into some of Canton's history and preserve at least a few of the stories that have made Canton a great place for 200 years. We are especially fortunate to have the enthusiasm and commitment of three women who have spent scores of hours collecting, researching, and writing about the wonderful variety of images in this book. Judy Liscum, a native of Canton, who devoted much of her career in education to developing in her students a true interest in their own heritage; Julie Grayson, a native who spent many years away but then returned when she felt a need to come back to her roots; and Linda Casserly, a transplant in the 1970s, who has become passionate about the history of the town and village and lives it every day. Their work (and this book in particular) is a very special birthday gift to Canton.

—Varick A. Chittenden

One
RIVERS, MILLS, AND FACTORIES

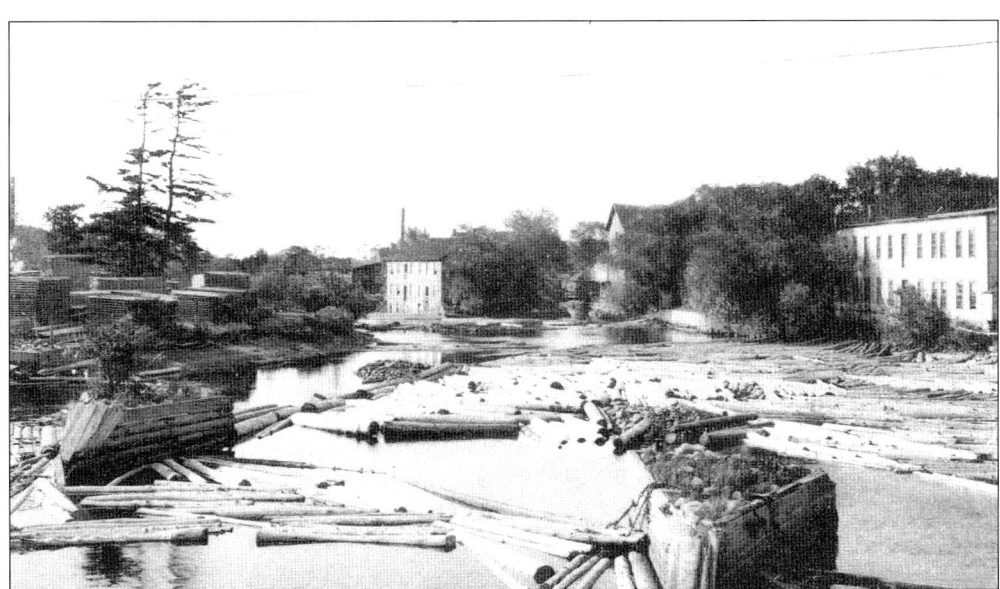

GROWING UP AROUND THE OLD MILL STREAM. Canton's 200 years of history sprang from the rocks that dammed the Grasse River. The falls, over which the water runs freely today instead of through sluices, provided waterpower for mills, both grist and lumber, and for the town's early industries. These industries turned out sashes, doors, and even the boxes for butter and cheese produced on area farms. Stillman Foote, who emigrated from Middlebury, Vermont, built the first gristmill. He rode a saddle horse to the area in the summer of 1800. His vision encouraged him to buy the mile square tract, which is the site of today's Canton village. There is no trace of the old dam or the busy sluices, the runs of stones, or the stone wheels of the grinding mills. Tourists are lulled to sleep by the roar of the Grasse River's free waters running over their rocks, as they did when Stillman Foote first looked upon the spot 200 years ago.

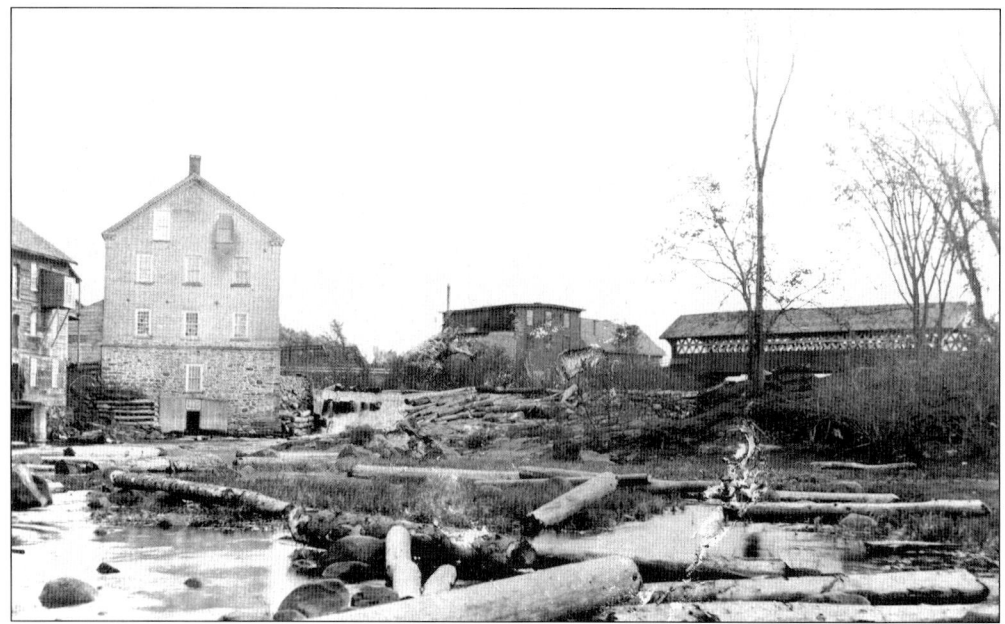

COVERED BRIDGE. Milton D. Packard, supervisor of the town of Canton, built this covered bridge over the West Channel of the Grasse River during Civil War days. Demolished in 1904, it was replaced with a concrete one. The covered bridge was the first river-crossing at that site to be lifted well above the river level.

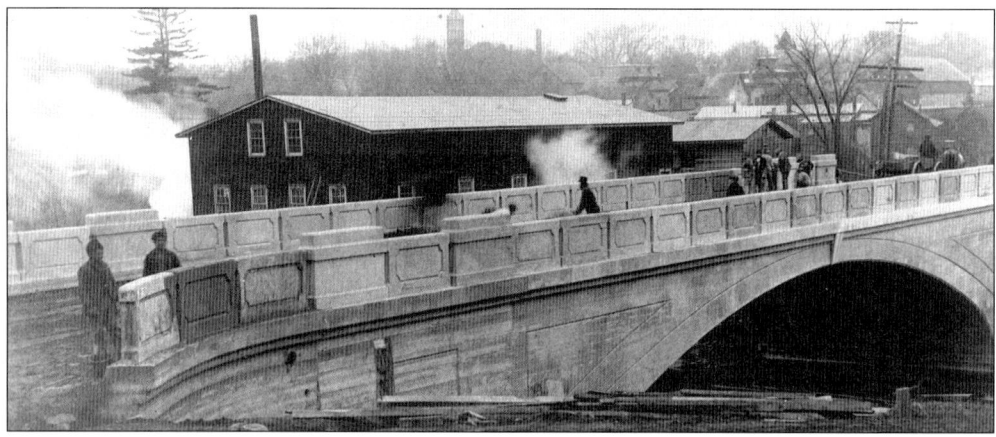

EARLY CEMENT BRIDGE, 1904. This is the concrete bridge which replaced the wooden one at the west side of the Grasse River. Signs at both ends read, "$5 fine for driving through this bridge faster than a walk," and this was part of a village ordinance. Notice the county courthouse tower in the background.

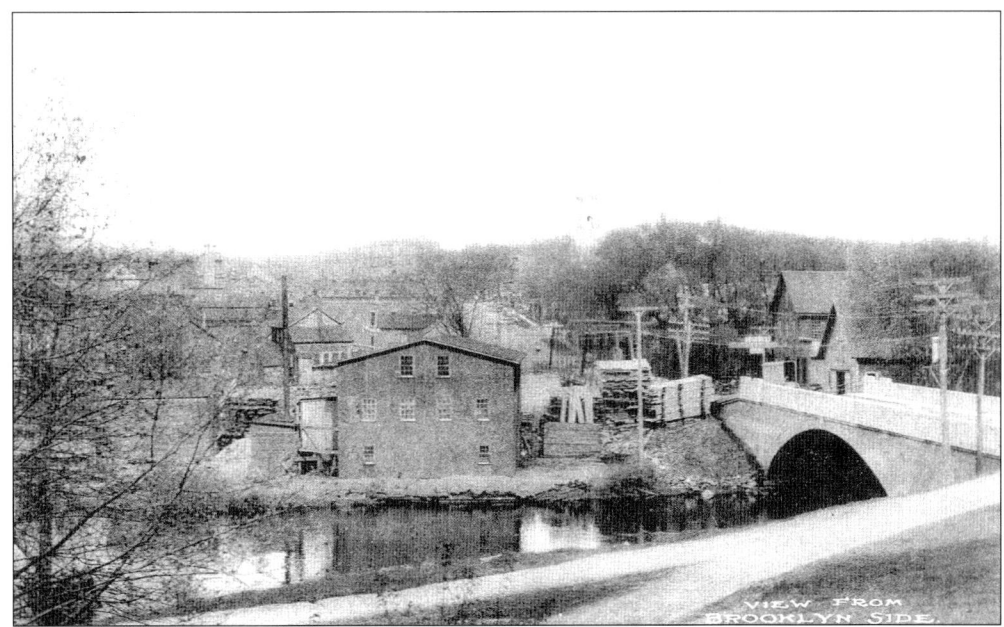

VIEW FROM BROOKLYN SIDE. Several early families living on the west side of the village came from Brooklyn. At this time two bridges spanned the Grasse River; one was cement and the other a King Iron Bridge. The back island is known as Falls Island. A carpentry shop, which made and repaired wagons, was located on the front island, later known as Coakley's Island. A livery stable and blacksmith shop were located on the right side of the bridge.

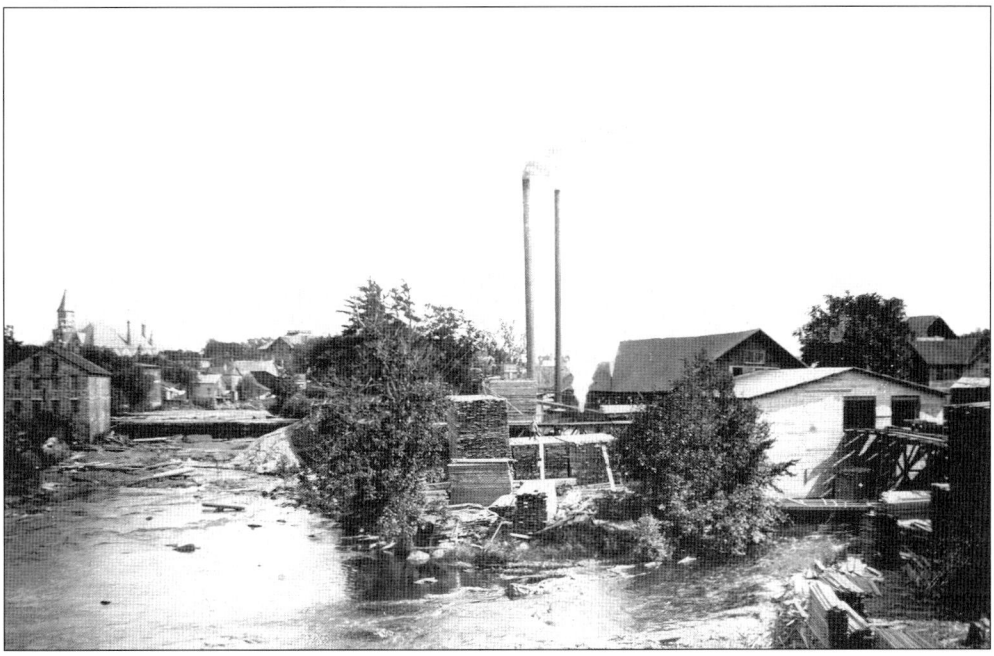

FALLS ISLAND. At the beginning of the century, this lower part of the back island was a beehive of industry. The sawmill, lumberyard, and gristmill were water-powered. A cheese box factory, tannery, and foundry were also located on the islands. Bear in mind that all traffic to and from the island was by horse.

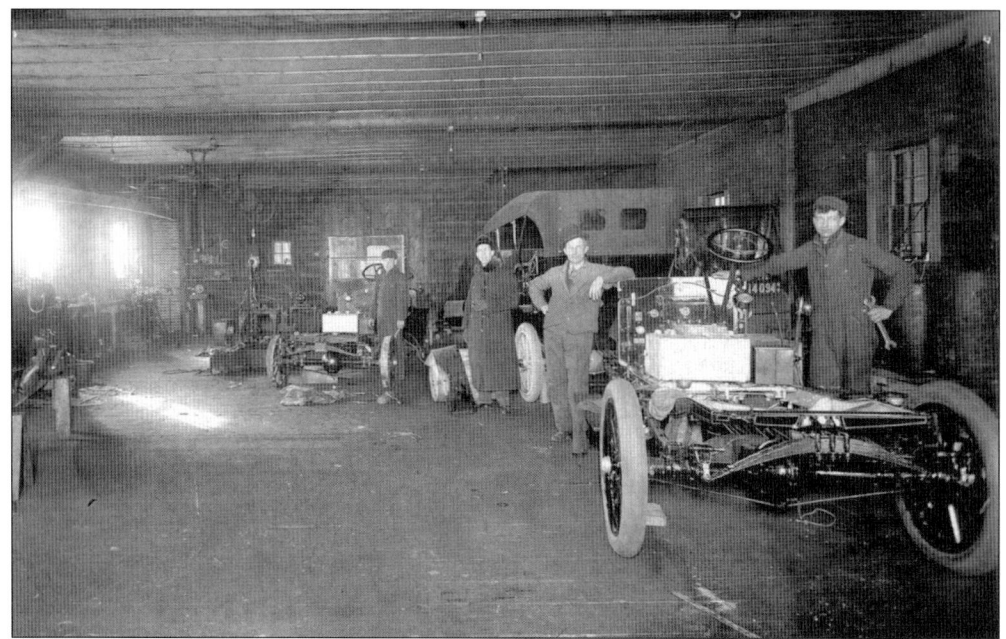

CHARLIE COOK'S GARAGE. Charles Cook and W. B. Barlow's garage was located downstairs in a two-story building on the left side of Main Street as one crossed the bridge. Cook was Canton's first and leading mechanic. Stanley Barber worked for Cook in the business, which was eventually sold to Horace Bartman.

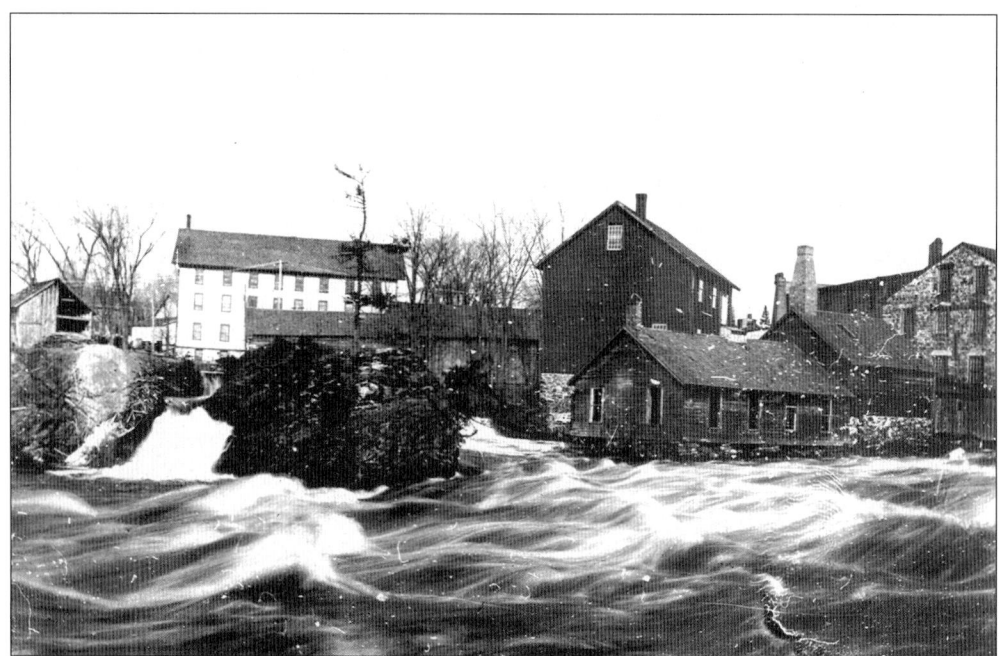

RUSHTON'S FACTORY. This picture shows the frothing waters of the Grasse River from the west bank of the river in early spring. A man-made flume took in water from the west branch of the river down to the lower part of the island. The four-story Rushton Canoe Factory stands in the background, located on the corner of Water and State Streets.

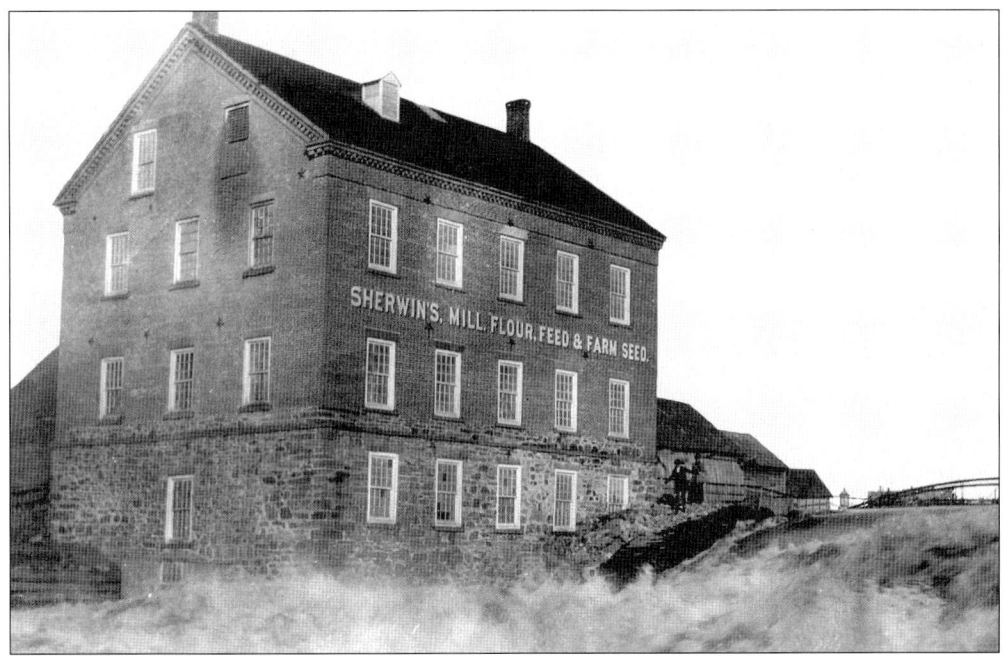

SHERWIN'S MILL. A three-story brick mill was built by Lucius Moody in 1860 and called the St. Lawrence Mill. It became the property of Nathaniel Hodskin and D. W. Sherwin in 1888. Sherwin was a veteran of the Civil War. Alongside the mill stood George Gilmore's furniture shop, followed by Henry Stickles's sash and blind business.

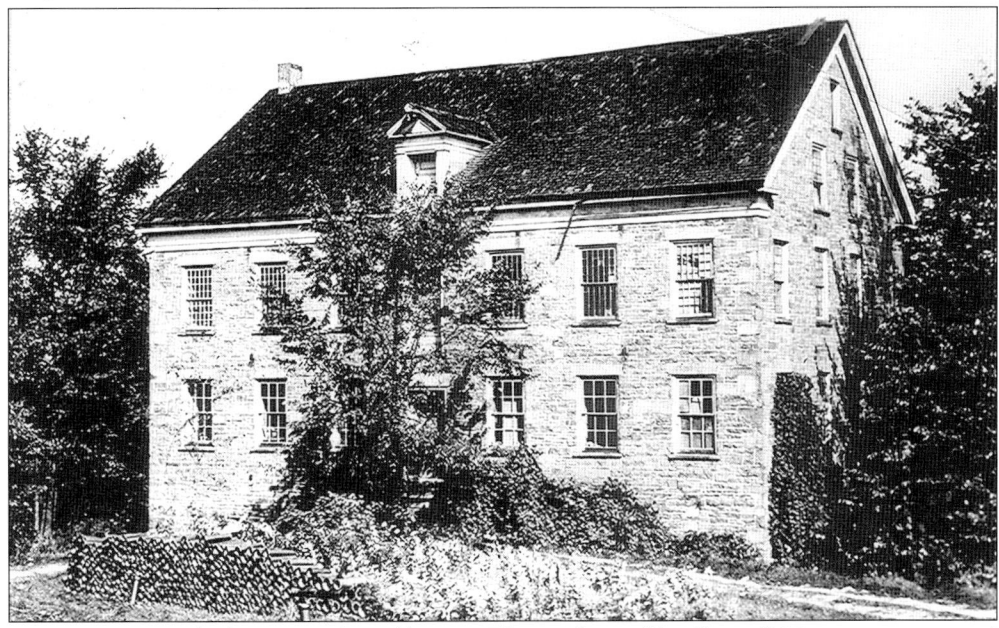

EAGLE MILL. In the language of an old song, "The creaking old mill is still Maggie since you and I were young." The four story Eagle Mill was built of Potsdam red sandstone in 1842 by Henry Van Rensselaer. The first large grist mill with four runs of stones, it had a capacity of 600 bushels of grain a day. It was also known as Bullis Mill with ownership eventually passing to John Coakley. The stones of the Eagle Mill now lie under the Cascade Inn parking lot.

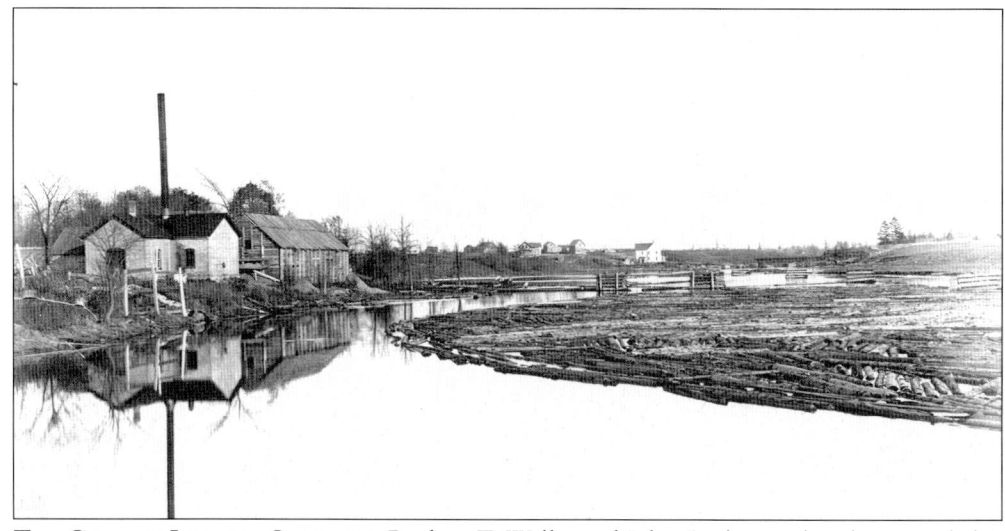

THE CANTON LUMBER COMPANY. Reuben T. Wells, and John Bird owned and operated this lumber company after A. Barton Hepburn sold his shares. Lumbering was big business for Canton, and the logs floated down from the north and middle branches of the Grasse River in the town of Clare. The Canton Lumber Company was located at the rapids, near Leigh Falls.

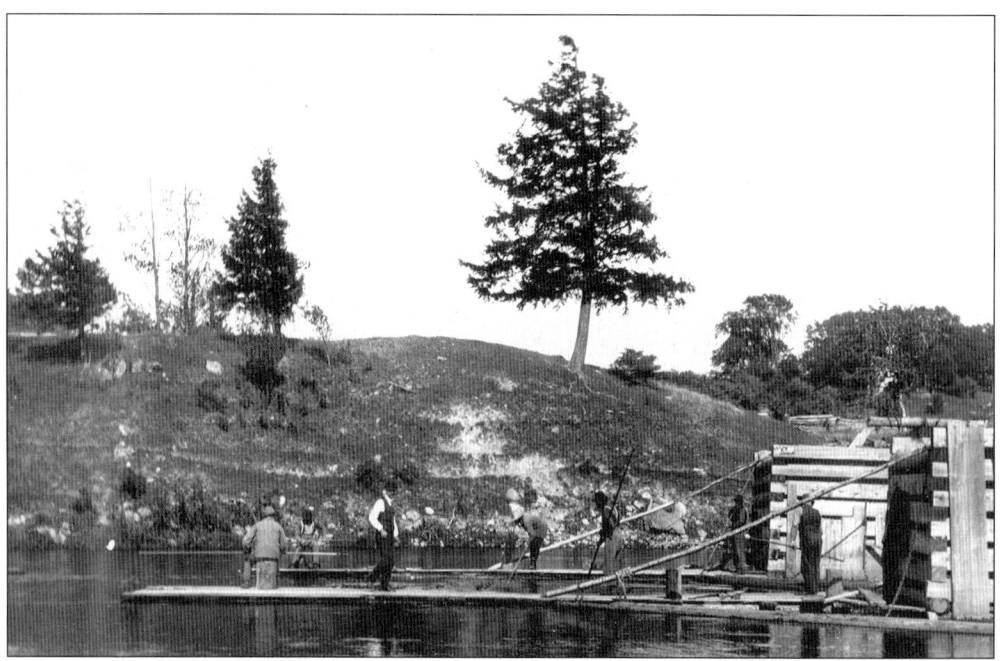

LOG-SORTING BOOM, 1900. One of several booms, this log boom was located on the Grasse River beside the Glen Hurlbut farm. The logs were corralled for sorting at the booms with the lumbermen using their cant hooks or peaveys to break up log jams. Logs were branded with an owner's insignia by burning it into the log.

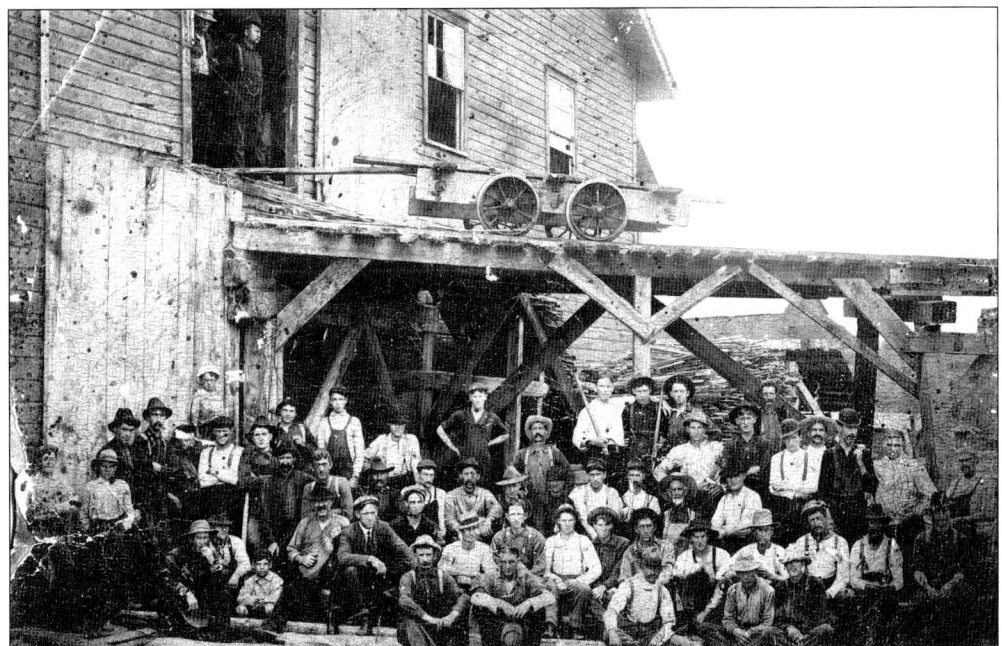

JIMMY SPEARS SAWMILL. Spears lumber mill was located north of the Main Street bridge. The mill was powered by both water and steam. The lumbermen worked in the woods for several weeks, came to town, and drank until all their hard earned money was gone. It has been said that women of the village were not seen during the lumbering season.

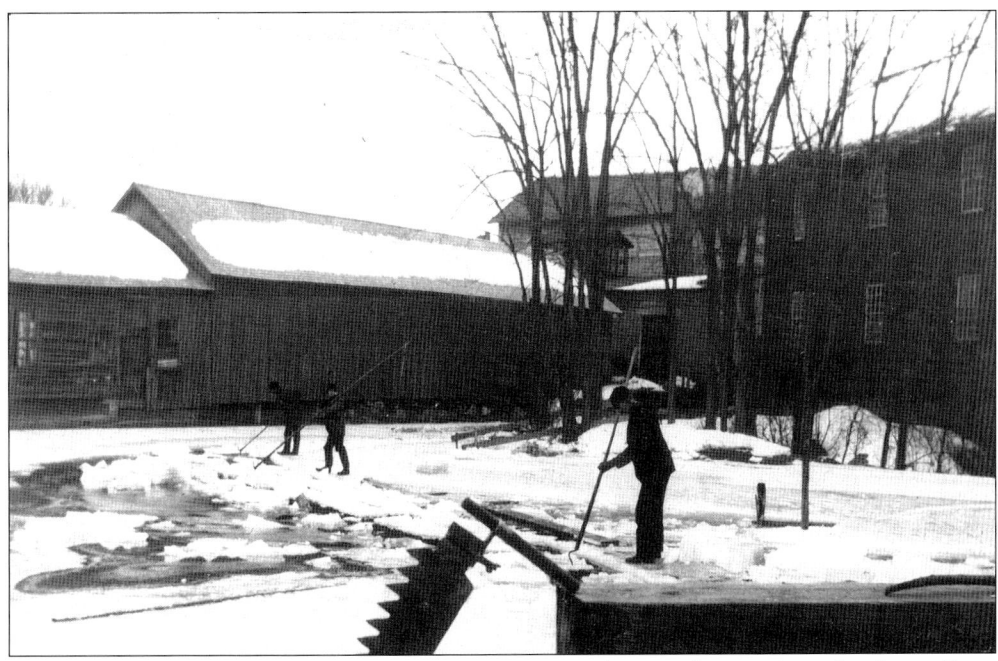

ICE HARVESTING. Long before refrigeration, ice was stored in warehouses along the Grasse River for use throughout the year. Many farmers used the winter to harvest ice and worked day and night, marking and cutting the ice into blocks. Ice was shipped to the cities by train in ice cars.

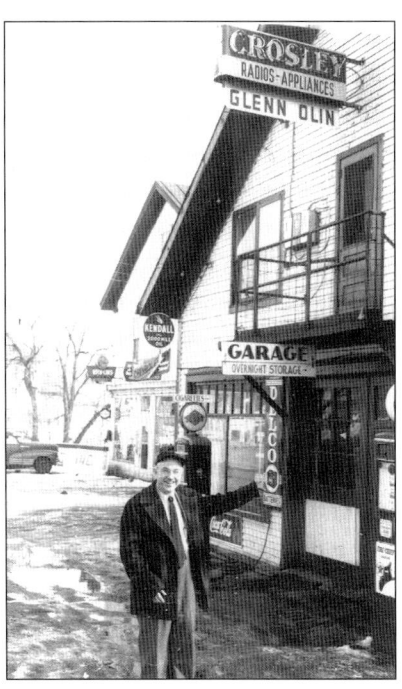

OLIN'S GARAGE, THE 1950s. Glenn Olin along with his brother Mark ran a very successful gas station and garage on Canton Island Park (formerly the Willow Island Restaurant site). The Olins were distributors of Crosley refrigerators and appliances. To accommodate his customers, Glenn actually moved his whole building back so cars could pull up on both sides of the pump. Snyder's car shop was located next door.

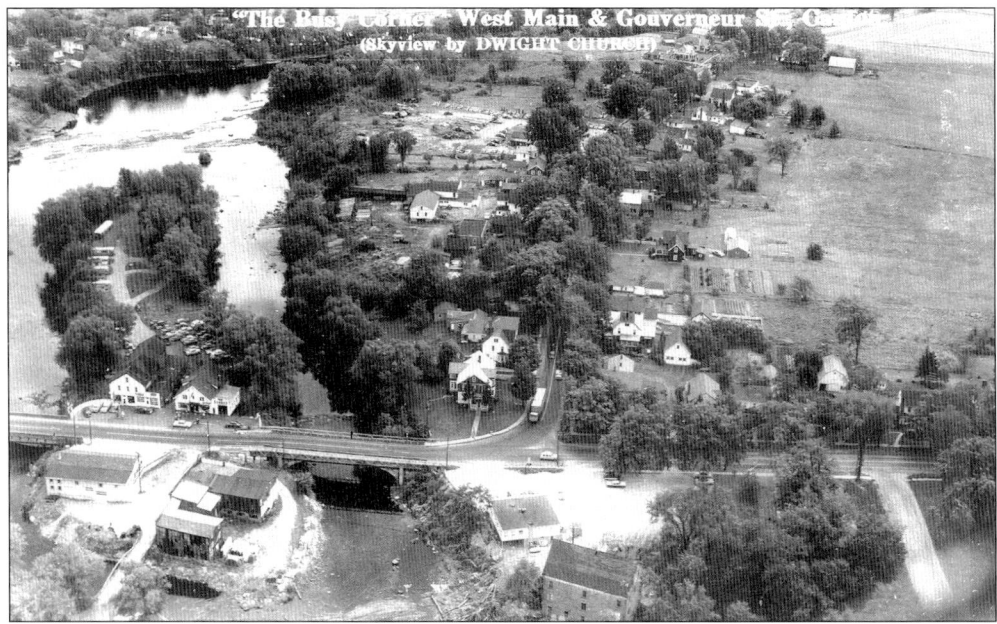

AERIAL VIEW. This is a D. P. Church photograph of the islands with camps located on the Grasse River behind Olin and Snyder's businesses. Across Main Street is the John P. Coakley and Sons' building and construction business. The Eagle Mill is still standing with the Cascade Inn in front, and D. P. Church's $5 Photo Studio House across the street.

Two

Family Farms

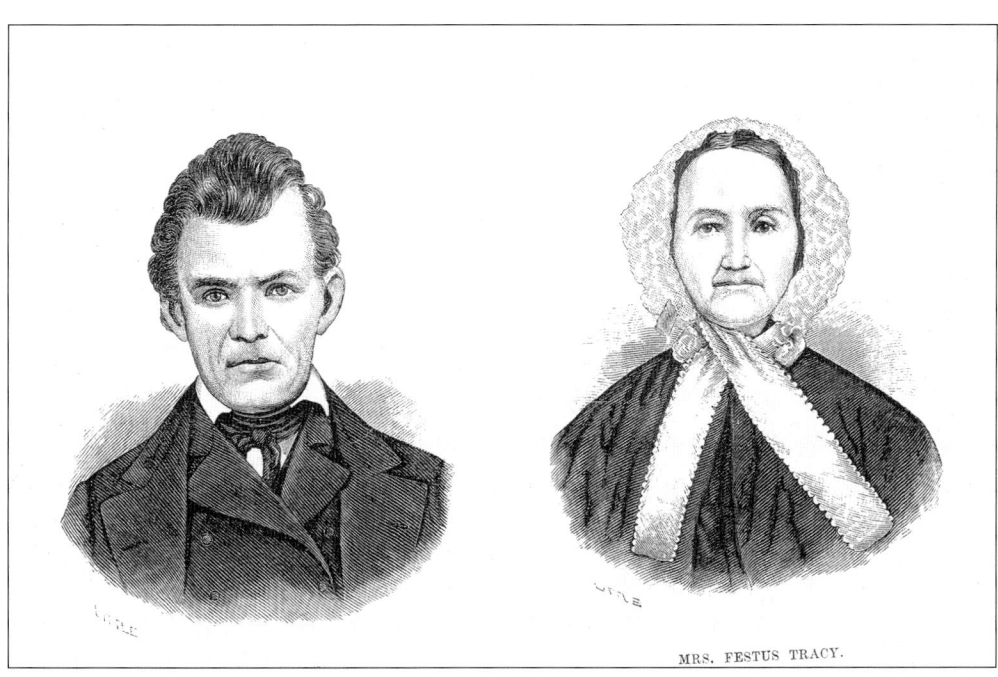

Festus Tracy, First Landholder in the Town of Canton. Festus Tracy, a native Vermonter and member of the surveying party, claimed his farmland in 1799 before anybody else did. This farm is located on Route 68, on the knoll just past the St. Lawrence University riding stables. According to legend, Tracy scooped up a handful of soil and declared it the richest he had seen. He brought his bride Elizabeth to the farm in 1802 and built a log cabin, at first without windows or a door. Blankets hung over the openings that first winter.

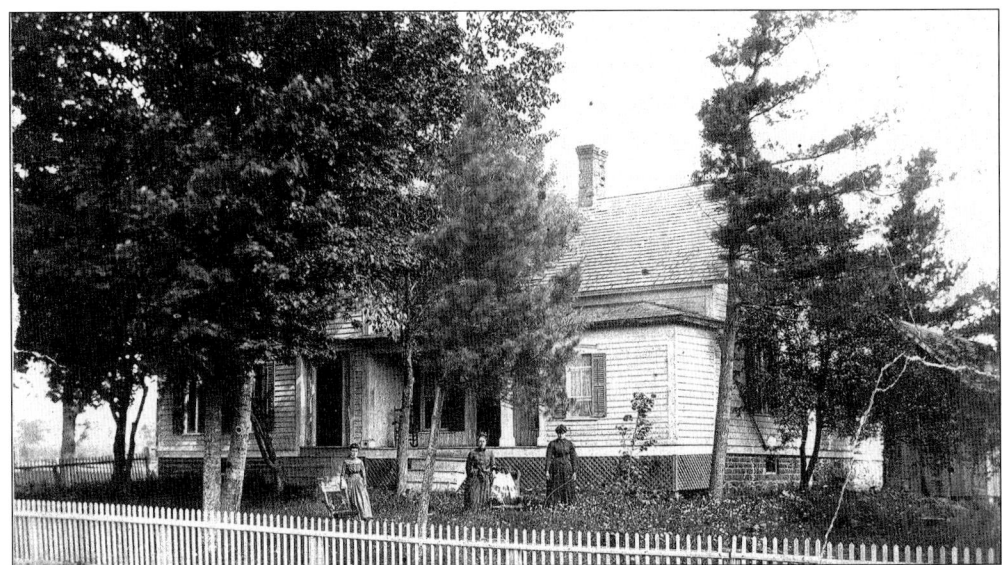

JUDD-MARTYN-THOMPSON FARM. The large red barn built in 1820 by Elmeron Thompson still stands on this property. First settled by Dan Judd (c. 1804), this farm is located on Route 11, across from the Best Western University Inn. The ownership passed from the Judds to the Tyler and Elisha Martyn families. The last to farm this land was the Thompson family. Elmeron's son Stanley sold the farm to St. Lawrence University in 1973. SeaComm Credit Union bought the property for a new bank, but retained Elmeron Thompson's stately red barn. (Courtesy of David Thompson.)

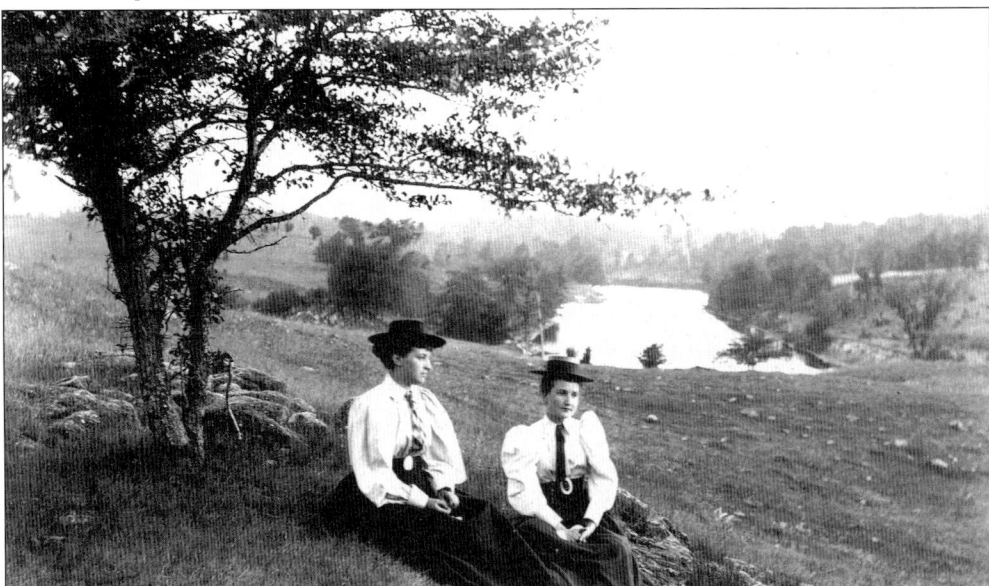

JOHN HEATON FARM. This hilltop farm is located just beyond Brewer Road on Route 68, toward Pierrepont. The farm was purchased by John Heaton of Addison, Vermont, in 1814 for $5 an acre. A log house was completed first, followed by a large farmhouse and, later, a smaller farmhouse. Heaton's three wives gave him seven children. His granddaughter, Lucia Heaton, was the first woman physician in St. Lawrence County. Pictured are two of John Heaton's daughters in the farmyard. (Courtesy of SLCHA.)

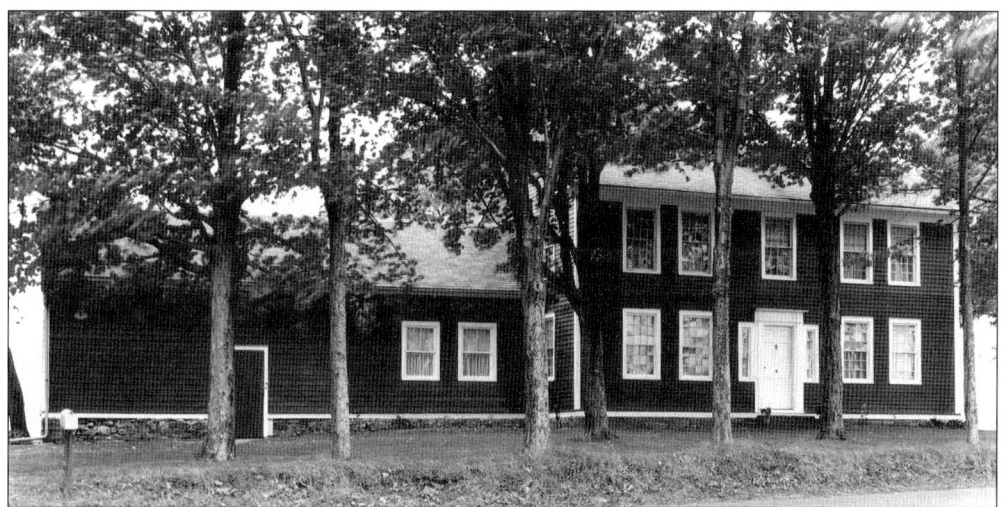

THE SANDERSON FARM. Two miles from the village on Heaton Hill, stands one of the oldest homes in Canton. Married in 1814, Ebenezer Sanderson and his bride Lucy traveled from Vermont to New York. The larger house was constructed around 1833 on the first 50 acres Sanderson purchased. Built to last, a hand-hewn oak frame was pegged together with wooden pins. Four fireplaces heated the home, and massive stone partitions divided the cellar. Growing to over 200 acres, ownership has never passed from the Sanderson family (Courtesy of Eileen Elmer.)

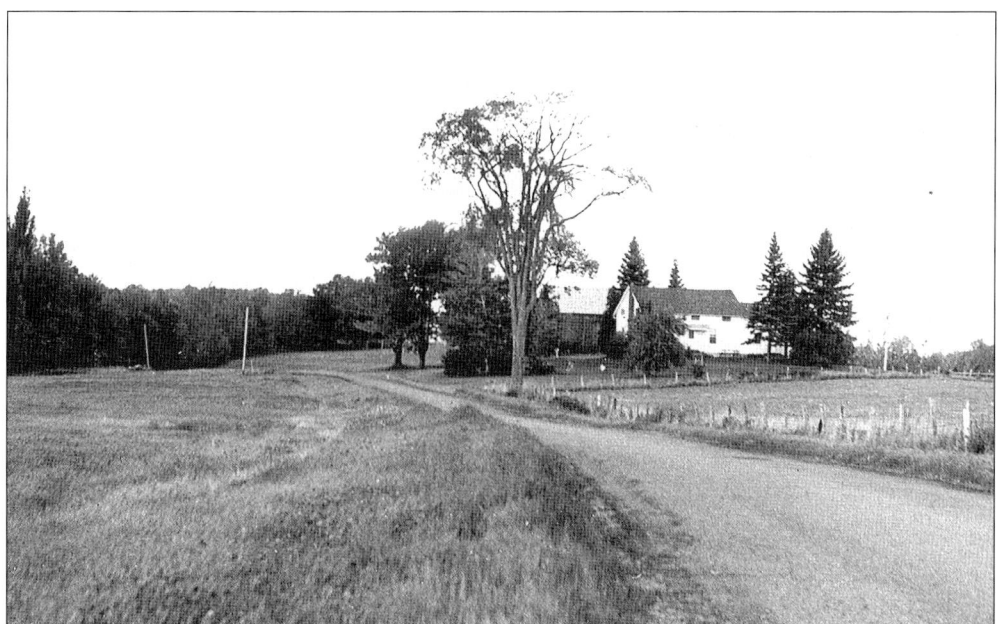

PIKE FARM. From Heaton Hill toward the village, the first left turn brings the traveler to the Pike farm. John Farwell purchased the property from land baron Richard Harison in 1811. After several owners, Albert Pike bought the property on October 18, 1912, and conveyed it to Doris (née Pike) and Ted Gibson in 1947. The present owners are Albert's grandson and his wife, David and Lora Gibson. (Courtesy of David and Lora Gibson.)

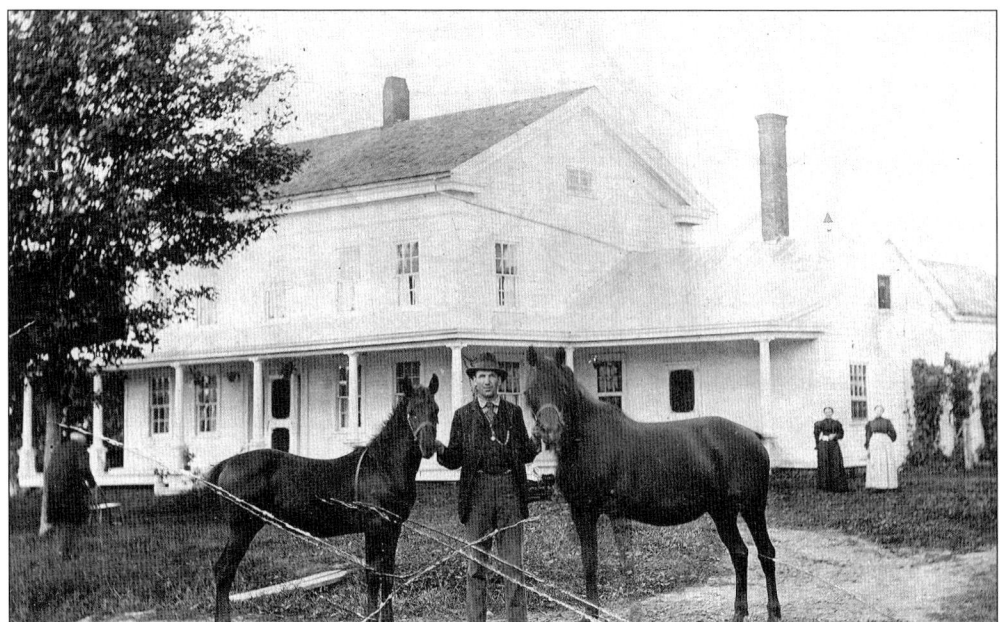

THE LANGDON FARM. When traveling south on Route 68, about five miles from the village is Langdon's Corners, one of the finest farms in the township. Peter Langdon and his wife came to the region from Dorset, Vermont, around 1807. As with most of the pioneers, a log cabin appeared that first year. After building the barn, a small frame house was constructed. Finally, in 1855, Peter's son Albert built this large farmhouse.

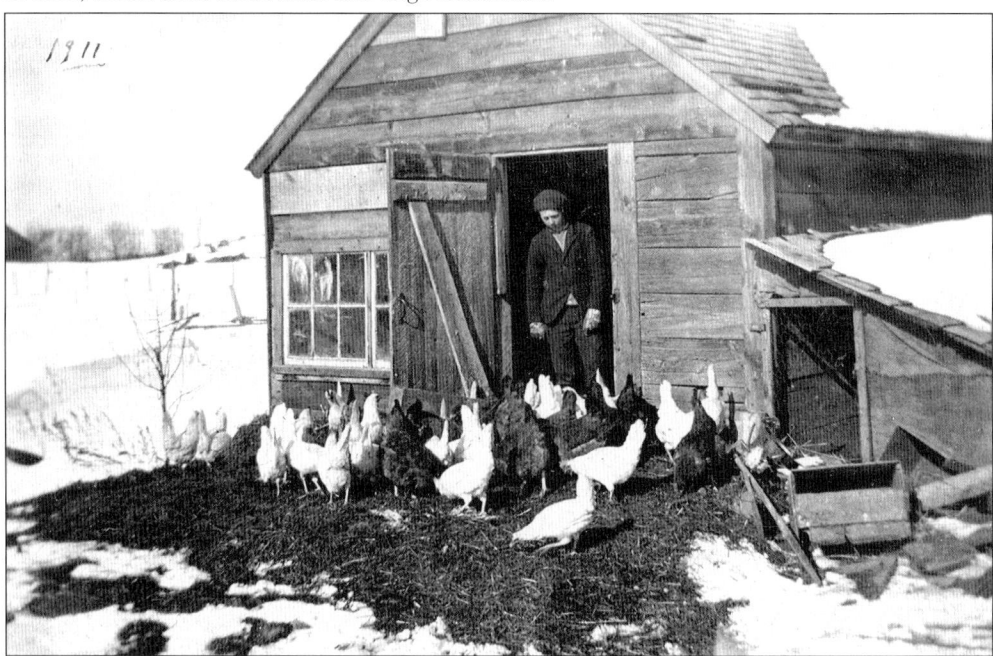

W. E. CHURCH'S HENNERY. In this photograph, W. E. Church can be seen in the doorway of the chicken coop, feeding his prized R. C. Rhode Island Reds. Most farms in the 1800s and early 1900s built henneries to house their brood. Usually, the women and children fed the chickens daily and collected the eggs. (Courtesy of SLCHA.)

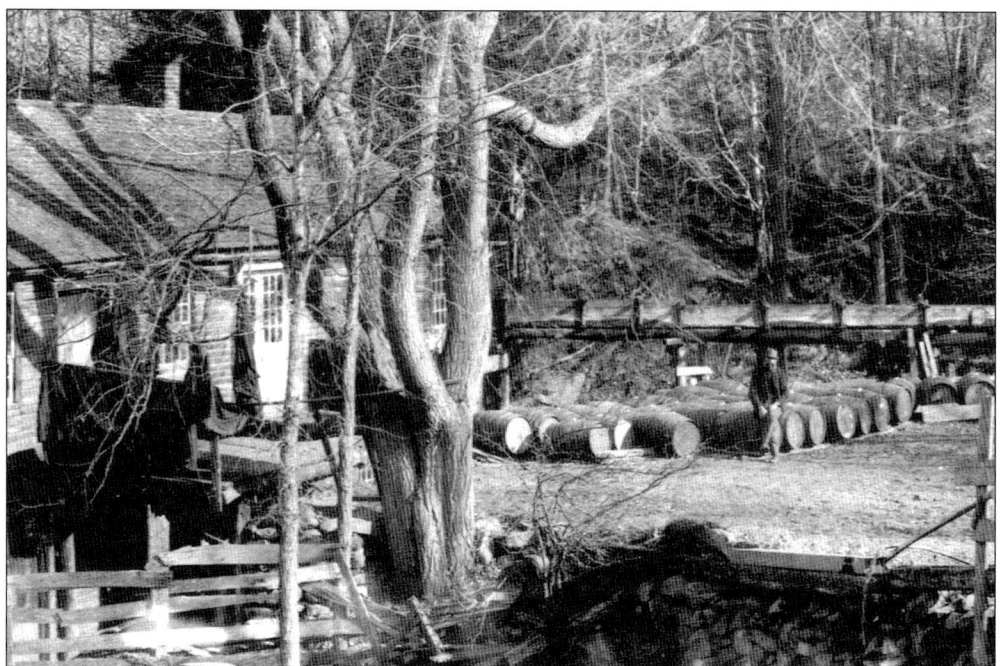

BOYDEN CIDER MILL. The sign on the side of the Boyden Cider Mill announces, "Wool Carding and Cider Making." Seated on a barrel is J. Herbert McLellan. McLellan was the maternal grandfather of Herb Judd, on Farnes Road, in Canton. (Courtesy of SLCHA.)

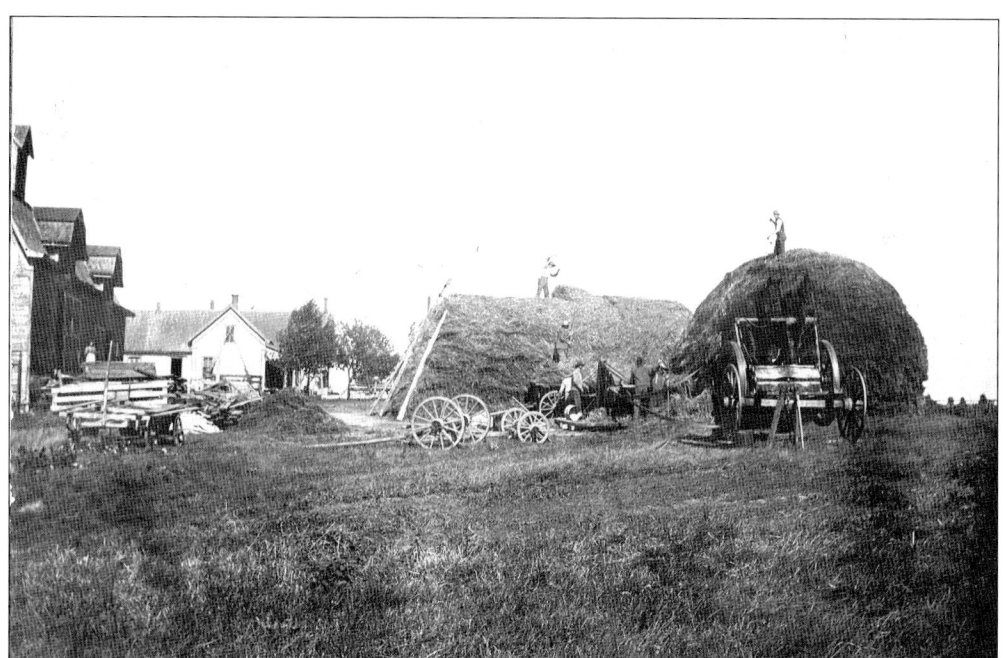

HAYING THE OLD WAY. Pictured here is a typical scene of the early 1900s. Every farm in the North Country used a team to mow, rake, and collect hay from the fields. Excused from school in May and June, the older boys in the family were expected to help in the fields.

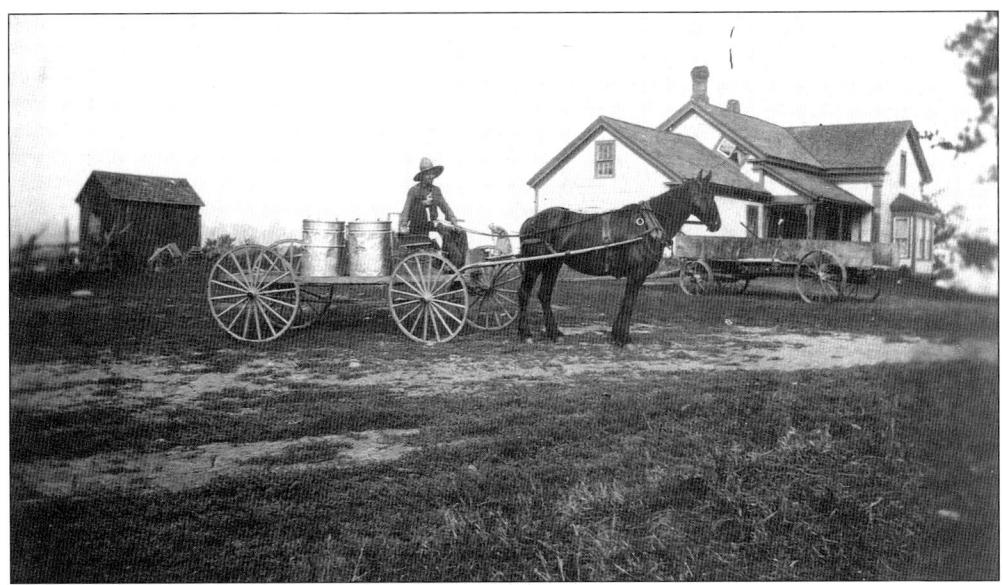

THE RODEE FARM OF BRICK CHAPEL. Seven generations of Rodees have operated this farm. In this photograph, Bernard Rodee, father of Bill, is seen here with his hired man's daughter. Hiram Rodee and his wife, Maria, established the farm in 1845 and built two houses, one on the west side of the road and the other directly across from it. Today, William and Marilyn's son, Elliott, operates the family farm and lives in the remodeled schoolhouse next door with his wife and children. (Courtesy of Marilyn and Bill Rodee.)

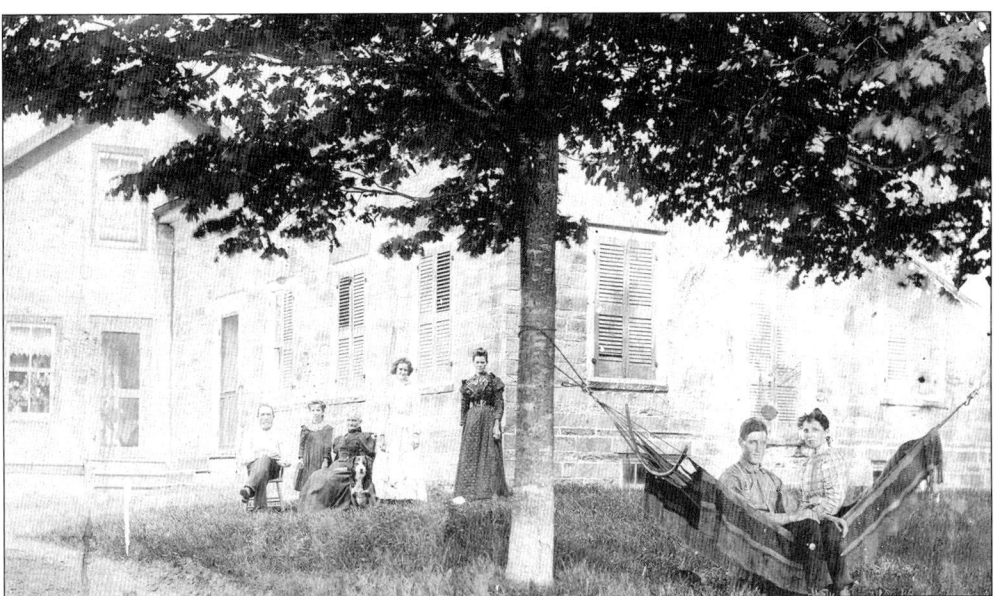

BULLIS FARM. Five generations of the Bullis family have lived at Waterman Hill. In 1842, John Wheaton Bullis, his wife, Mercy, and their eight children took the northern trail from Beadle Hill near Plattsburgh to the early settlement of Brick Chapel. Their son James, pictured on the far left, purchased the farm at the foot of Waterman Hill in 1867. Presently, Ira (Pete) Bullis and his wife, Janet, own the property and live in the beautiful sandstone house. (Courtesy of Janet and Pete Bullis.)

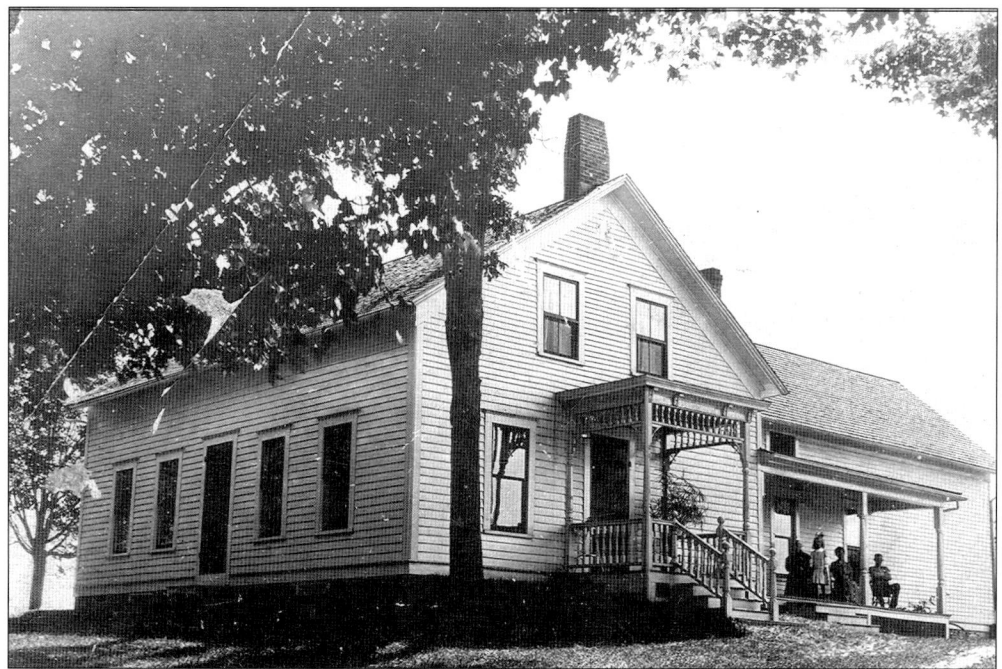

DRURY-BLOUNT-FAVRO HOME AT BRICK CHAPEL. Just before reaching Brick Chapel from Canton, and turning right onto the Barnes Road, a traveler would find this seventh generation homestead. Janet Favro is the great-great-great-great granddaughter of one of Brick Chapel's founders, John Richardson. He was the settler who donated the land for the church and cemetery. Favro runs the 240 acres as a hobby farm and still operates the sugar bush, as did generations of her ancestors. The remodeled house has been updated, but, in case of an emergency, the privy is still attached to the back of the house. (Courtesy of Janet Favro.)

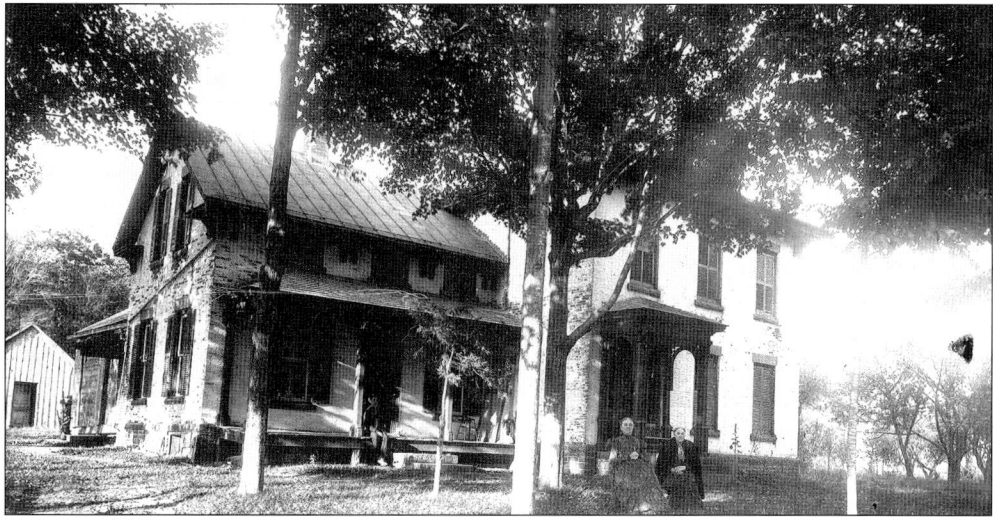

BARNES FARM. Continuing up Barnes Road, the impressive Barnes farmhouse sits on the right. Jesse Barnes traveled to Canton from Connecticut on foot, carrying on his back whatever he needed. Having located the site for his homestead, he returned to New England for his wife and child. Several generations of the Barnes family continued on this fine farm. In recent years, when it was sold, the neighboring Favros bought the barn, sugar bush, and several acres of land.

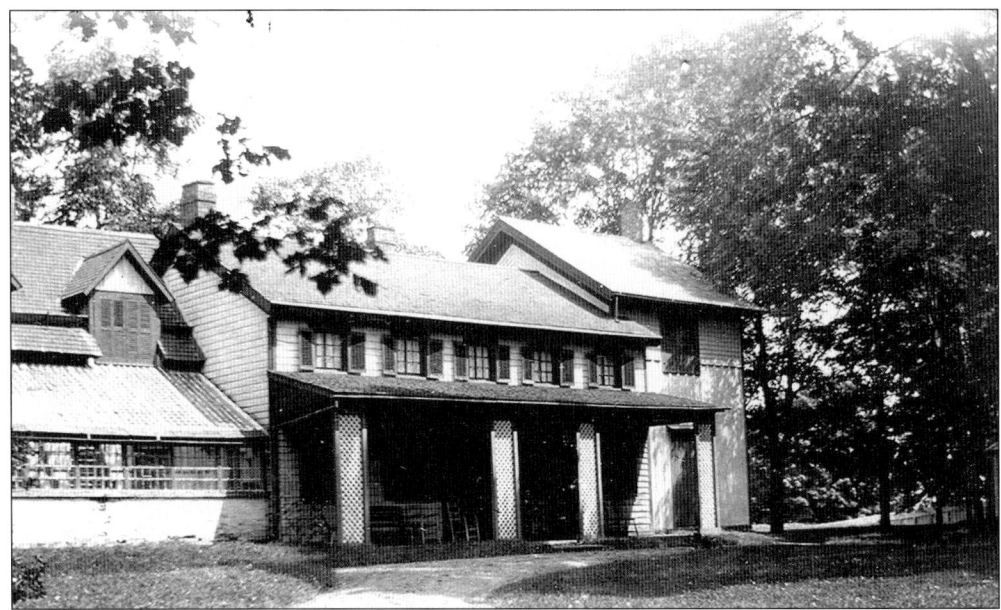

TOM HARISON PLACE. The farm pictured here was built by Thomas Ludlow Harison, who also built Morley's grist mill, Trinity Episcopal Chapel, and the Morley school. This well-kept farm is located on the Slick Street Road, just at the edge of the Morley hamlet. Owned by the Jordan family, it is still a working farm, and they take pride in keeping their property one of the loveliest in the township. (Courtesy of SLCHA.)

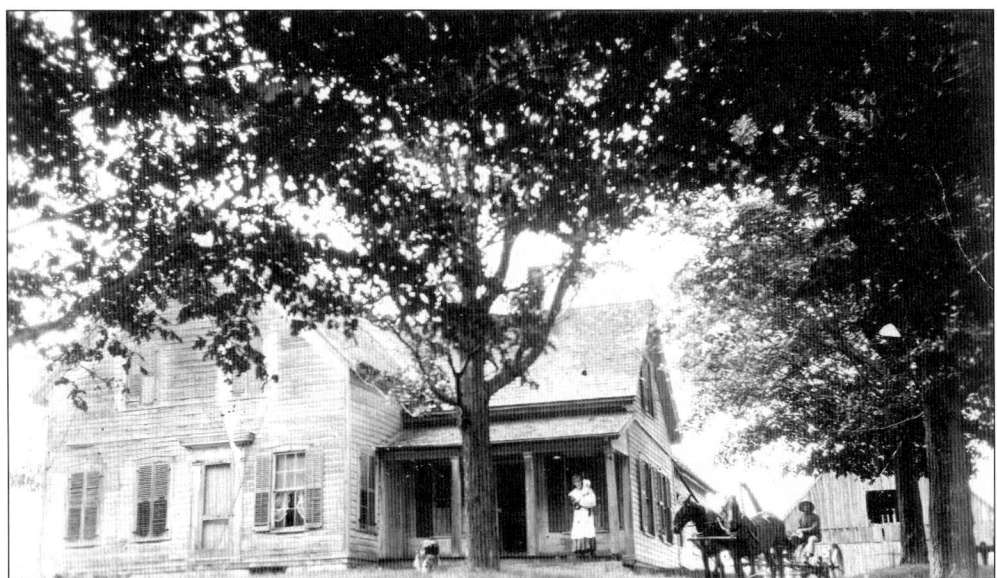

WALTER PERRY'S PLACE, C. 1912. This farmhouse, owned by Walter and Abbie Ginn Perry, is located on the South Road outside Rensselaer Falls. The Perrys bought the farm soon after their marriage in 1910. The baby in the photograph is Eunice Perry Shepherd. She later graduated from Rensselaer Falls High School, taught for many years, and was one of the founders of the Rensselaer Falls Historical Society. (Courtesy of Jacqueline Lane.)

Three
FROM ONE-ROOM SCHOOLS TO CAMPUSES

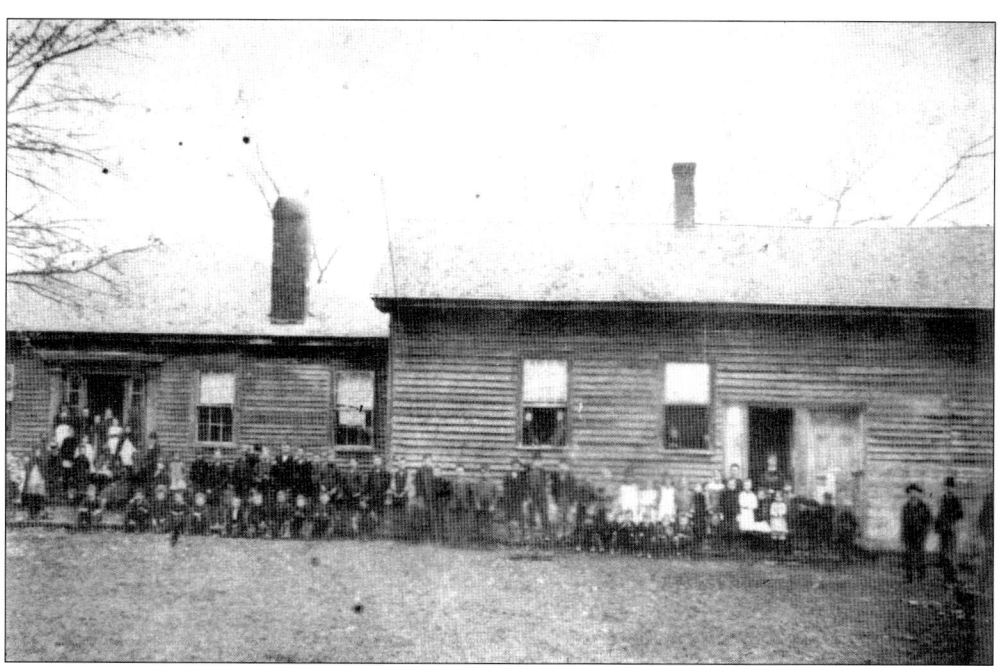

THE CANTON ACADEMY. This early school, built on Pearl Street in 1831, was Canton's first attempt to have a sturdy, permanent school in the village. Twenty-five residents paid $1,250 toward its construction, thus charging tuition to those who attended. Until 1839, the academy admitted only boys. Sold years later, it became a private residence.

TEACHING CERTIFICATE. Even in the early 1800s, teachers were awarded papers stating their qualifications to teach. This certificate was issued to Miss Lucy Shepard in 1834, and reads, "We the subscribers Inspectors of Common Schools for the Town of Canton St. Lawrence County do certify that at a meeting of the Inspectors called for that purpose; we have examined Miss Lucy Shepard and do believe her well qualified in respect to moral character, learning and ability to teach a common school in this town for the term of one year from the date here of given under our hands at Canton this 10th day of May 1834."

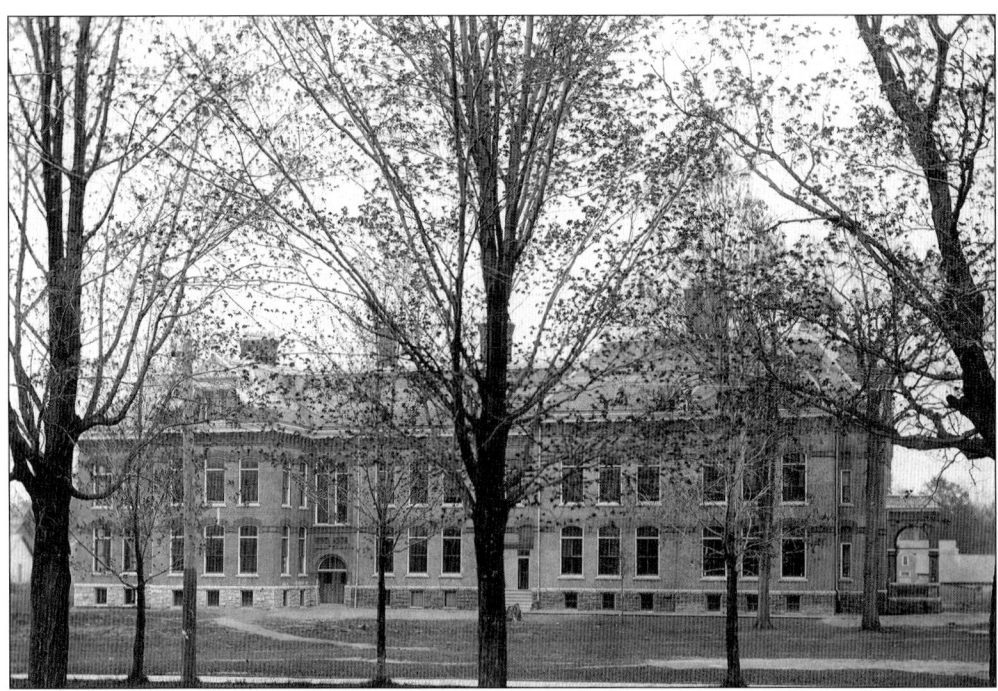

THE CANTON UNION FREE SCHOOL (GRAMMAR SCHOOL). Built in 1883, this school occupied the site of the John Leslie Russell home on Court Street in the village. For 25 years, it housed all of the students from grades 1 through 12. The addition of a wing in 1896 offered the school plenty of room. When the high school was built in 1908, the name changed to the Grammar School. However, in January 1925, fire destroyed a good portion of the building.

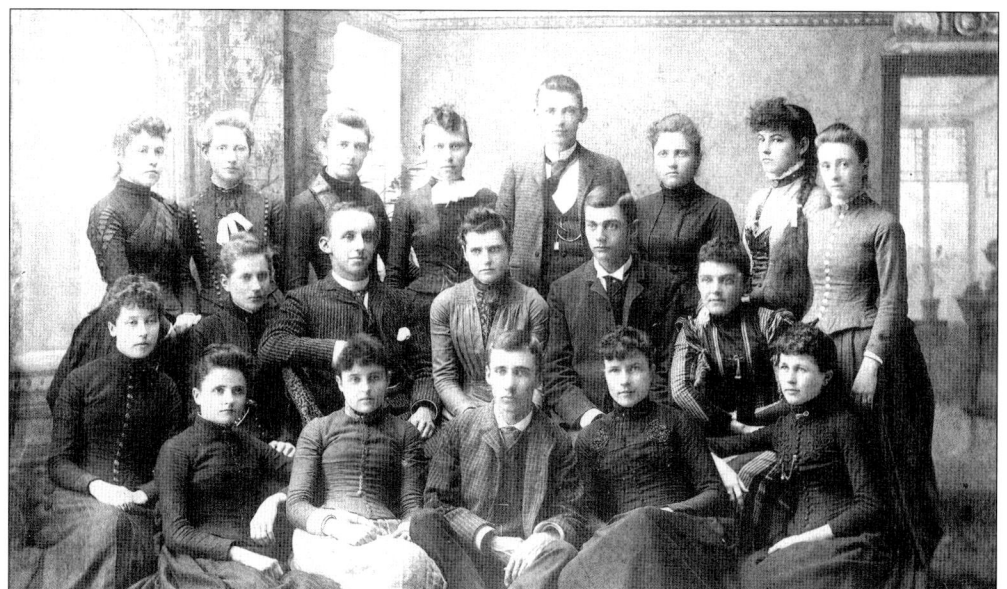

UNION FREE SCHOOL, CLASS OF 1889. Seen here is the graduating class of the Canton Union Free School, six years after the new school was built. From left to right, they are (first row) Margaret Woods, Mina Emerson, John Finnigan, Julia Woods, and Gertrude Pierce; (second row) Katie Burke, Annie Murray, Elon Lovewell, Grace Lynde Ransom Empey, and Helen Jackson; (third row) Mary Woodcock, Jennie Merritt, Jessie Farmer, Fanny Dailey, Fred Meade, Nellie Baker, Minnie Sautmay, and Bridget Mahoney.

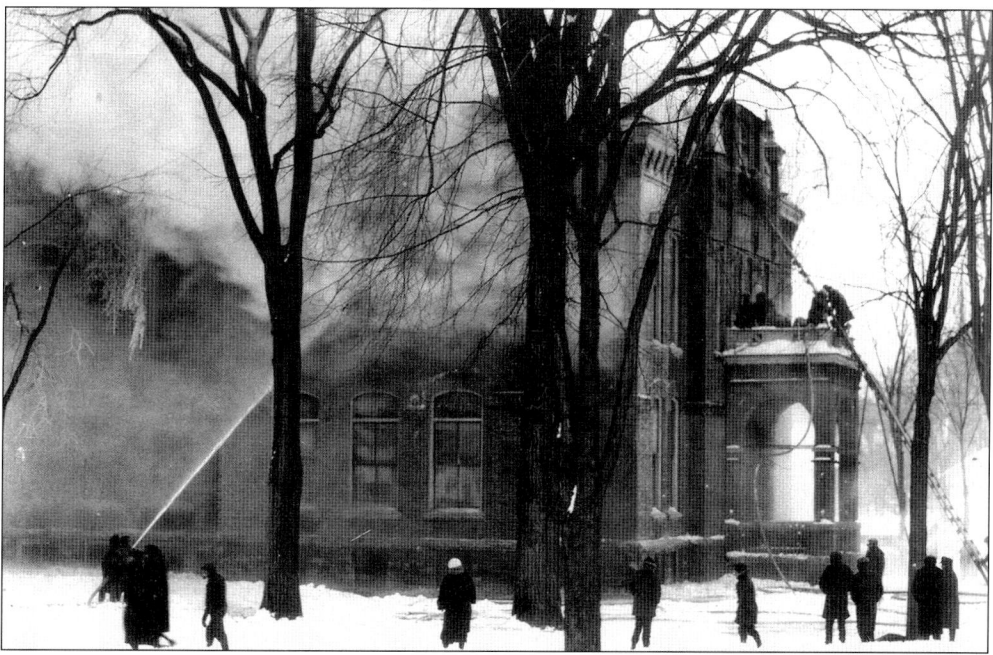

FIRE DESTROYS THE GRAMMAR SCHOOL. On a Sunday morning in January 1925, a fire broke out at 7:00 a.m. at the grammar school on Court Street. The temperature that morning was 32 degrees below zero. Nearly destroyed, the school sustained considerable damage. A faulty furnace was thought to be the cause of the fire.

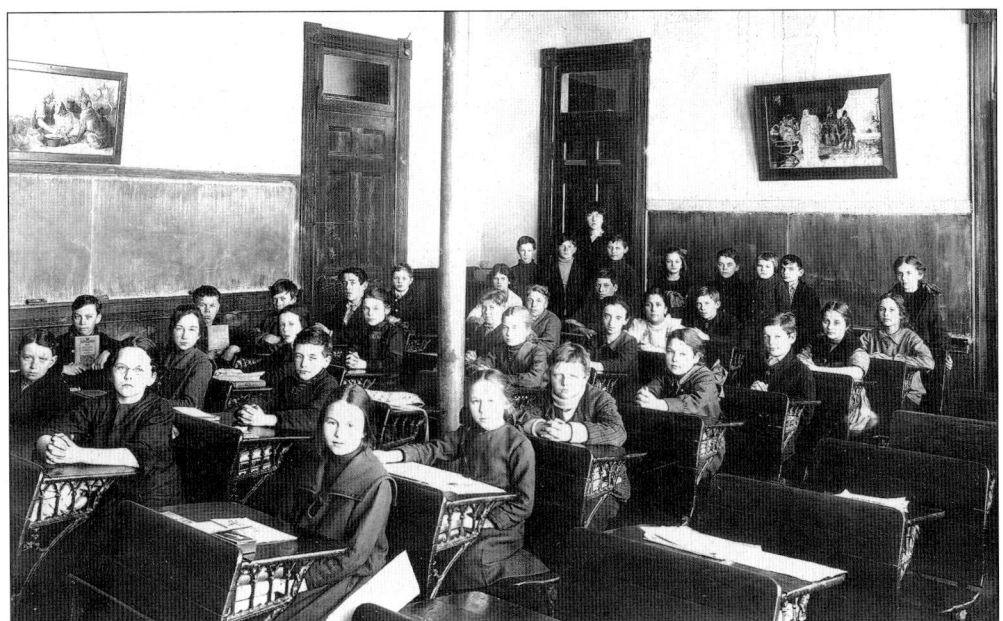

INSIDE THE GRAMMAR SCHOOL. This rare photograph of the inside of a classroom was probably taken in the Union Free School after the disastrous fire of 1925. Immediately rebuilt, this magnificent building had large spacious classrooms trimmed with dark mahogany woodwork. The grammar school met its demise in 1973 when St. Lawrence County bought the property for the Harold B. Smith office building.

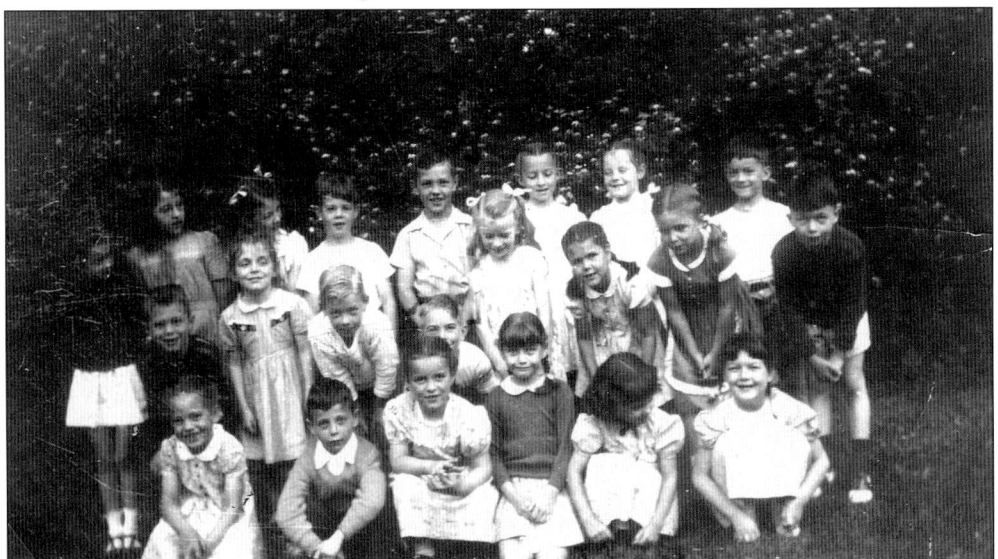

MARGARET MYERS' KINDERGARTEN CLASS. Margaret Myers taught kindergarten at the Grammar School for 23 years and was loved by all of her students. This photograph shows a group of her 1946 kindergartners. They are, from left to right, (first row) Connie Shatraw, Michael Kitay, Carol McCarthy, Nan Jones, Sherry Jones, and Judy Todd; (second row) John McKenney, Nancy Houk, Wayne Mousaw, unidentified, Judy Comstock, Roxanna Thorbahn, Barbara Dommeyer, and John Caneen; (third row) Sandra Hall, Marie Trathen, Natalie Clark, Duane Briggs, Barry Young, Janet Butterfield, Beverly Welsh, and John Stauffer. (Courtesy of Carol Johnson.)

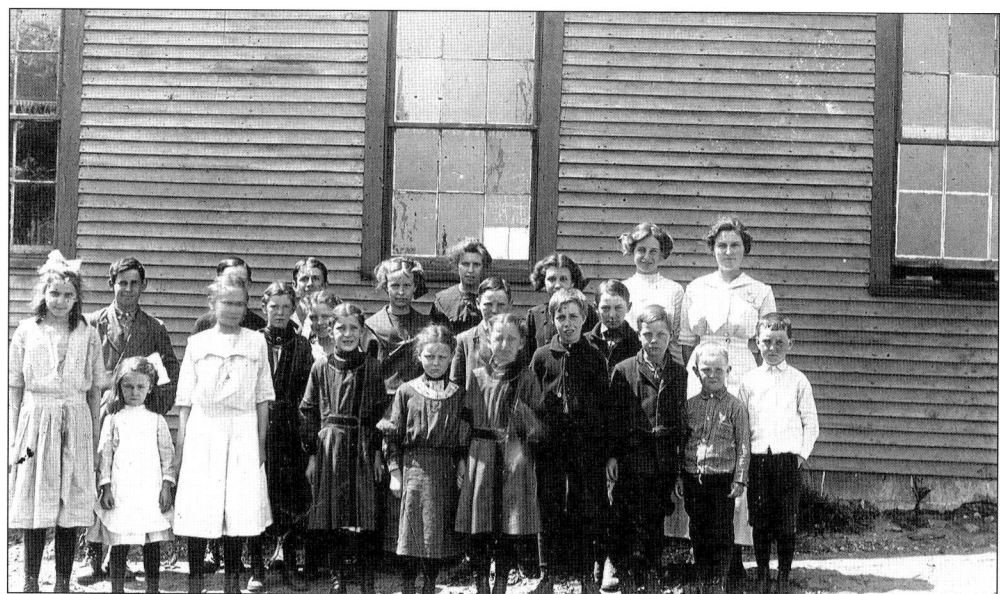

THE WOODBRIDGE CORNERS SCHOOL. The District Seven one-room school was built in 1881. Larger than most other rural schools in the town, its seating capacity was 30. Former students remember morning devotions with Bible readings and the Lord's Prayer recited in unison. Apparently, the separation of church and state ruling did not reach the rural schools. Closed in June 1945, the schoolhouse received a new foundation, and was expanded as a private home. Flossie Todd is fourth from the left in the first row. (Photograph Courtesy of James Todd.)

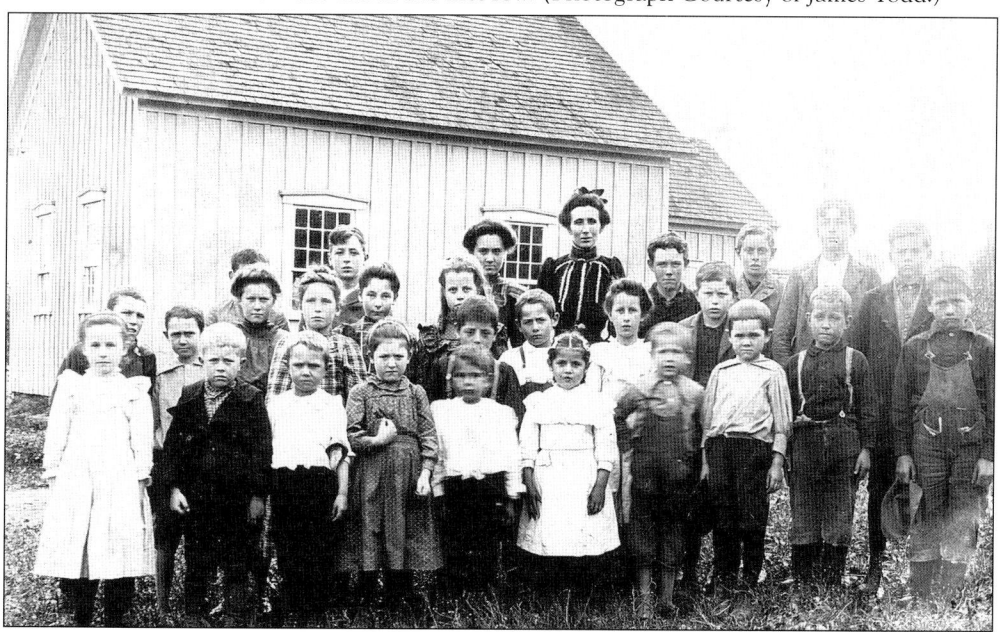

THE PINK SCHOOLHOUSE, NEAR PYRITES. All students attending the Pink Schoolhouse in 1900 lived on area farms. Most had to trudge a mile or two to go to school. Few students attended high school for two reasons: there was no daily transportation into the village, and boys were needed to help on the farm. Teachers were unmarried, had very little training, and salaries were only $10.00 a week. They boarded at one student's farm for a term, and then moved to another.

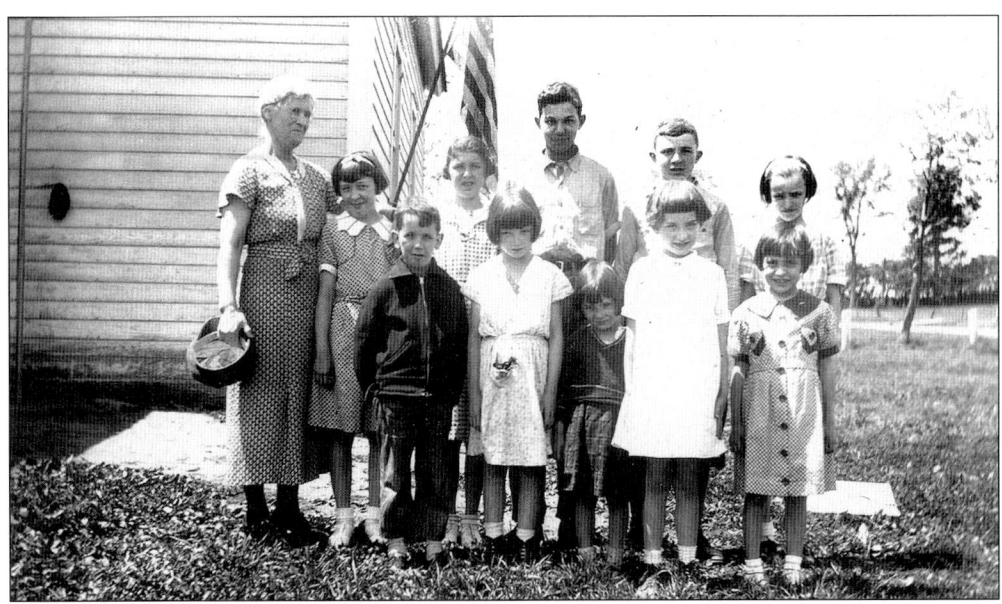

TEACHER AND CHILDREN AT THE KNOX SCHOOL. Nona Kennedy and her students are pictured in 1936 outside the Knox School. Thought to have been one of Canton's oldest, the land was donated by the Knox family. From left to right are (first row) Gerald Pike, Mary Brown, Frances Brown, Hope Robinson, and ? Brooks; (second row) teacher Nona Kennedy, Gladys Brooks, Marjorie Brooks, Keith Johnson, Hollis Brown, and Jean Brown. This school was located on the corner of Pike Road and Route 68. (Courtesy of Hope Mayhew.)

CERTIFICATE OF ACHIEVEMENT. Clarence Armstrong, superintendent of all Canton schools from 1923 to 1964, visited each rural school several times a year. He lived in town, and traveled the back roads on horseback, by horse and carriage, or automobile. This is a certificate signed by Armstrong, indicating the child had passed the state exams in the seventh grade.

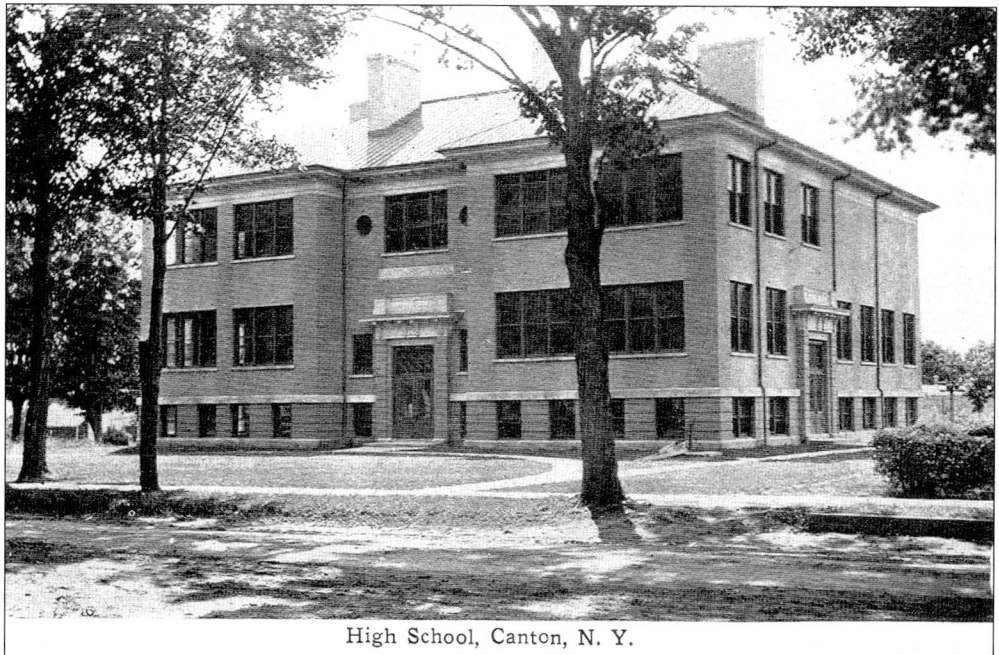

High School, Canton, N. Y.

OLD HIGH SCHOOL. In 1908, the yellow brick building known as the Old High School was built on the site of Dr. John Bassette's residence. Constructed on the corner of Pearl and Court Streets, students adhered to certain standards. The boys' door was on one side of the school, while the girls' door was on the other. No student dared use the wrong door.

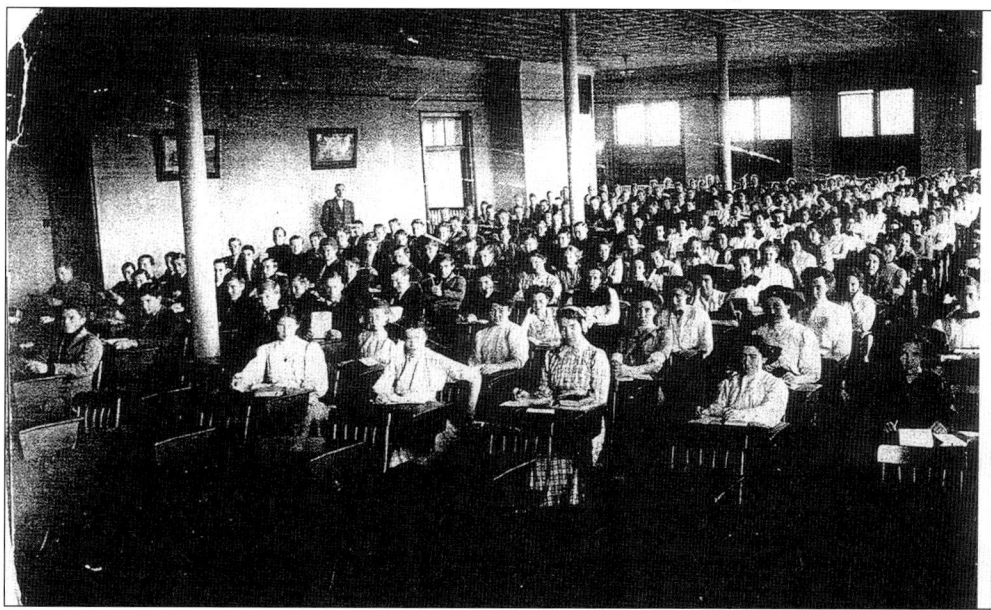

STUDY HALL, OLD HIGH SCHOOL. This picture shows the enormous size of the study hall on the second floor of the high school. The school served grades 7 through 12 until 1954, when the new Junior-Senior High School opened. For the next few years, this building housed several elementary grades and was demolished in 1961. Today the St. Lawrence County Public Safety Building stands on this site.

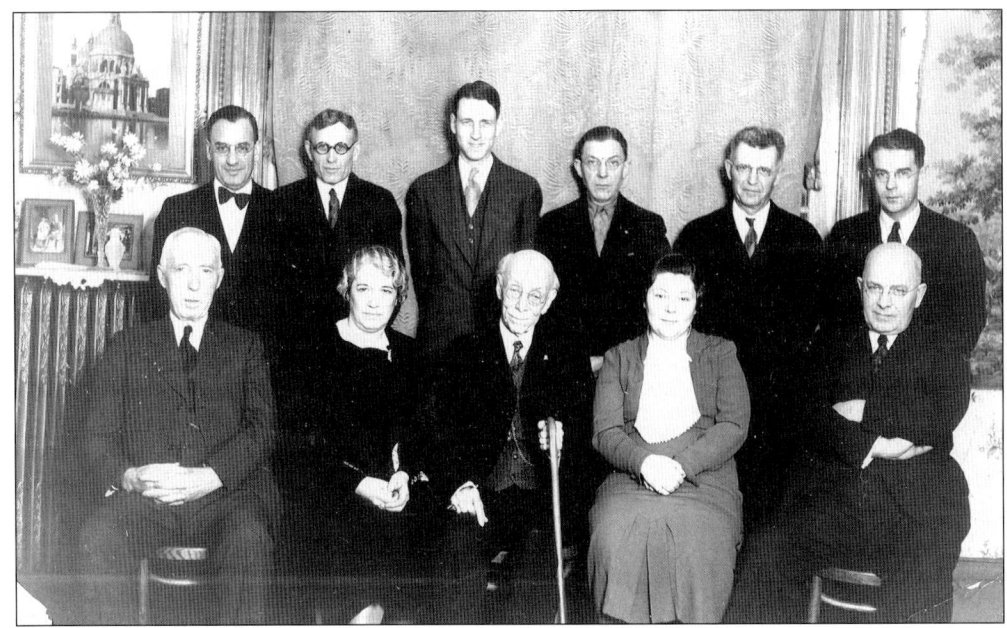

CANTON SCHOOL BOARD. Pictured here are the Canton School Board members in 1928. From left to right, they are (first row) Charles Bird, Edith Wight, Dr. James Payson, Grace Barr, and Ward Hamilton; (second row) Roy Pike, Thad Melrose, Lewis Cook, George Robinson, Charles Tait, and supervising principal Hugh C. Williams. Most of these people were either prominent business-owners or professors.

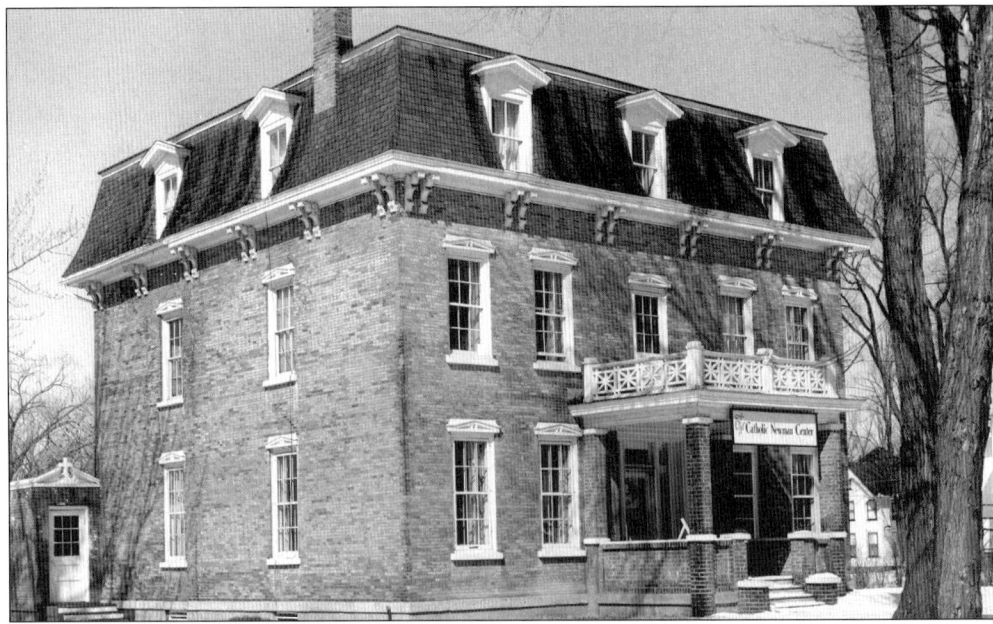

FIRST CATHOLIC SCHOOL. Constructed in 1928 on Court Street, St. Mary's Parochial School served its parishioners for 30 years. Taught by four Sisters of Charity, St. Mary's offered a Catholic education to the first eight grades. A new school was built adjacent to St. Mary's Church and the Rectory in 1958. Presently, children in pre-kindergarten through grade six attend. St. Mary's School celebrated its 75th anniversary in August 2005.

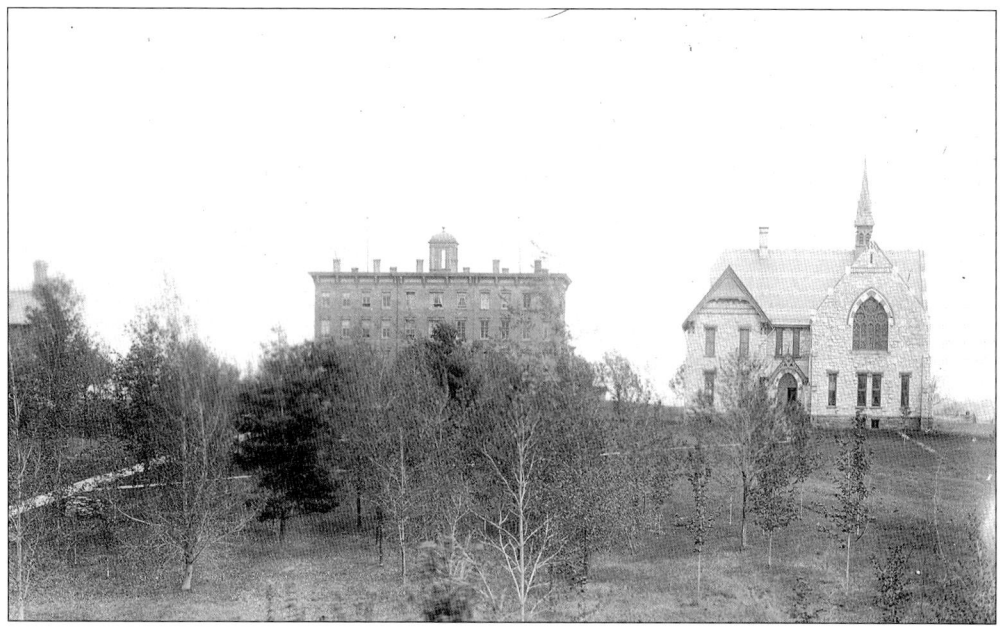

VIEW OF THE ST. LAWRENCE CAMPUS, MID-1800S. Pictured here is the St. Lawrence University campus in its early days. At the Universalist State Convention in 1852, plans were made to establish a Universalist Theological School, and Canton was selected as the site. Three years later, 26 acres of land were purchased in the name of the Universalist Educational Society. Today university property includes thousands of acres, and 2,100 students are enrolled.

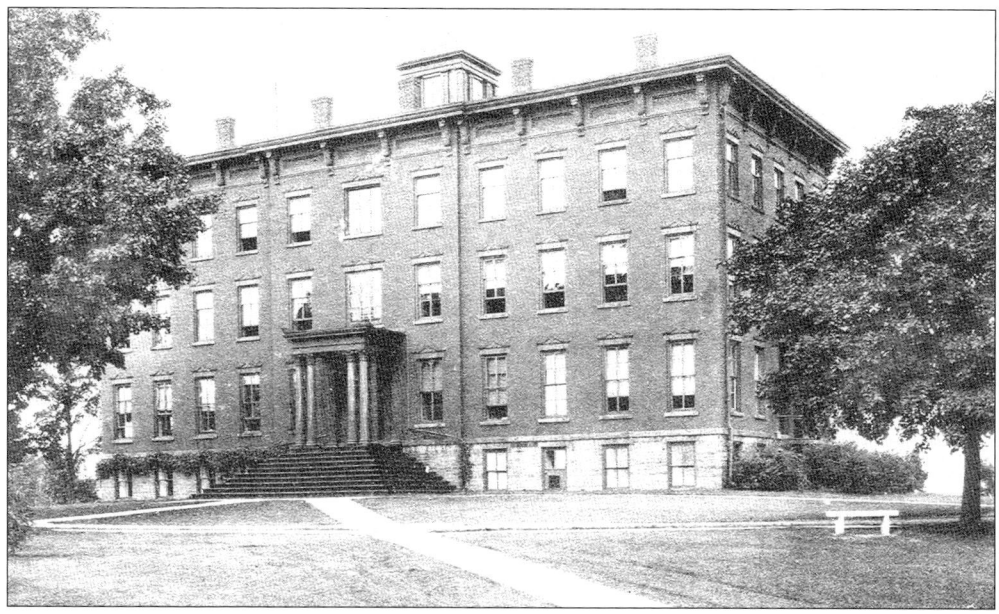

RICHARDSON HALL, ST. LAWRENCE UNIVERSITY'S FIRST BUILDING. The state legislature granted the charter to "The St. Lawrence University and the Universalist Theological School" in 1856, and Richardson Hall, pictured above, was constructed the same year. Both schools met in the same building for a time, and the first commencement graduated five students.

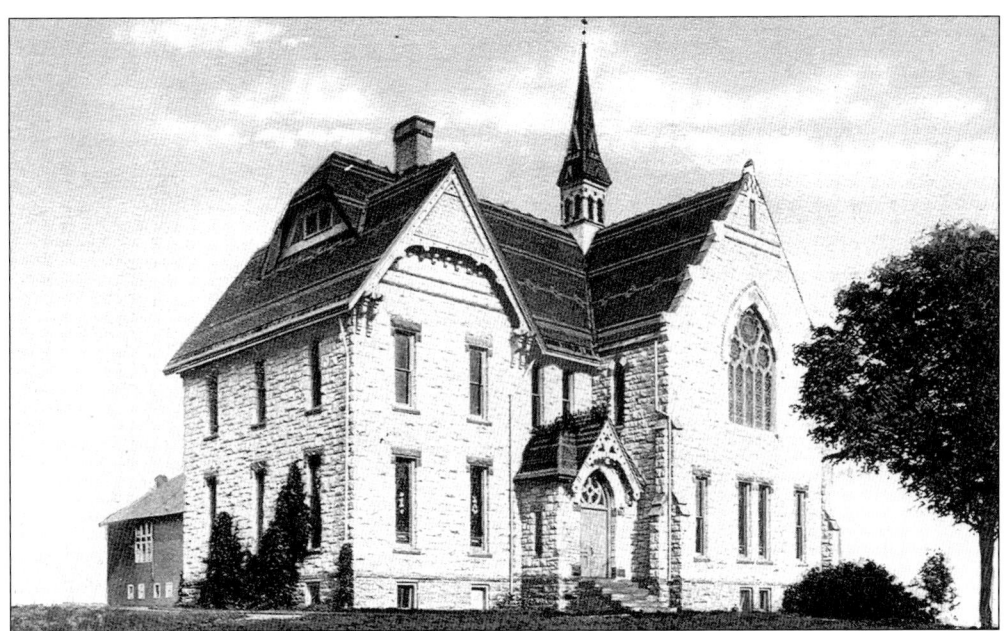

DR. EBENEZER FISHER HEADS THE THEOLOGICAL SCHOOL. The first class of the new Theological School met in the fall of 1858, with Dr. Ebenezer Fisher at the helm. The new building to house this school was built in 1881. The school continued to graduate theologians until the 1950s. Fisher Hall burned in 1951, but a new structure, Atwood Hall, still stands on the St. Lawrence University campus.

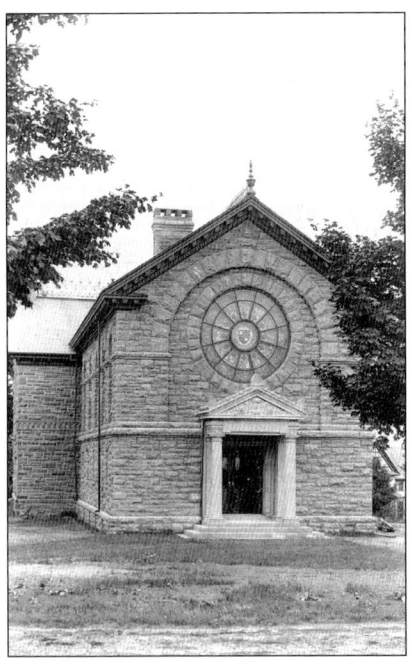

HERRING COLE. This beautiful building still graces the campus of St. Lawrence University. Built in 1869, thirteen years after Richardson Hall, Silas Herring of New York City financed the building of a new library. The library was used as a governmental repository, and before long, a wing had to be added. In 1889, Edward H. Cole financed the renovation and the addition of the Cole Reading Room.

GUNNISON MEMORIAL CHAPEL. Gunnison Chapel, a non-denominational campus church, is probably the most beautiful on any university campus. Almon Gunnison became president of St. Lawrence University in 1899. The campus was still small with few buildings, but that was soon to change. President Gunnison proved to be the first large fund-raiser in the university's history. He raised $200,000 in endowments and remodeled several of the existing buildings. Gunnison also founded the agricultural school. The chapel was named in his honor.

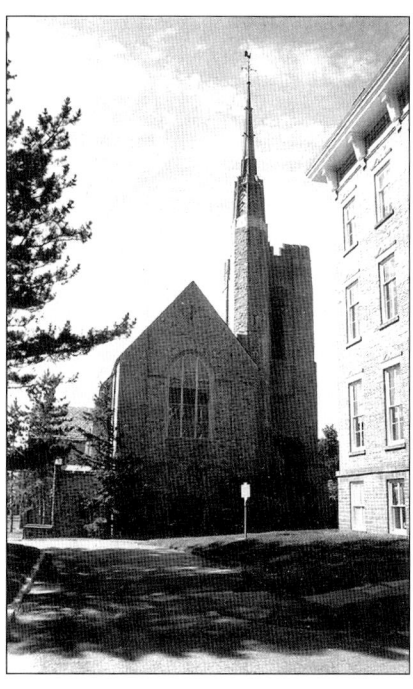

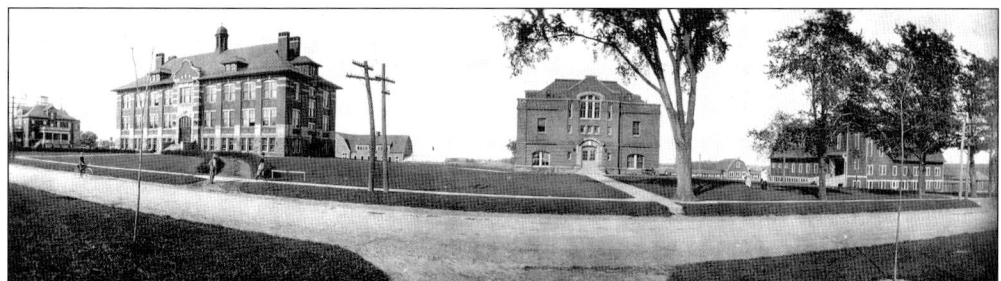

ARRIVAL OF THE AGGIE SCHOOL. In this photograph, one can see the first four buildings of the State School in Canton. From left to right is the Weather Station, Cook Hall, Payson Hall, and the school barn. In 1906, the state legislature passed a bill that created the agricultural college. First called the Agricultural School at St. Lawrence University, home economics was also taught. In 1925, the school became independent from the university and technical courses were added in 1937.

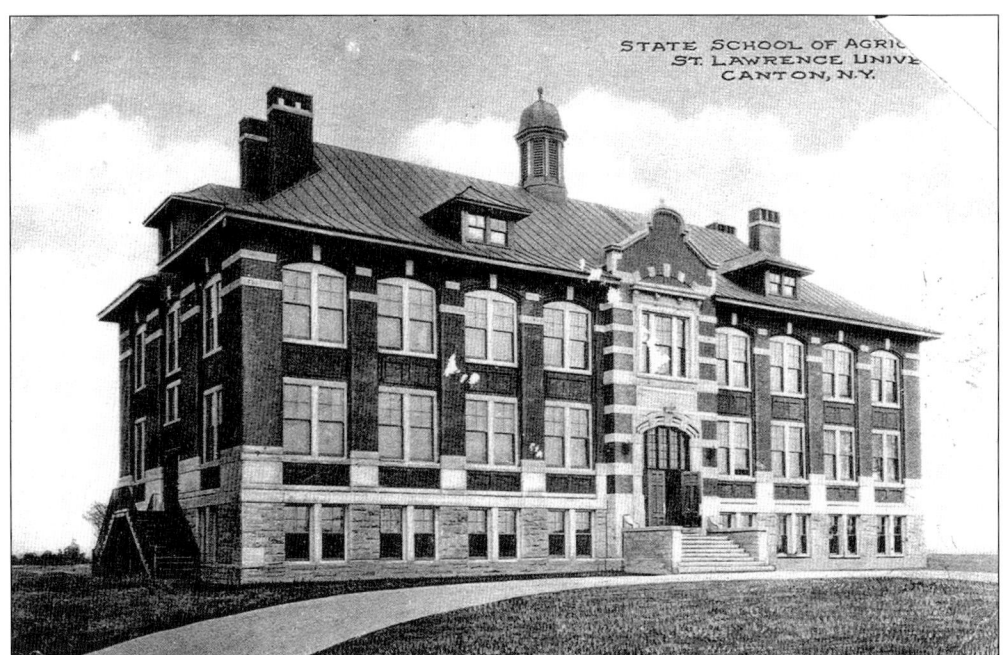

HEYDAY OF THE AGGIE SCHOOL. Cook Hall was named in honor of Dean Herbert Ellis Cook. Before the agricultural depression in the North Country, the Aggie School grew by leaps and bounds. Much of its success was due to Dean Cook. He offered great experience in practical farming and had a wide acquaintance with the leading agriculturalists in the state.

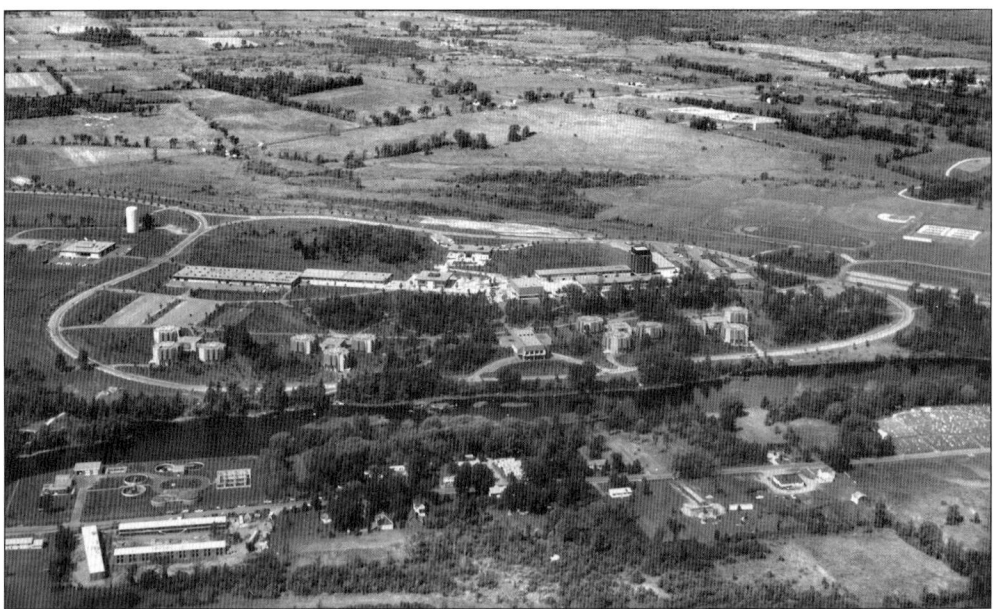

NEW CAMPUS AT CANTON COLLEGE. This picture shows the beautiful new campus, situated west of the village, along the Grasse River. The spacious 555-acre campus was acquired in 1962, mostly through the generosity of Anne and Edson A. Martin. The name changed to the State University Agricultural and Technical College at Canton. Today, there are 2,600 students, and the official name is the State University of New York College of Technology at Canton.

Four

MAIN STREET AND SIDE STREET BUSINESSES

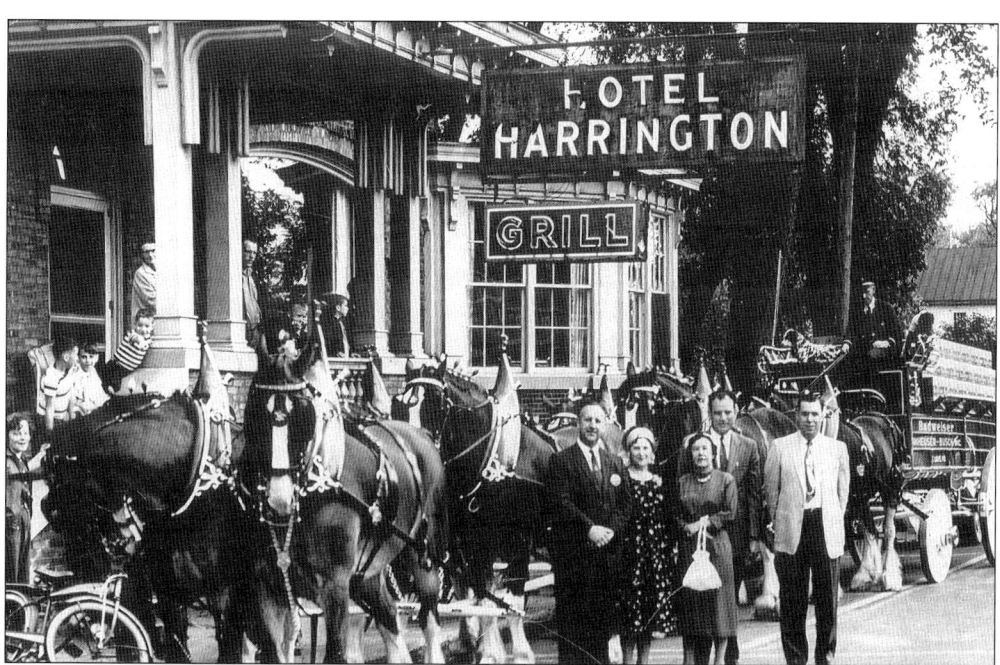

HOTEL HARRINGTON, CLYDESDALES COME TO CANTON. The grandest hotel in The North Country is the perfect setting for a Clydesdales photograph opportunity. People identified in the photograph are Phil McMasters, who may be the young man partially behind the pillar on the left; Beverly Welsh, the young woman on the patio; and Verda Bailey and Thelma Bushaw, owners of the DeKalb Hotel, are the women standing next to the horses.

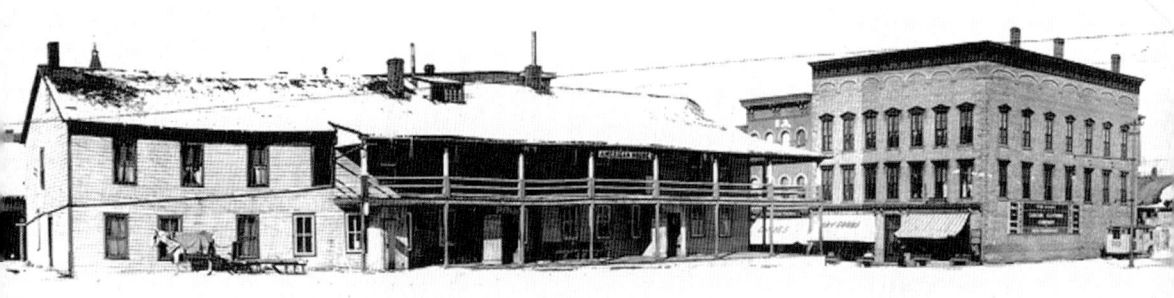

MAIN STREET PANORAMA, EARLY 1900S. Please note that the horse in front of the hotel is the only living creature in this photograph on this obviously very cold winter day. Pictured from the left are the American House, the E. M. Kirland Pharmacy, the Safford and Eastman dry goods store, and Jeremiah O'Brien's quaint, miniature diner on wheels. Across Court Street from left to right is the G. J. Duskas fruit and ice cream store, the W. E. Dunn and Son grocery and crockery store, and the Bing S. Stevens Book and Stationery store. The next block is pictured

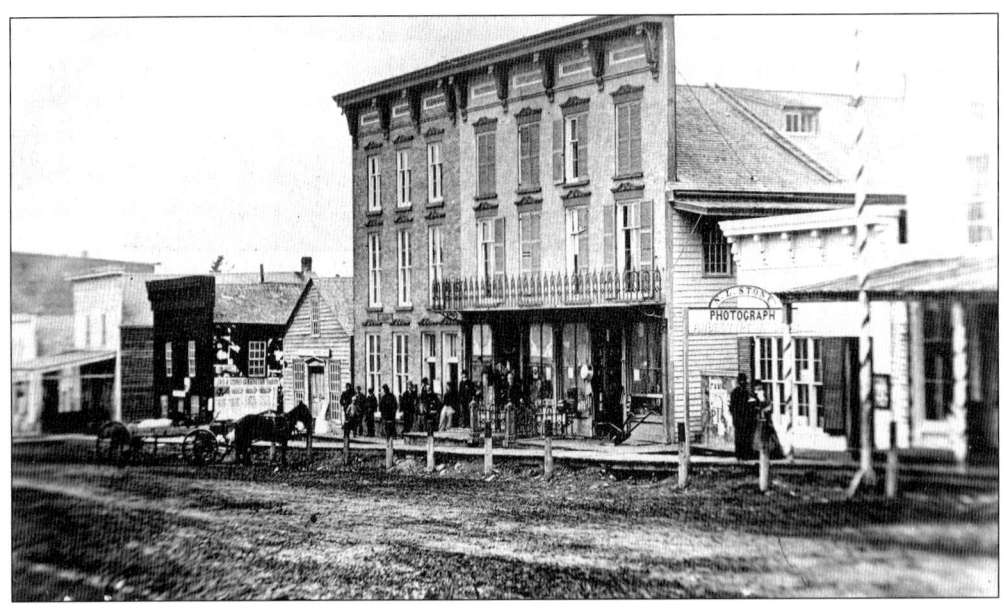

NORTH SIDE OF MAIN STREET, PRIOR TO 1869 AND 1870 FIRES. There has been much controversy over the historical accuracy of the physical location of this picture. Most agree this set of buildings was between Hodskin and Water Street (Riverside Drive). It was rumored that Walter Van Valkenberg rescued George Stone from the sewer hole in the foreground of this picture. George fell into the sewer at the park.

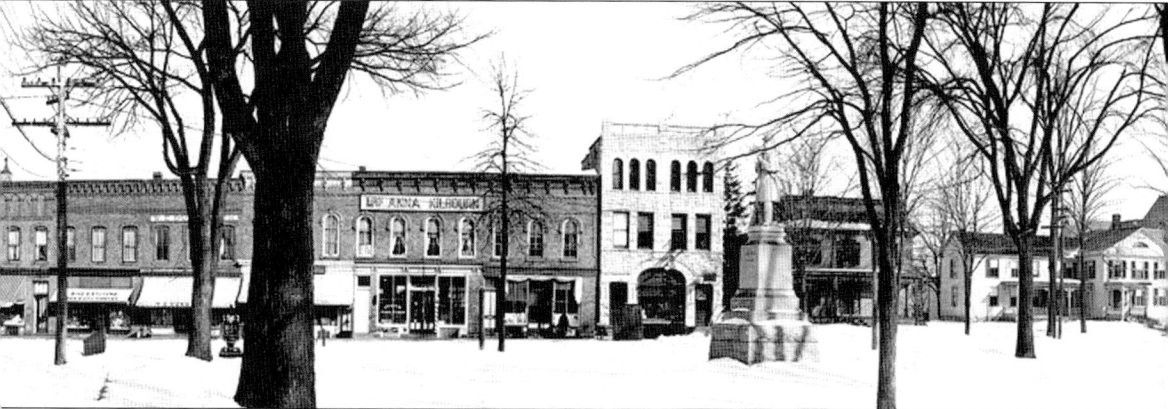

with Fraser's Pool Room and a barbershop at street level, with Mrs. Anna Kilbourn millinery store on the second floor. Next may have been the optometrist office of Charles W. Liggio. The impressive three story building on the end was built by Dr. Fred Drury and at one time housed Thomas Miller's furniture store on the ground floor and the Copeland and Kip photograph gallery on the second floor. To the right is the stately Duskas/Drury home built by Minerva Dunn with the home of Silas Wright at the far right.

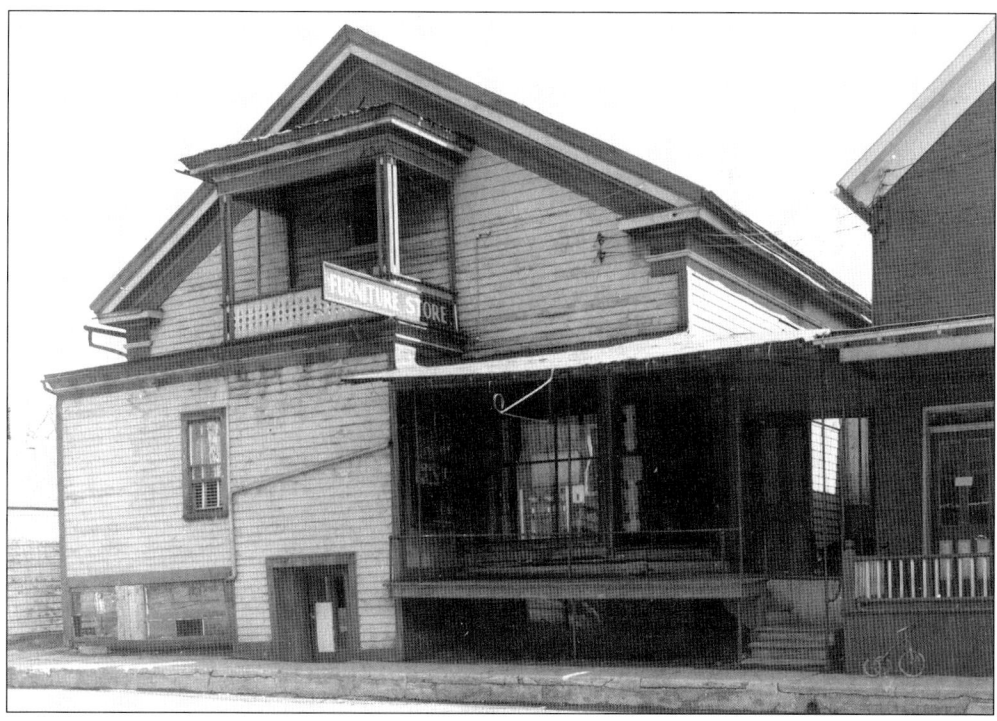

GILMORE FURNITURE STORE. Established in 1867, this business was remodeled and became Gilmore's Furniture and Undertaking Rooms. As the "Hodskin Opera House," this building was previously home to Canton's first opera house. The First Baptist Church of Canton worshipped here in the 1860s.

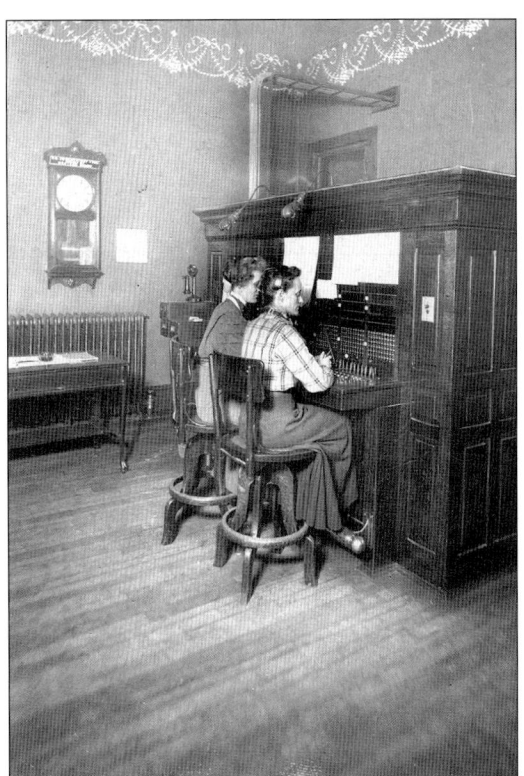

MOUNTAIN HOME TELEPHONE COMPANY. This business was first located in the library room of the old town hall and then moved to the ground floor of the Drury Block. One of these women may have been either chief operator Nora Potter or later, Mary Sawyer.

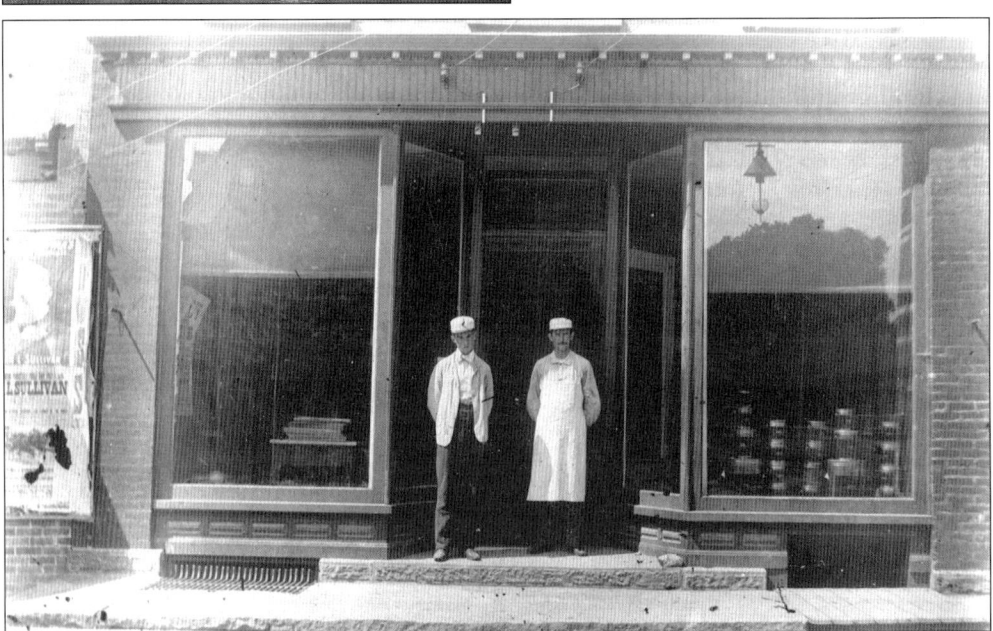

SOUTH SIDE OF MAIN STREET, DONIHEE AND BAKER BLOCK. James Donihee is the butcher on the right, in the doorway of his meat market in the late 1890s. The Canton Club occupied the second floor prior to moving to its Court Street location, and the third floor was occupied at various times by the Odd Fellows Lodge, the American Legion, and the Legion Auxiliary. This building and the Billy's Restaurant block were destroyed by a fire in April 1974.

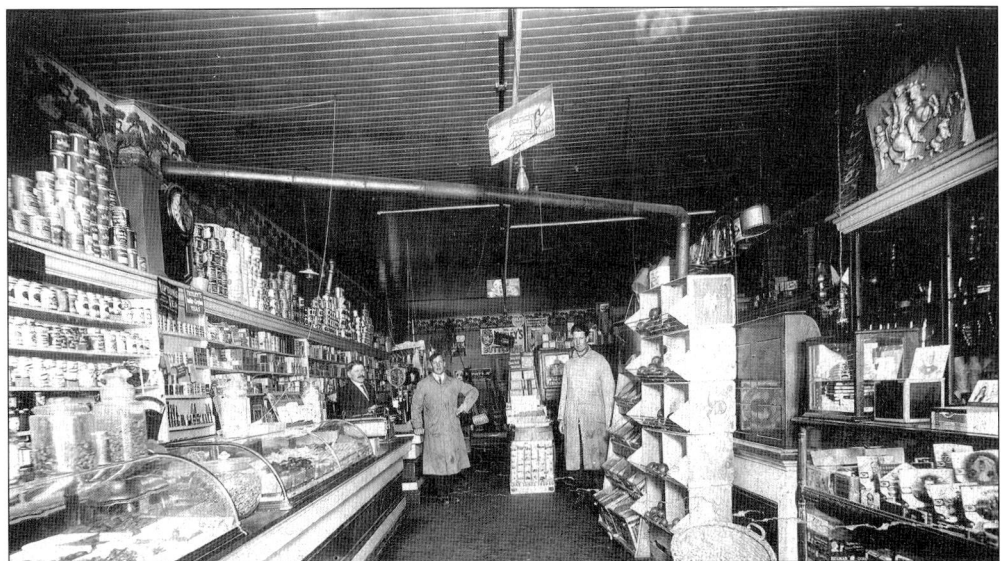

KINGSLEY GROCERY STORE. Pictured here in the 1890s, from left to right, are Thomas Kingsley, George Todd, and Frank Harmer. Built in 1871, it was first the L. L. Jackson grocery store. As the Sugar Bowl, it was owned by George Duskas and later by his nephew, William Duskas. Subsequent owners were Peter Neragin and Charles Clark. Most notably, it was Ralph's Restaurant during the 1960s and 1970s, owned by Ralph Ensby. The second floor of this building was occupied at various times by lawyers and a dentist. It is now home to the One Stop Mail Shop.

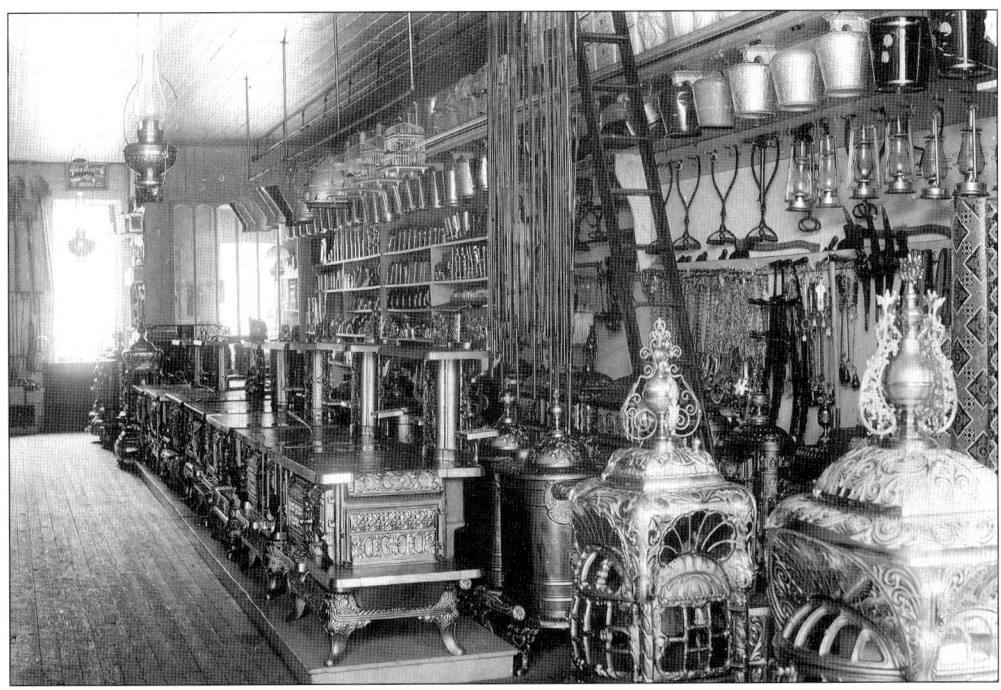

CANTON HARDWARE COMPANY. As is evident in this beautifully detailed photograph from the early 1900s, cooking and keeping warm were the two main concerns of Canton's early hardware store.

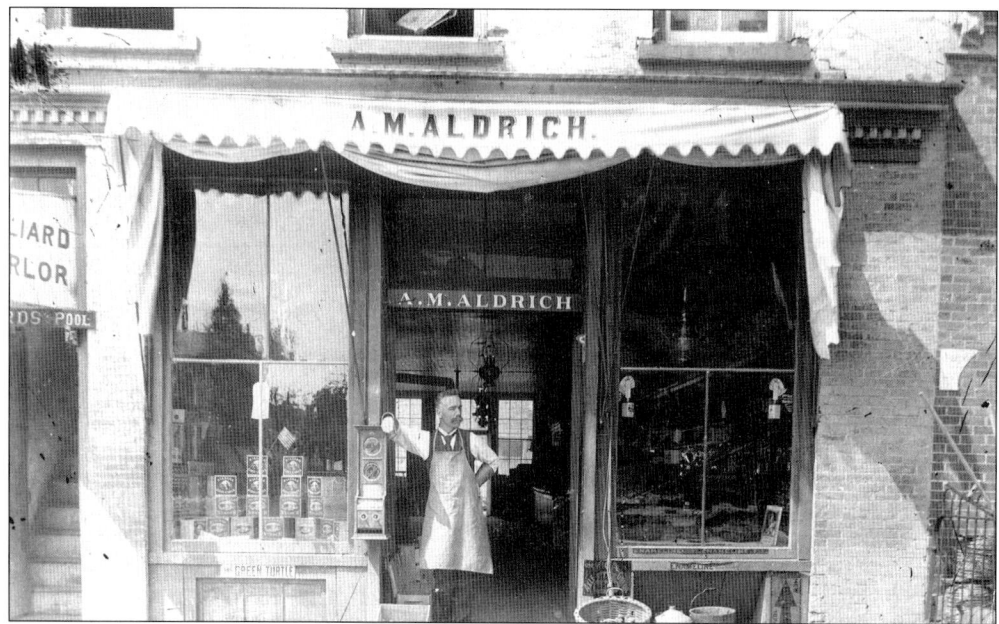

A. M. Aldrich Grocery Store. Wilber Wallace, clerk, stands in the doorway of the grocery store. Later, this building housed a furniture and undertaking business, which was owned and operated by Lorenzo and Millard Lawrence. Russell B. Lawrence III, the fifth generation of this family, continues the funeral home business at 21 Park Street. Before moving to the Miner Block in the 1950s, Pearl's Department Store was located here, followed by the Noble Shoe Store.

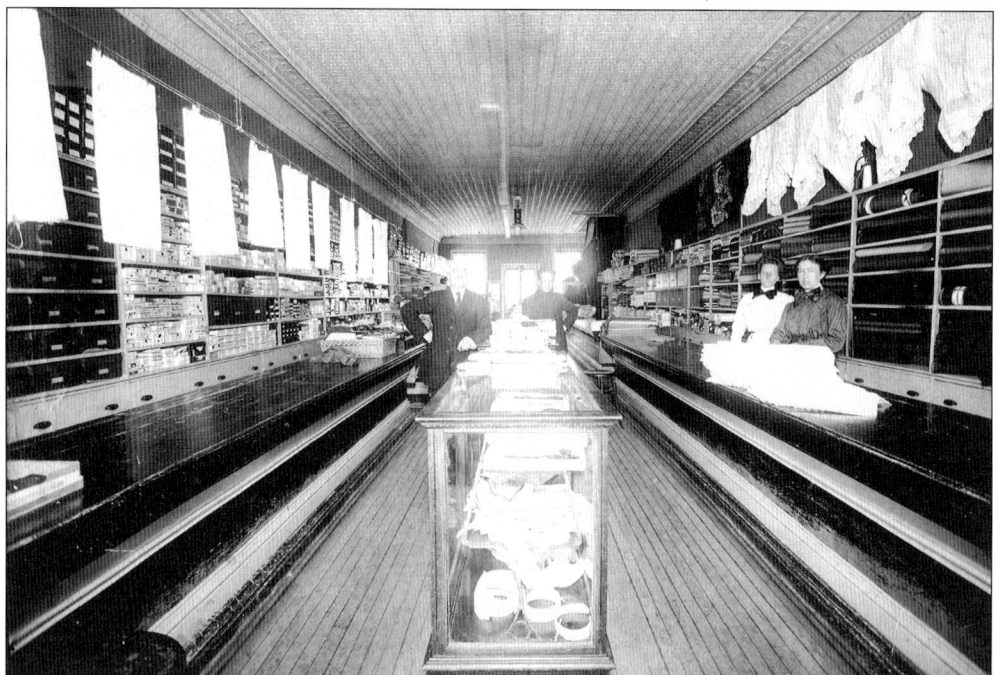

Austin's Dry Goods Store. Located on the north side of East Main Street in the early 1900s, pictured here, from left to right, are G. William Lewis (store manager), Harry Wheeler, Nellie O'Brien Peggs, and Alice M. Haley.

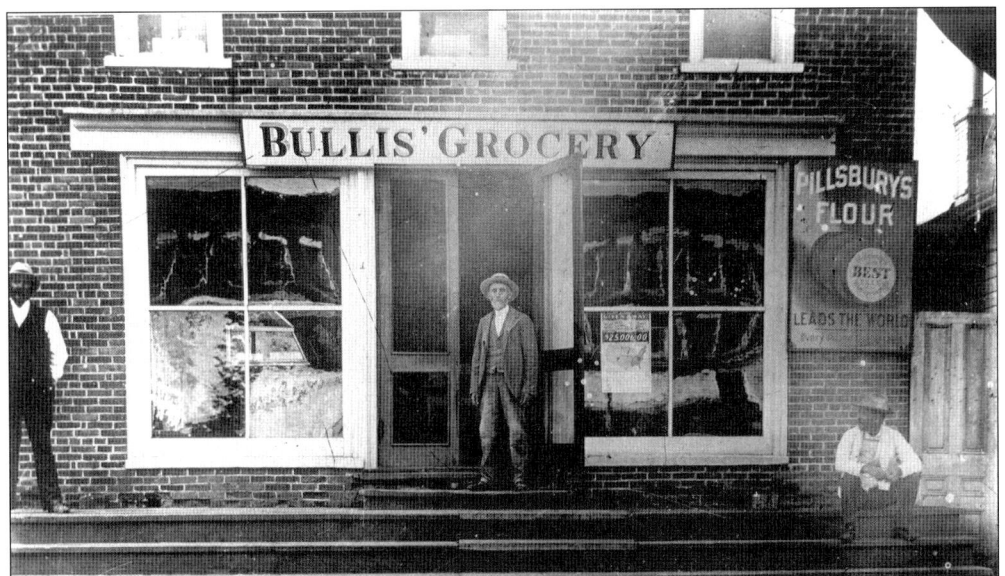

BULLIS GROCERY STORE. Located where Community Bank now stands, this storefront was a grocery store with a feed store in the rear. Henry Bullis was one of the founders of the First National Bank, which was also located on this site, and served as a director for 40 years. The second floor housed the commercial printing business of Vic Chaney.

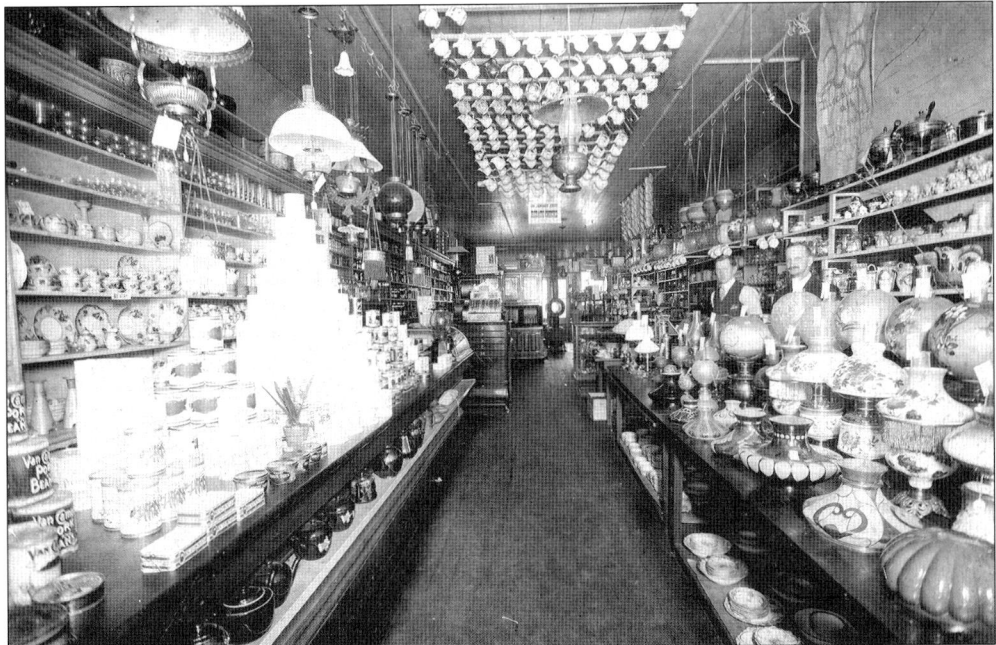

W. E. DUNN AND SON, C. 1910. Located on the north side of East Main Street, George W. Dunn, owner of this grocery and fine china store, is on the right with Roy H. Bassett (later secretary of Canton Savings and Loan) on the left. Subsequently this location was occupied by the Oneida Creamery Company and by the Reasoner television and radio business.

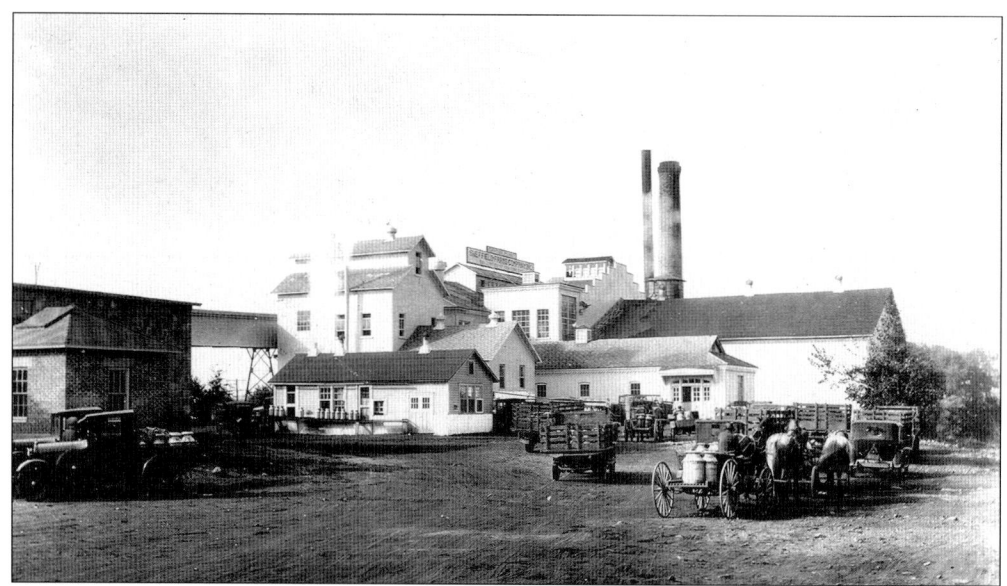

SHEFFIELD FARMS COMPANY, 1915–1920. The Canton Milk Plant first functioned as a fluid milk bottling plant supplying New York City. The Page Condensed Milk Company purchased the plant in 1914 and produced goods for the World War I over-seas markets. Purchased by Sheffield Condensed Milk Company, production soared to 600,000 pounds per day. Over the next 40 years the plant produced evaporated milk, sweet cream, and casein. Kraft Foods Division purchased the plant in 1951, converting it to American cheese production and storage. The plant continued operation until 2004.

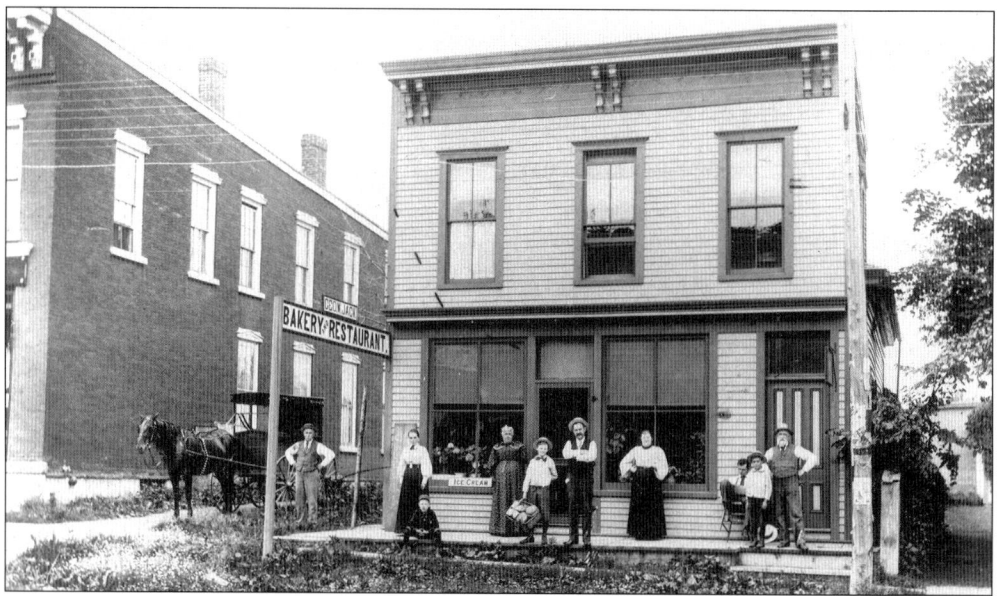

GEORGE W. JACK BAKERY AND RESTAURANT, C. 1915. The bakery and restaurant were located on the long-time site of Merrill Brothers Hardware, The Bicycle Post, and now Swirls. The building is one of the oldest and the only wooden building left on commercial Main Street. Jack also sold bakery goods around the village every afternoon from a cart; loaves of bread were 5¢ and coffee and donuts were 10¢.

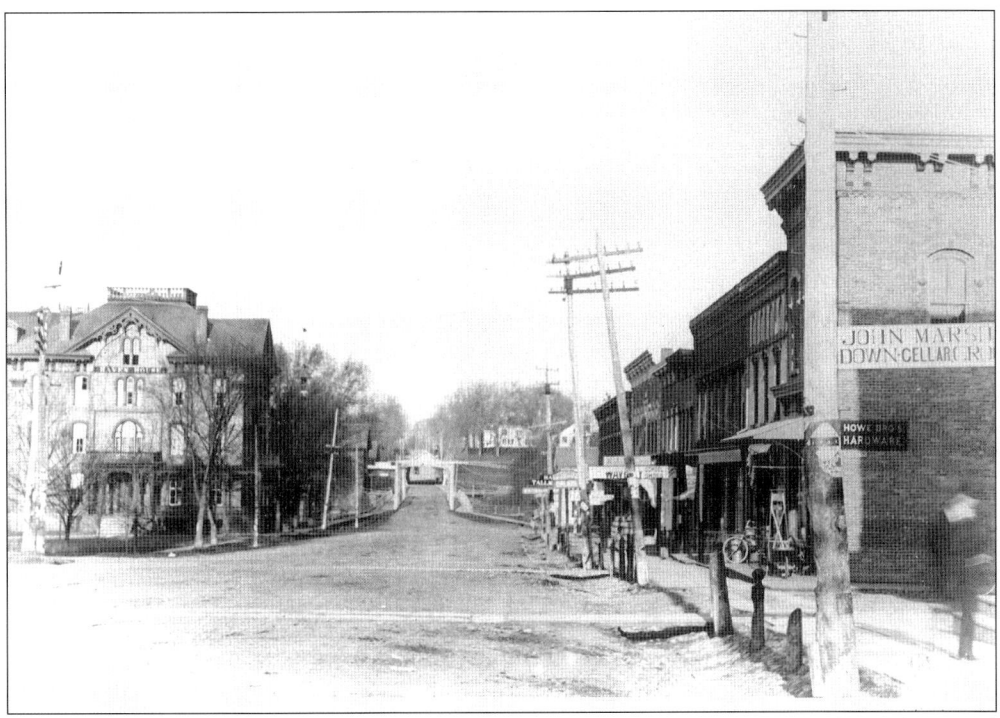

LOWER MAIN STREET LOOKING WEST, BEFORE 1919. The Haven House, later the Hotel Harrington, is shown on the left, with the covered bridge and the Stillman Foote House in the background. Howe Brothers Hardware is at the right on the site of Canton's first hardware store, which was owned by Deacon Sackrider. Rebuilt after the Great Fire of 1870, Howe Brothers purchased the store in the early 1890s and continued its operation for 29 years.

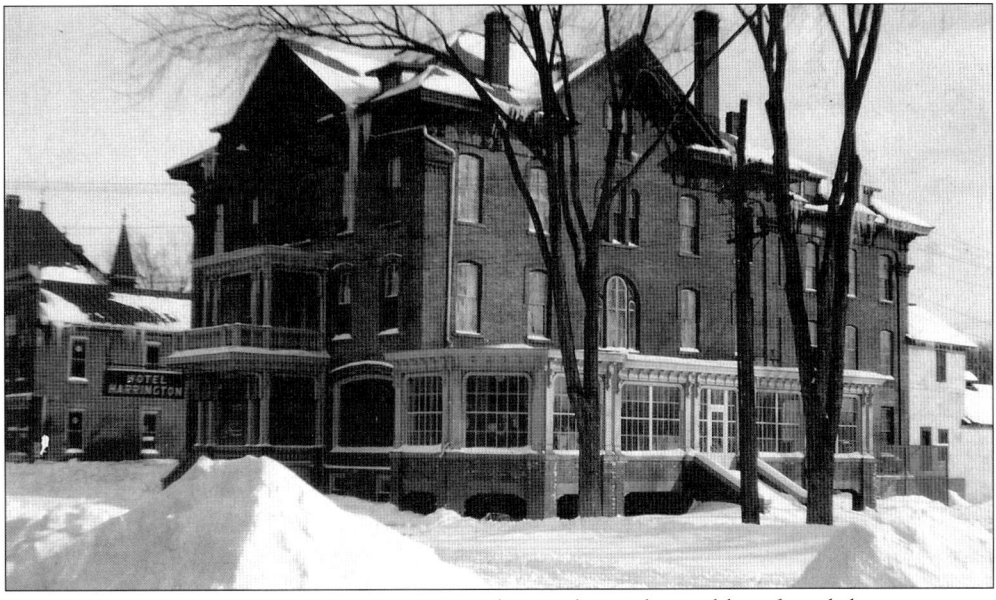

HOTEL HARRINGTON. It is easy to imagine reading in front of a crackling fire while anticipating an evening of fine dining, or looking at the winter wonderland from these beautiful windows of one of the most luxurious hotels in New York State. This was one way to be snow bound in style.

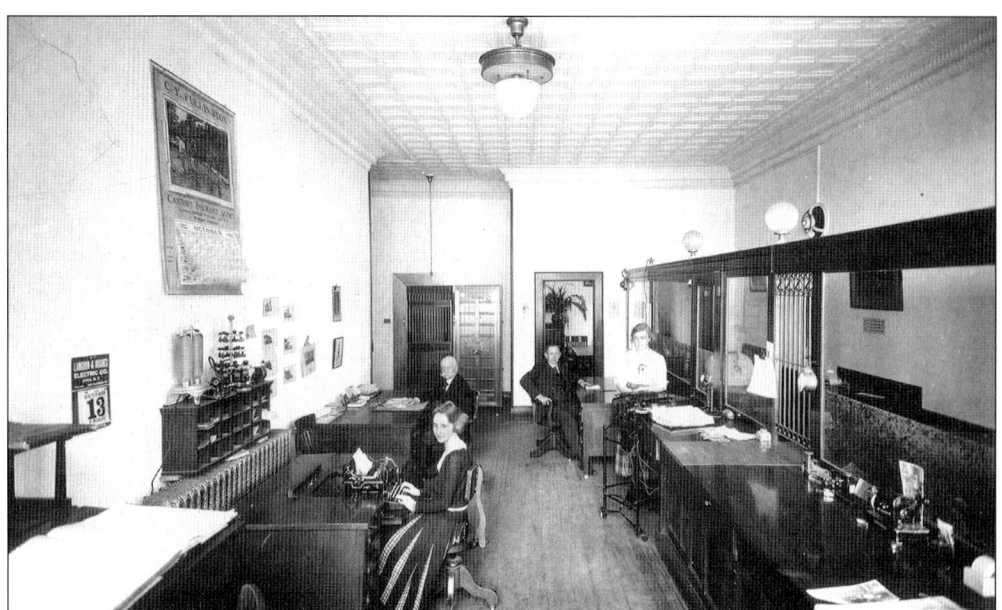

CANTON SAVINGS AND LOAN. Pictured from left to right are G. William Lewis, president; Myrtle Sullivan; Roy H. Bassett, secretary; and Fannie S. Bassett on October 13, 1922. In 1899, a little band of Canton citizens organized and established this institution. Motivated by that good old American tradition of thrift, they wanted to guard their savings intelligently to use the money for the up-building and betterment of the community as a whole. The bank is now known as North Country Savings at the same location.

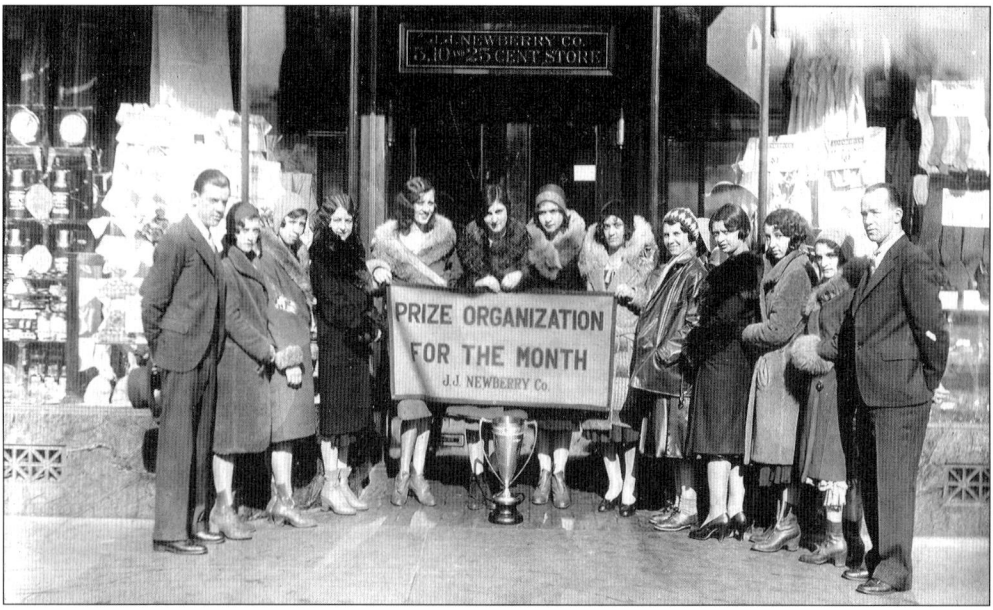

J. J. NEWBERRY 5-, 10-, AND 25-CENT STORE, ROARING TWENTIES. The employees of Newberrys Company received the Prize Organization for the Month award. Newberrys was established on Canton's Main Street in May 1931. Remembered fondly by many village children, Marion Lytle served the best ice-cream floats and sodas at the soda counter with its spinning chairs. The store closed in 1994 and is now the Home Front.

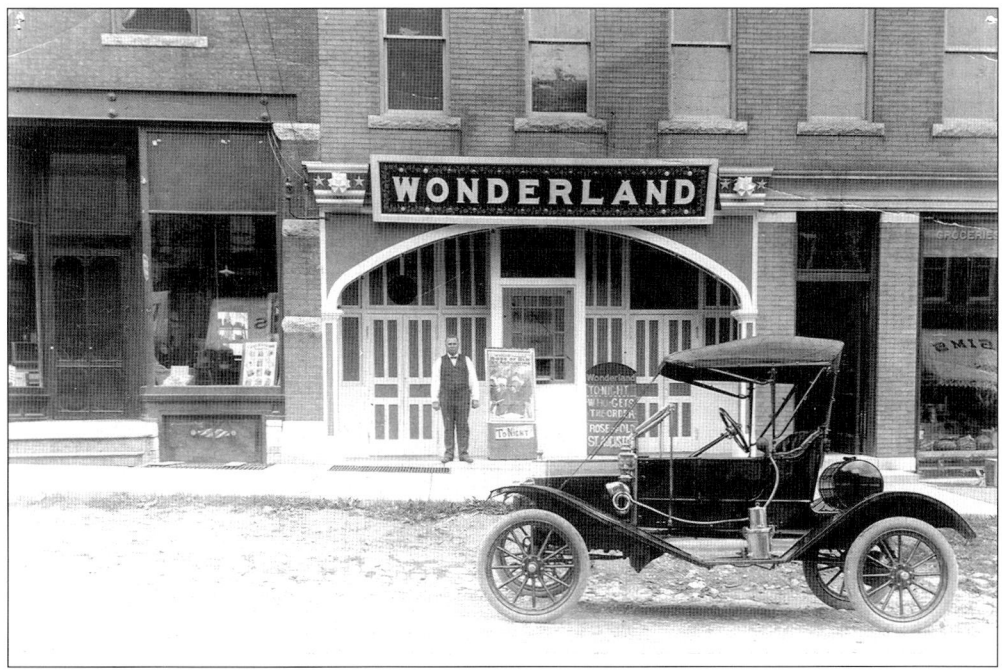

WONDERLAND THEATER, C. 1920. Close to the site of the present-day American Theater, the featured movie is *Rose of Old St. Augustine*, which was filmed in 1911. The man in front of the theater has been identified as Stan Southworth, and the car may be an 1895 Stanhope.

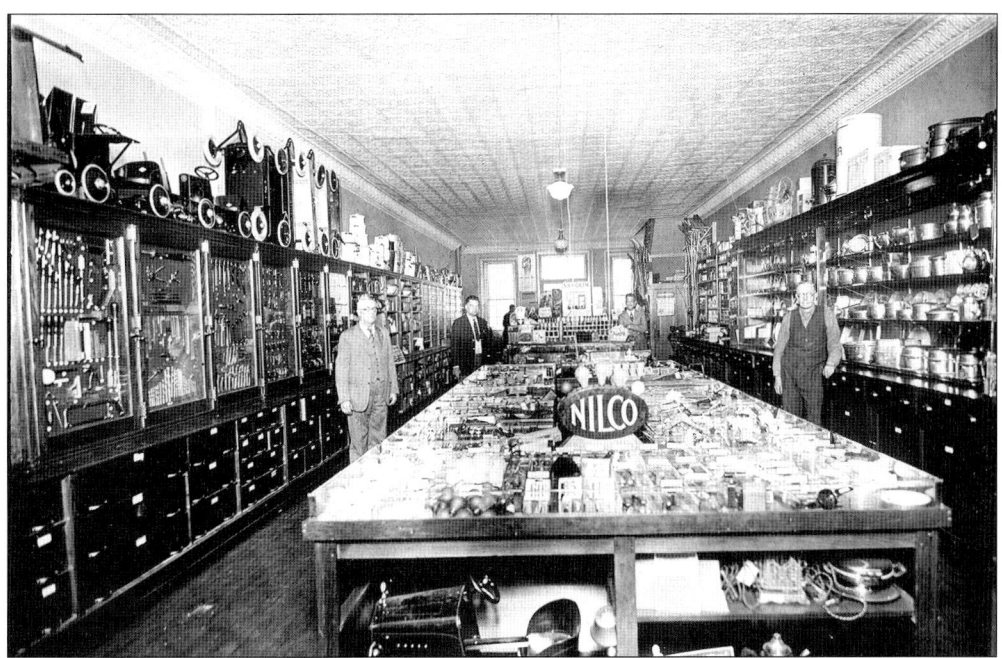

HOWE BROTHERS HARDWARE STORE, 1927. Shown in this photograph, standing left to right, are Floyd Pickerd (clerk), Mr. Calhoun (hardware sales clerk), Milford Howe and Charles P. Howe, (brothers and owners).

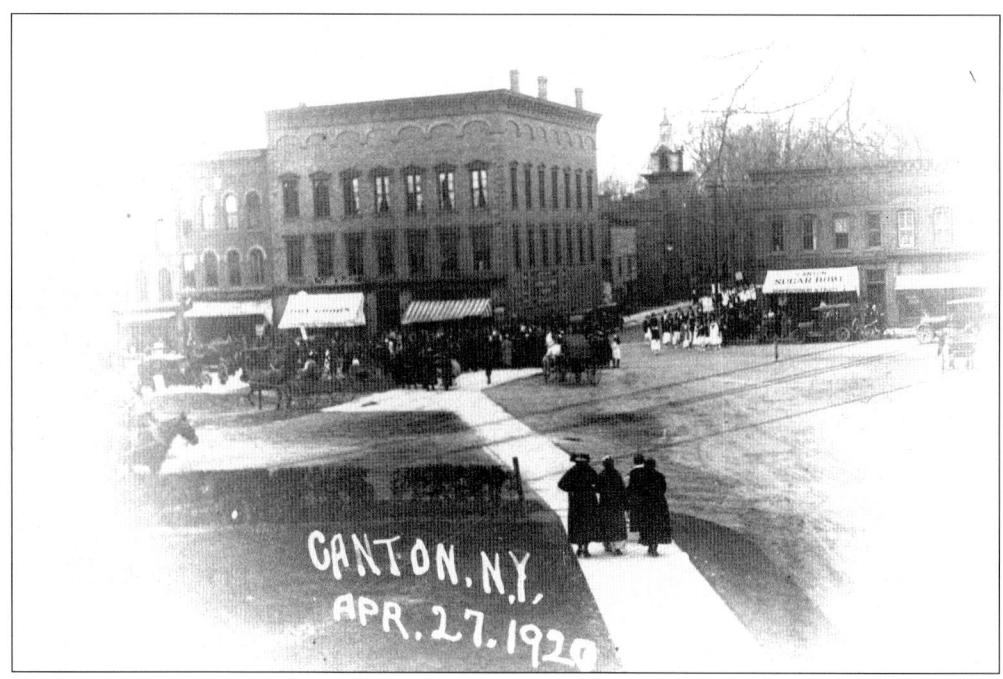

APRIL 27, 1920. A parade of graduates of Ogdensburg's first school of nursing approaches Main Street from Court Street.

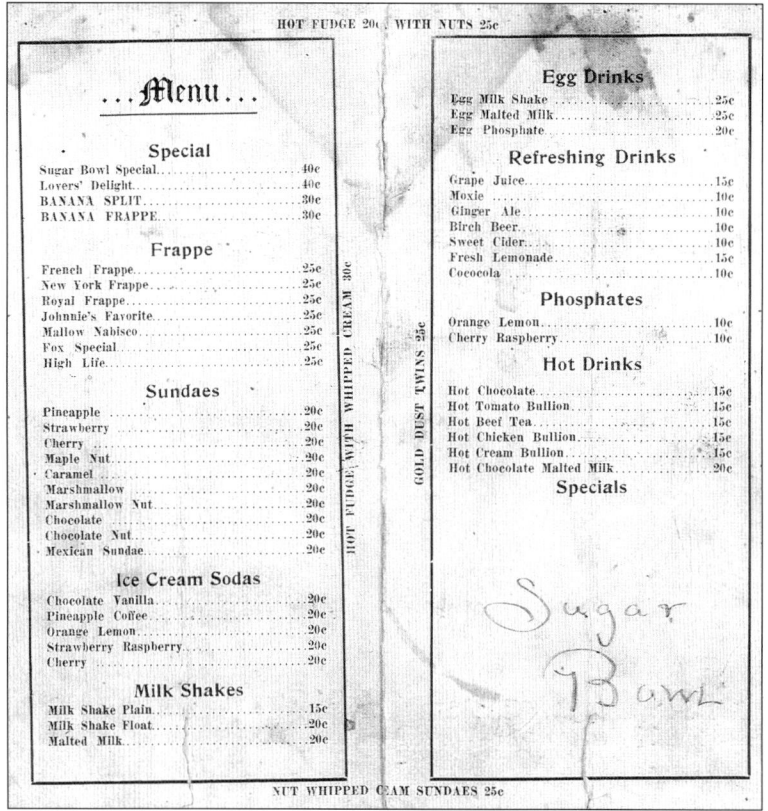

SUGAR BOWL MENU. Karl Keller provided this menu from the Sugar Bowl, a soda and confectioner's store at the corner of Main and Court Streets. Keller's mother kept it as a keepsake remembrance from the first date with her future husband. Imagine, milkshakes were 20¢, and sundaes were 25¢. Does "Refreshing Drinks" imply that "Egg Drinks" were not so refreshing?

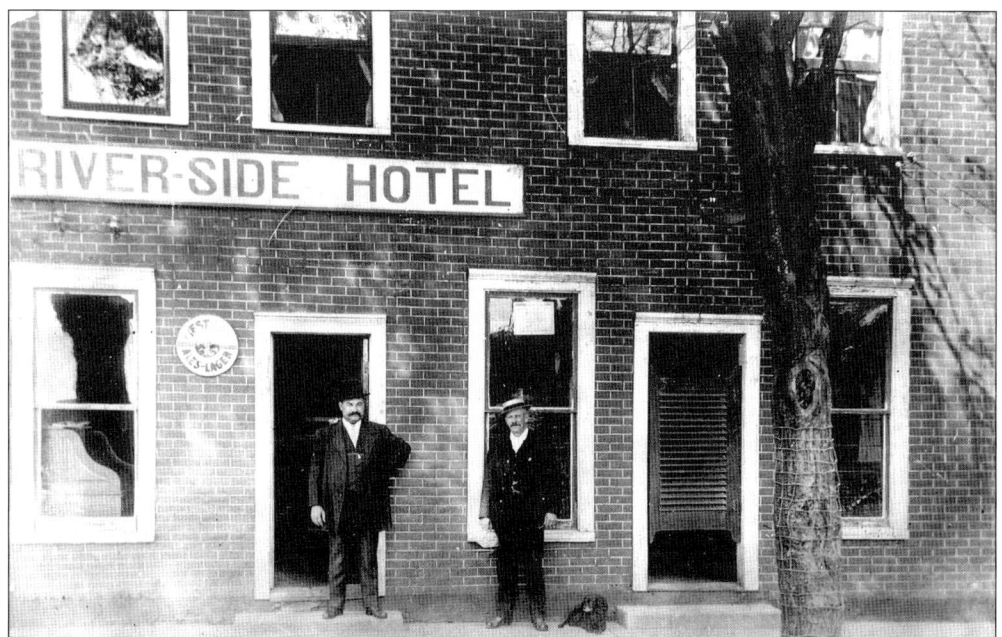

RIVERSIDE HOTEL. Located near the corner of Main and Water Streets, the hotel was owned in the 1920s by Fred Narrows and was reported to be one of many small brothels in the days of Prohibition. In the doorway stands William "Humpy" Womach, an "exceptionally fine mason" who did much of the stonework in the village.

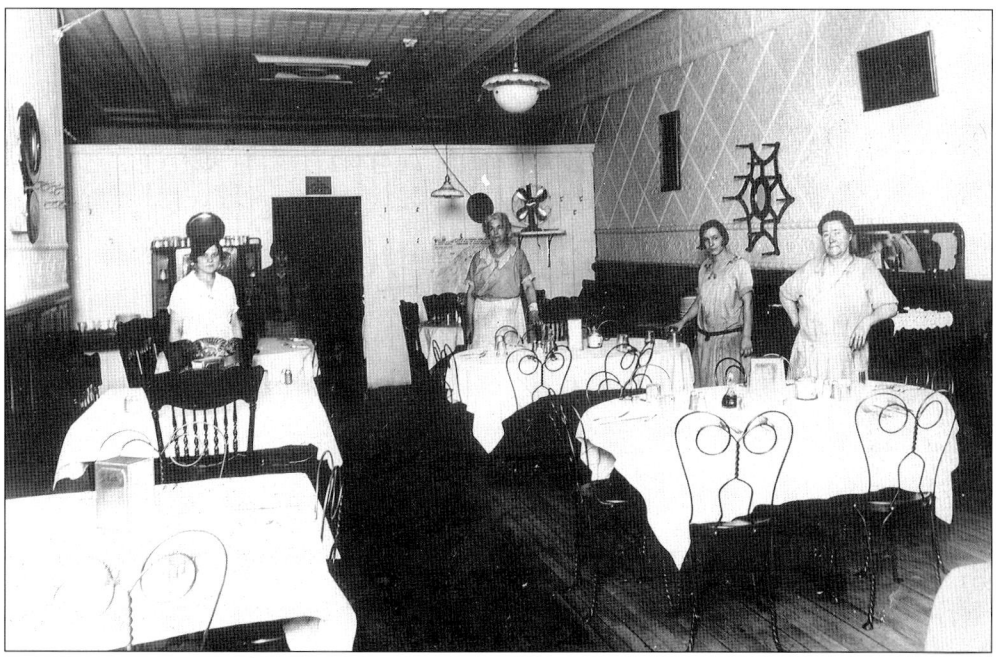

CLUB RESTAURANT. This restaurant was located at 17 Main Street (north side) in the 1930s. From left to right are Helen Collins, an unidentified St. Lawrence University student employee, Lib Ayers (owner), Jennie Carney, and Kit McLaughlin (owner).

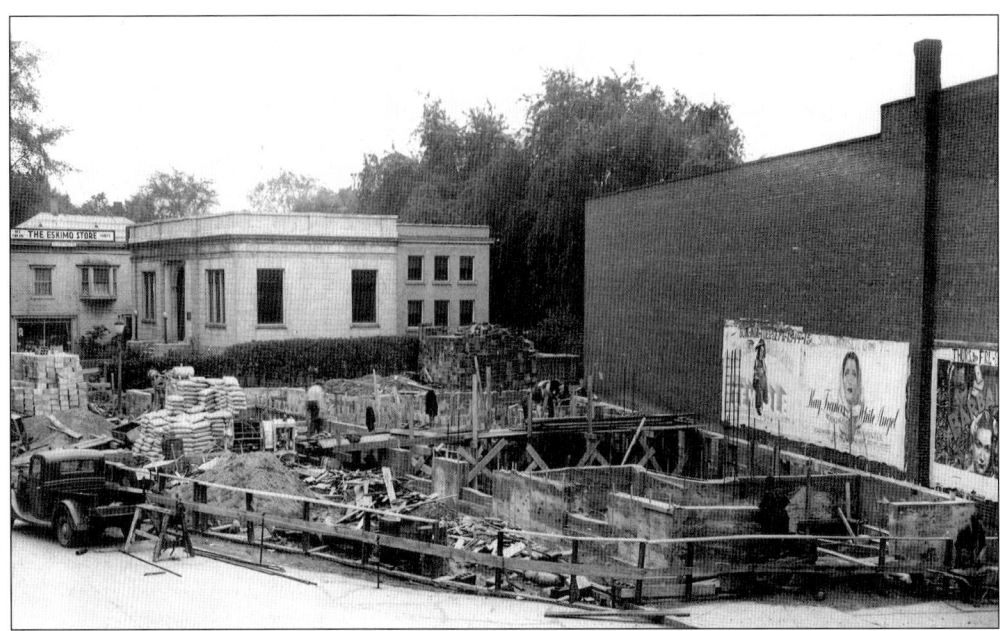

SEPTEMBER 1936. Pictured here is an early construction phase of the post office on the site of American House Hotel with the library and "The Eskimo" in the background. Postmistress Grace Sullivan placed several items in a metal box in the building's cornerstone: ceremonial invitations, stories of local papers reporting construction activities, construction pictures taken by Kip, historic photographs, and copies of the addresses delivered at the ceremony.

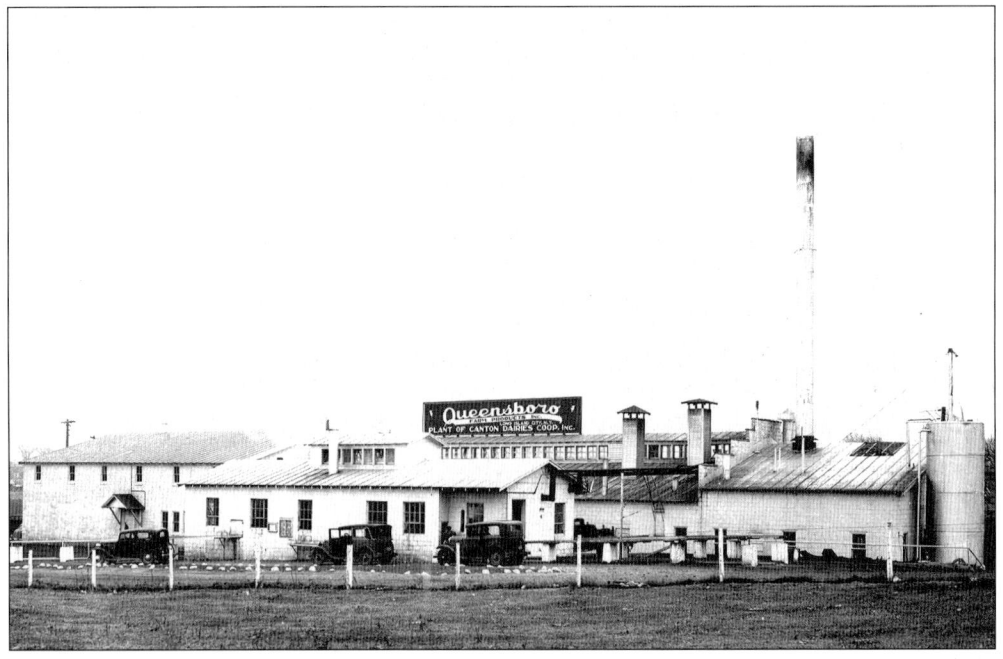

QUEENSBORO DAIRY COOPERATIVE. The Queensboro milk plant was built in 1938 to help St. Lawrence County dairy farmers market their milk for a fair price. This cooperative had over 300 patrons from local farms as well as those from Waddington, Stockholm, Edwards, and Brier Hill. The plant was sold in 1970 to Mace Motors, where Frank Mace stored his antique cars.

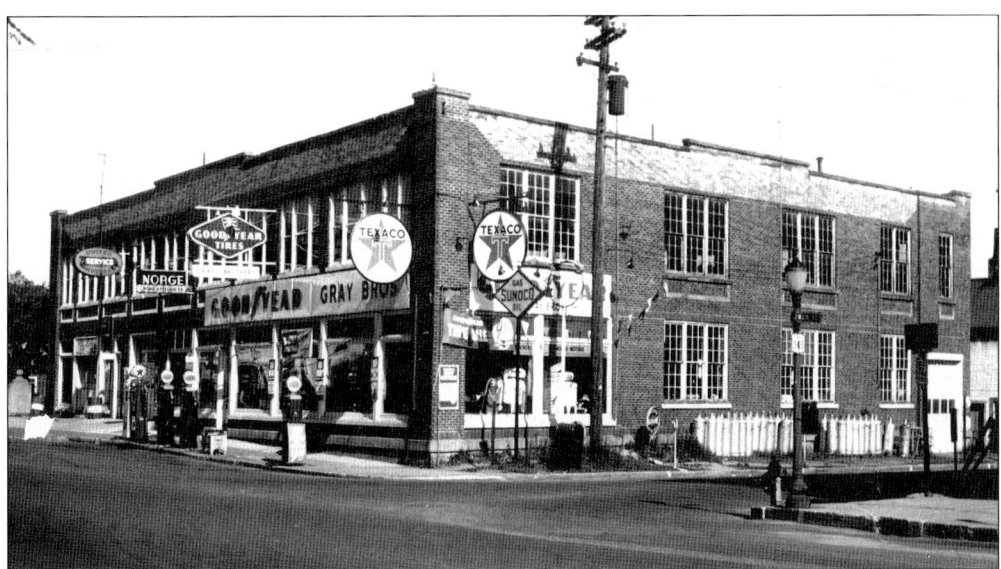

GRAY'S GARAGE, C. 1950. Roy Gray came to Canton in 1918 as a telegrapher and worked in the blacksmith shop owned by Darius Sullivan in 1928. He learned to vulcanize tires while working in the Water Street tire and battery shop owned by Norman McMasters. Forming a partnership with "Shorty" Powell, they also sold gasoline and repaired autos. The business became Gray Brothers when Roy's brother joined him. In 1942, they bought the Sullivan garage and expanded, renting frozen food lockers. As garages became more plentiful, the business became Gray Bowling Lanes.

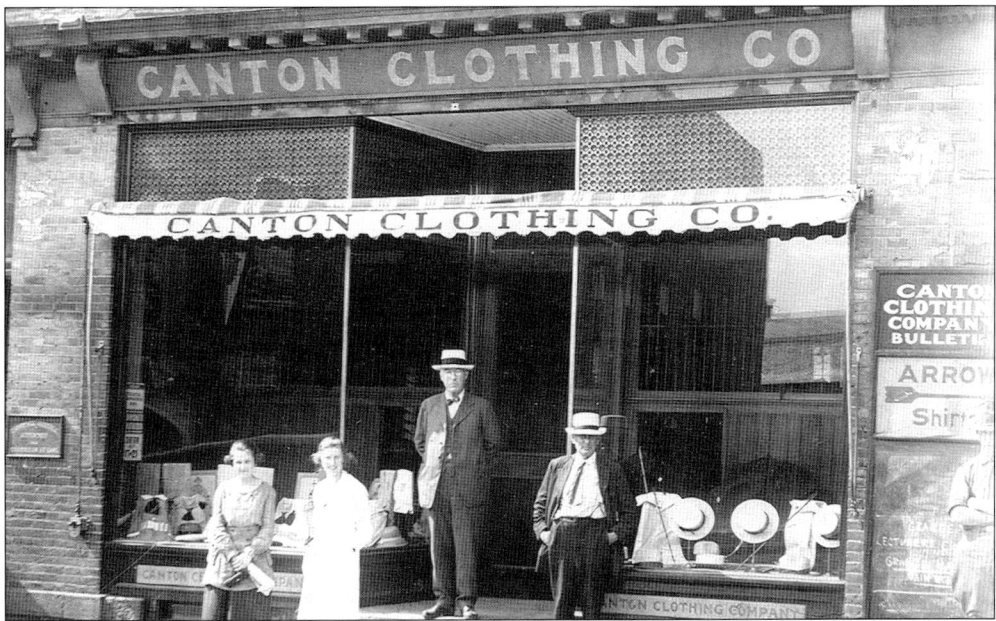

CANTON CLOTHING COMPANY. This store was located in the Miner Block at the corner of Main and Court Streets. From the early 1870s through 1960, the ground floor location continuously housed clothing stores. First was the Ellsworth and Wilson clothing store (1872), the Remington clothing store (c. 1894), the Canton Clothing Company (c. 1907), the Storrs Clothing Company (c. 1922) and Pearl's Department Store (1950).

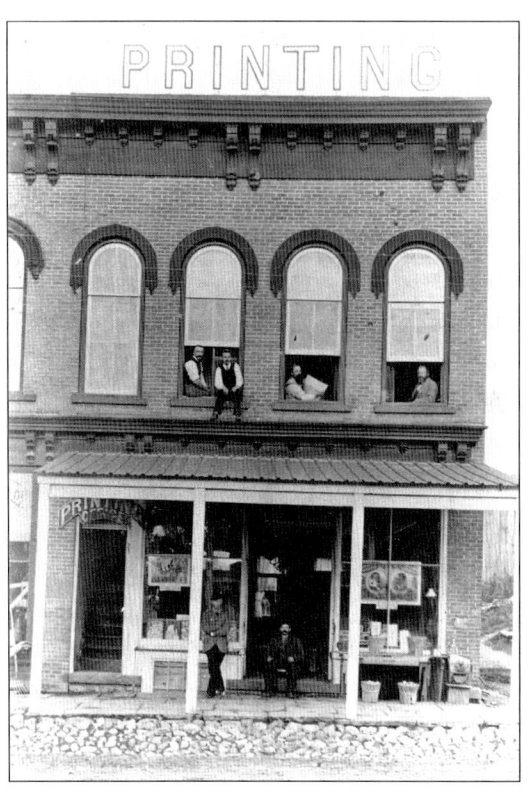

ST. LAWRENCE PLAINDEALER, THREE GENERATIONS OF MANLEYS. Seth Pierre Remington (Frederic Remington's father) and William B. Goodrich established the *St. Lawrence Plaindealer* in 1855. In 1873, George T. Manley, printing supervisor, purchased the paper with his nephew Gilbert Manley, the publisher-editor. Two subsequent generations of Manley editors appear in this early 1900s photograph including George's son Williston and grandson Gilbert Atwood Manley. Later owners include Mason Rossiter Smith, Mr. Garberson, Mr. and Mrs. Ralph Heinzen, Franklin R. Little, and the Northern New York Publishing Company.

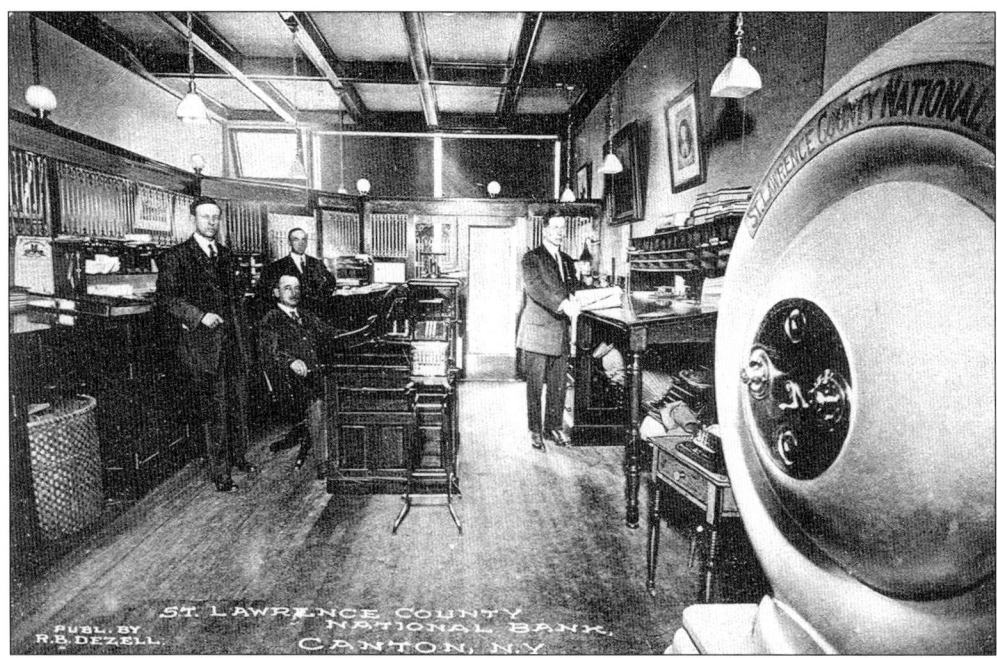

ST. LAWRENCE COUNTY NATIONAL BANK, C. 1944. This photograph shows the vault keeping Canton and St. Lawrence County's deposits safe. Community Bank currently owns this building as office space and files storage.

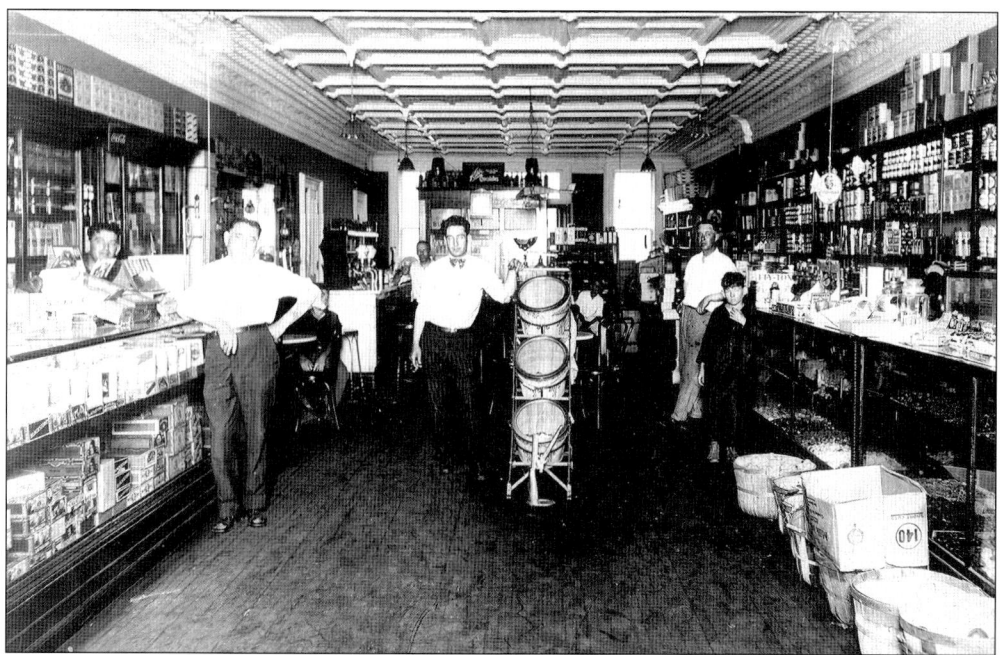

THOMAS INFANTINE'S GENERAL STORE AND GROCERIES. At 21 Main Street (north side, now Nature's Storehouse), this general store served as a grocery store and soda fountain. The store sold candies, fruits, and fresh roasted nuts. Pictured leaning against the left counter is owner and father Thomas Infantine, with son William in the middle. (Courtesy of Marilyn Mintener.)

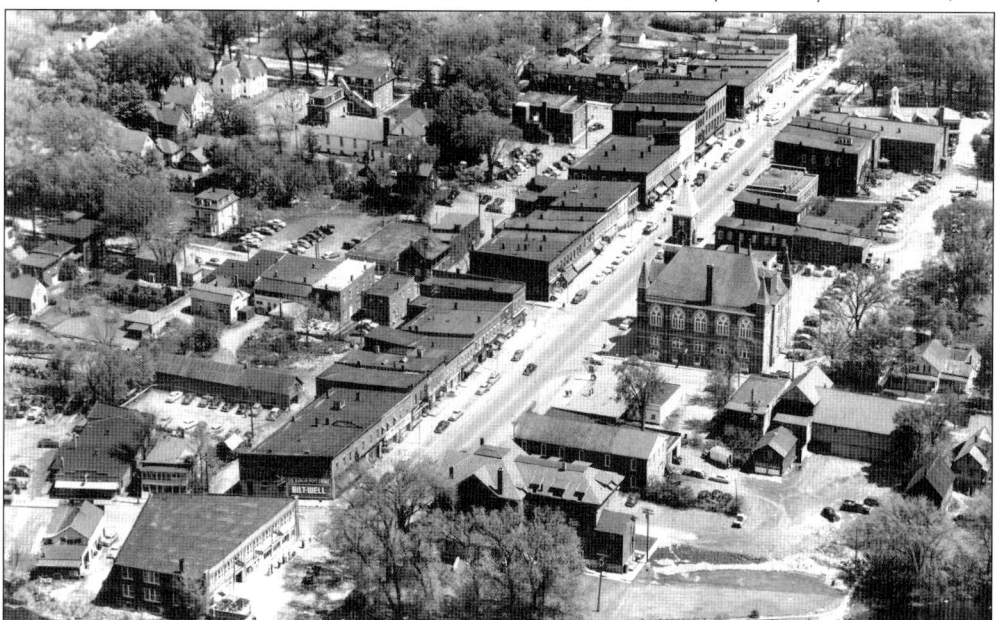

AERIAL MAIN STREET. This 1950s photograph, which looks north and eastward through the village, was snapped by Dwight P. Church, Canton's renowned aerial photographer. Today, sadly, much of Main Street's south side has disappeared. Gone are the Hotel Harrington, the town hall, Dawley's Garage, the Canton Diner, and Billy's Restaurant. Interestingly, with the exception of Gray Brothers Garage, much of the north side of Main Street remains unchanged.

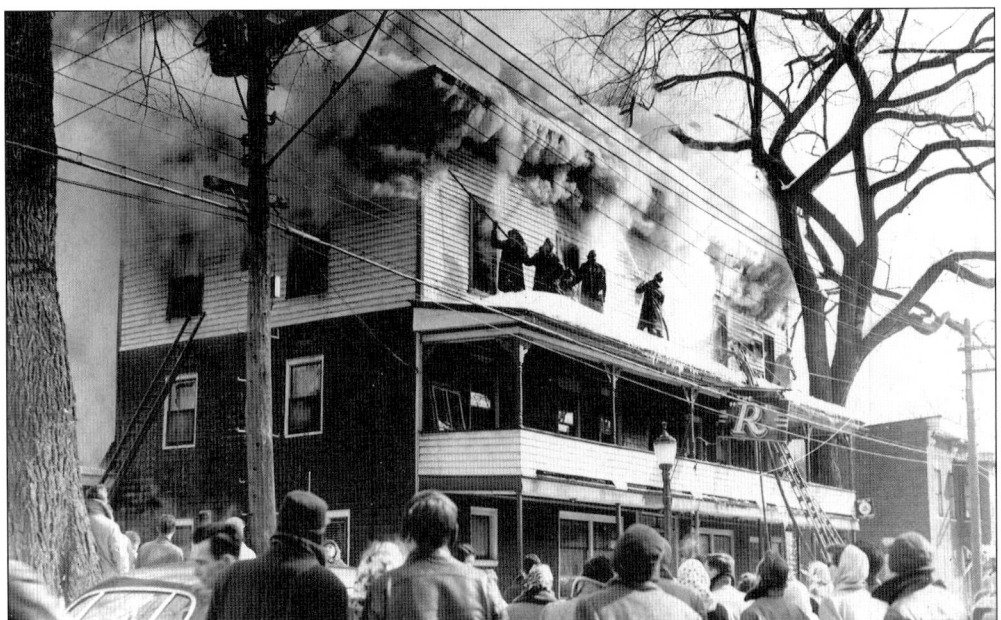

HOTEL "R" FIRE, MARCH 1950. The origins of this hotel can be traced to the mid-1800s. Dr. Elijah Baker built the structure as his home, then transformed it into a boarding house. It eventually became a hotel where the first twins in Canton were born. Purchased by several owners throughout its 150 years, it was known as the Stevens House, Commercial House, Erwin House, and the Hotel "R" for Hotel Russet, Canton. The hotel eventually became the St. Lawrence Inn. Having been torn down recently, the land is now owned by North Country Savings Bank and will become an office building and drive-through banking facility.

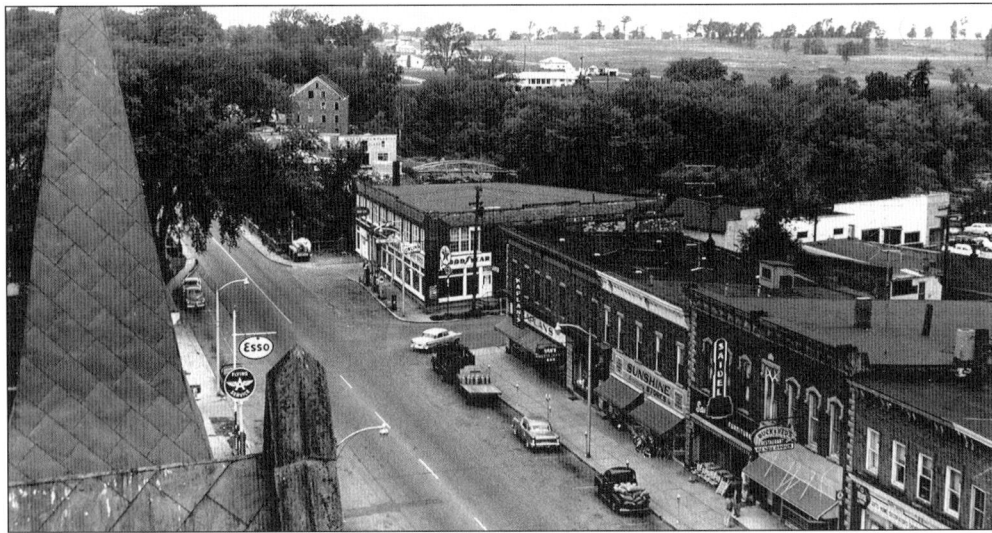

NORTH SIDE OF MAIN STREET, MID-1950S. From left at Riverside Drive and Main Streets are Gray Brothers Garage and Gray Bowling Lanes and Kaplan's Clothing Department Store. Proceeding to the right are Van's, Sunshine Hardware Stores, Saidel's Furniture, Buck and Red's Rendezvous, a gift and home decorator shop, and the A&P store before it moved to the Hotel Harrington site. The abandoned mill building in the background is the Eagle Mill. Built in 1845, it stood for 110 years until it was torn down to make way for The Cascade Inn.

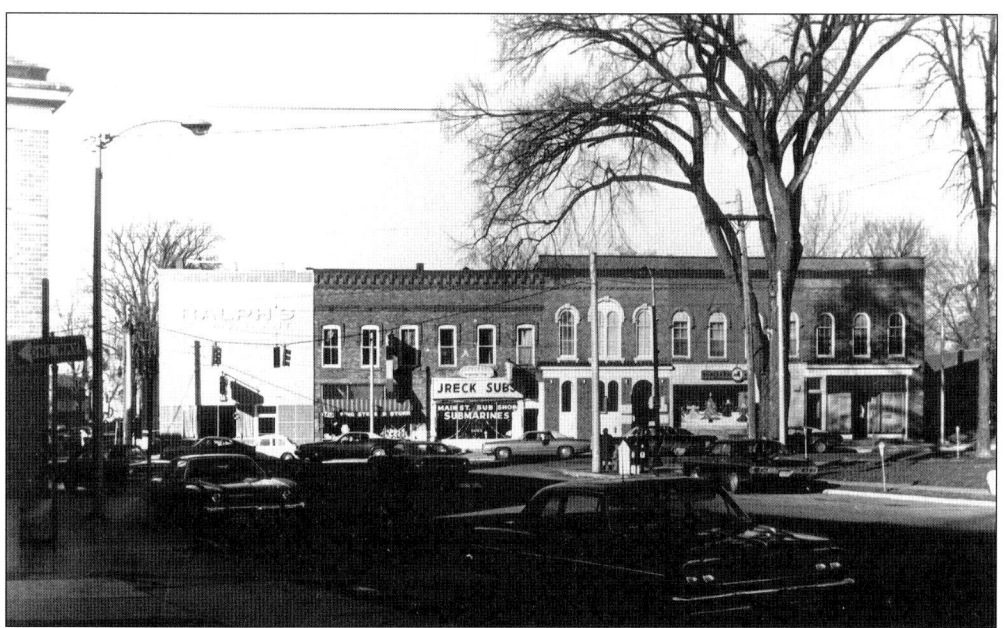

MAIN STREET BUSINESSES, MID-1960S. From left to right in this photograph is Ralph's Restaurant, the Bing Stevens Store, Jreck Subs, Oliver Law Firm, Niagara Mohawk, John Hardy optometrist, and the Canton Savings and Loan. Ralph's brilliant blue and orange storefront left a legacy for Canton's historic preservationists and business community—a legacy left to interpretation.

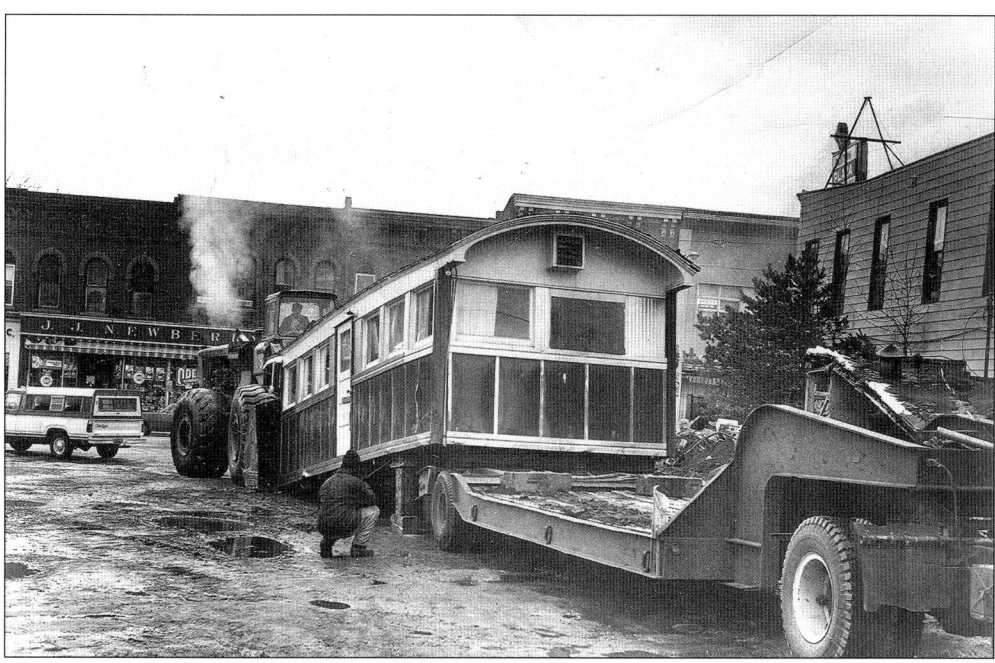

CANTON DINER. October 5, 1977, was the end of the line for the Canton Diner, which was located on the site of the present McDonald's. Paul Stiles of Rensselaer Falls, who had plans to relocate it to Morristown, purchased the diner. It is believed that he did not carry out those plans.

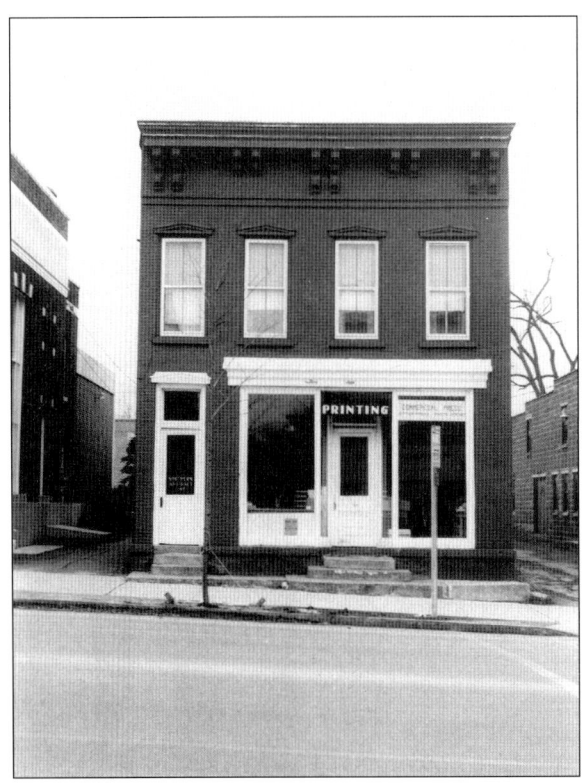

COMMERCIAL ADVERTISER, COMMERCIAL PRESS. In 1919, John A. Finnigan, famous Spanish American War reporter, Finnigan editor and author of the weekly column "Looking Through a Main Street Window," relocated the *Commercial Advertiser* newspaper to this building from its previous location on Hodskin Street. Tracy and David Charleson bought Commercial Press from Denzil Bowman, and occupied the building from February 20, 1990, until it moved to Cowen Road in 1999. Hair Designs now occupies this space.

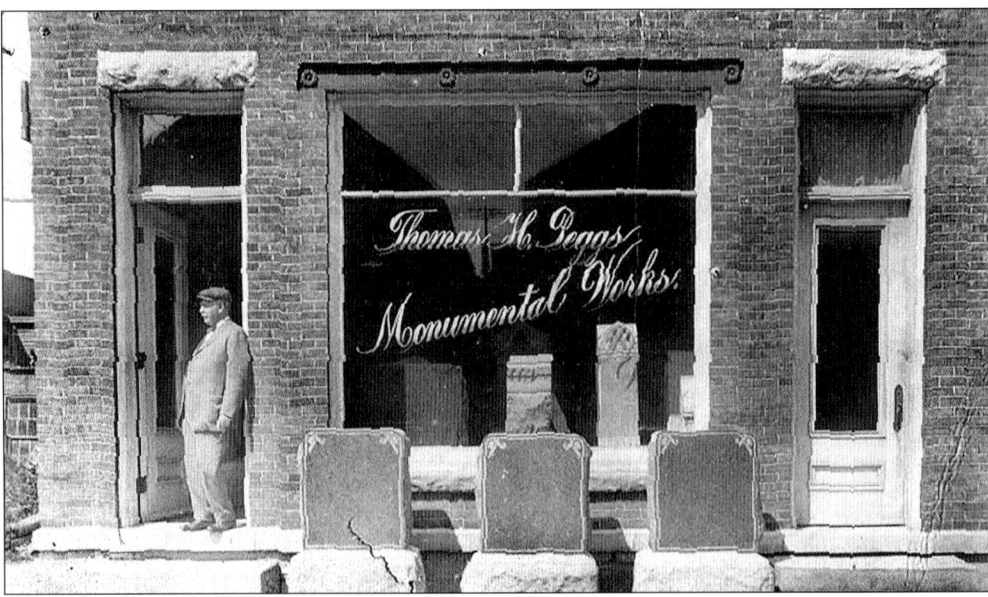

WITHERBEE AND WHALEN. Loyal Eldredge started this monument business on Court Street on the former fire station site. After Eldredge's death in 1915, the business was conducted under the name of Eldredge and Richardson until they sold it to George Martin, a long-time employee. Martin sold the business to another local monument firm, Witherbee and Whalen who moved it to their headquarters on Hodskin Street. Two other trusted and long-time Witherbee and Whalen employees were Henry Basilier and Julian Earl.

Five
HOUSES OF WORSHIP

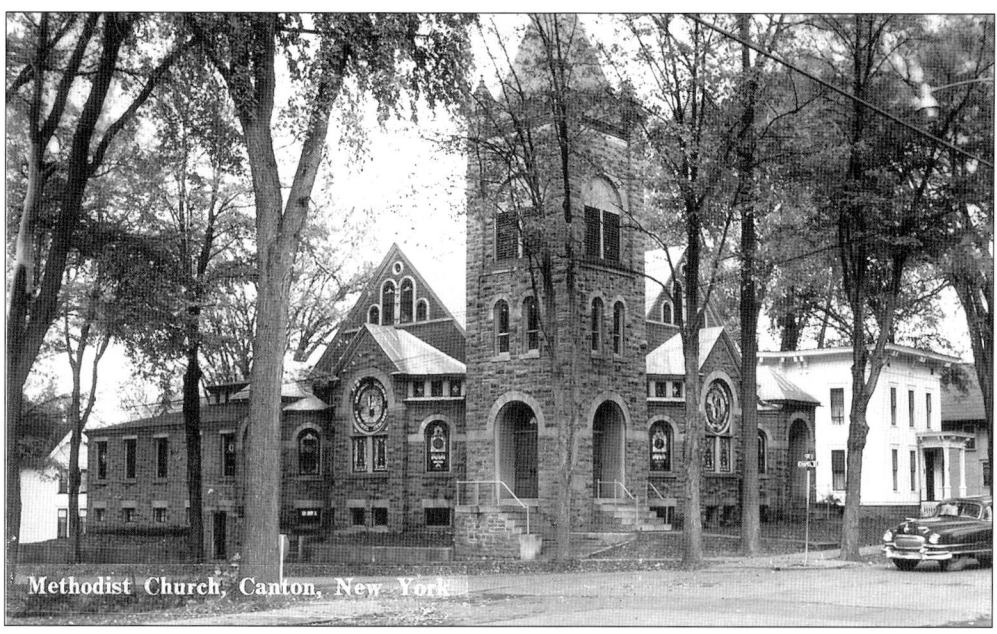

FIRST METHODIST CHURCH. Founded in 1819, meetings of the Methodist Religious Society were held in country schools. Built in 1823 in South Canton, now known as Brick Chapel, Canton's first Methodist church was turned over to the Presbyterians. A second Methodist Society was established in 1827, and in 1828 a wooden church was built at Chapel and Court Streets on a lot purchased from David C. Judson.

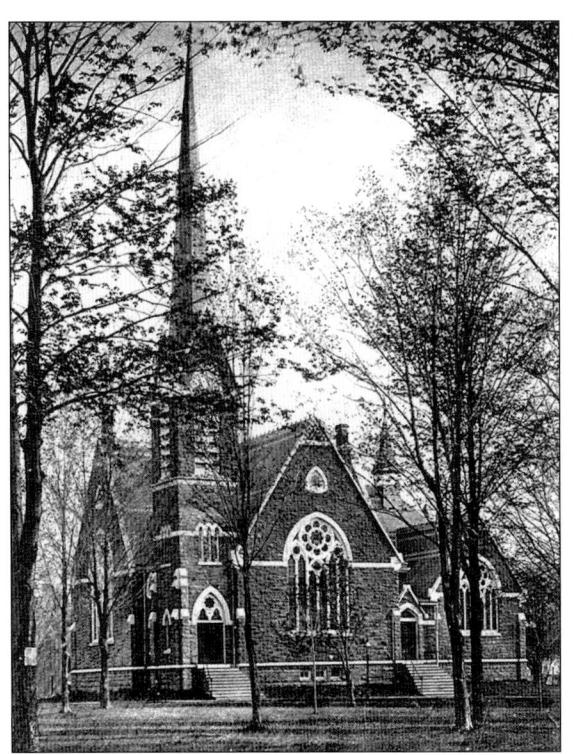

FIRST PRESBYTERIAN CHURCH. Founded as a congregational religious society in 1807, this church will celebrate its bicentennial in 2007. With a state-granted charter in 1821, the congregation became Presbyterian. In 1827, Silas Wright Jr. and Joseph Barnes donated land, a large portion of which became the Village Park and an adjacent plot for the church. A beautiful stone church was completed in 1830. The corner stone of that church is inlaid in the wall of the west vestibule of the present structure. A larger structure was completed in 1880, and in 1906, a new manse was built and remains in place today.

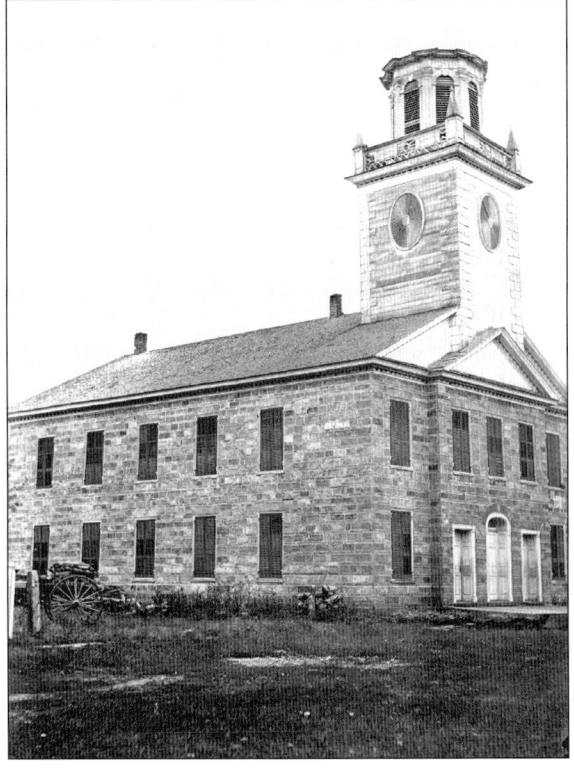

SEVENTH-DAY ADVENTIST CHURCH. First organized in 1914 as a Sabbath school, the Seventh-day Adventist congregation met on East Main Street until 1943. At that time, the Storrs' home on Court Street was purchased and converted into a church and manse. A new church was built on the same site and dedicated in 1967.

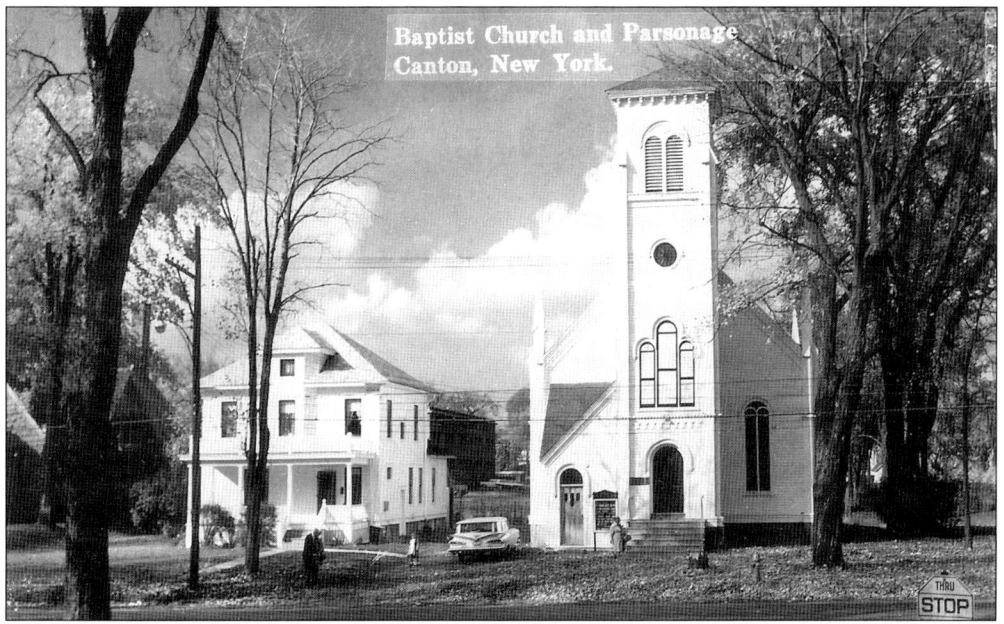

FIRST BAPTIST CHURCH. Established in 1823, the Baptist Evangelical Society agreed to build a brick church jointly with the Universalist Society. The two groups worshipped in the same church for 10 years until 1837 when the Baptist group built its own church on an adjacent lot. Two wooden structures preceded the present church, which was completed in 1871.

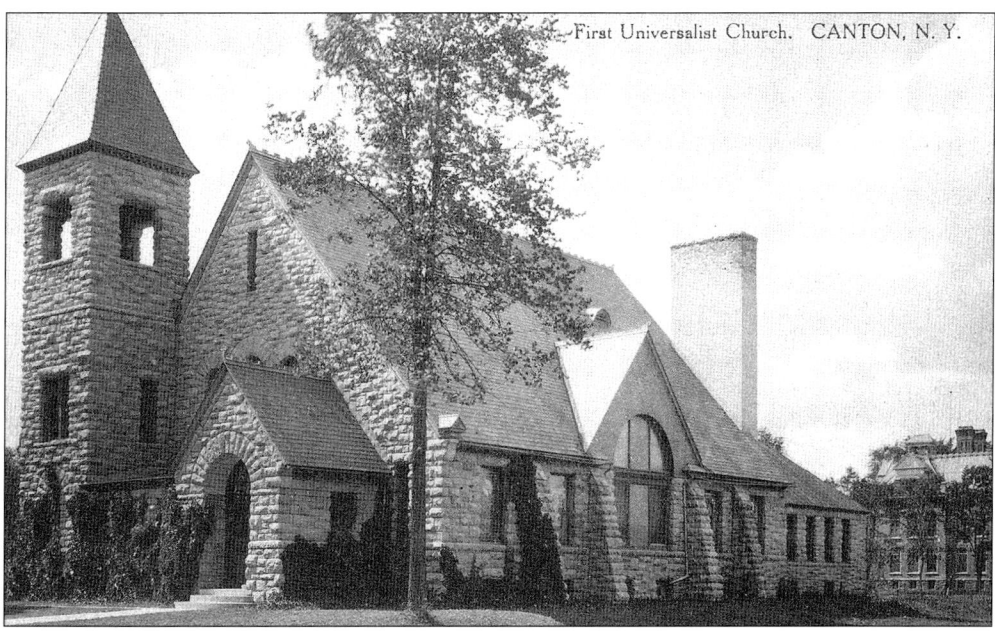

UNITARIAN UNIVERSALIST CHURCH. Formed by a circuit-riding New England missionary, the Unitarian Universalist Society built its first church in 1827 cooperatively with the Baptists. The two groups worshipped in the Union Church for 10 years until the Universalists bought out the Baptist Church, which built its own church next door. Universalist services were held at the Brick Church until 1896. This beautiful marble church was dedicated in 1897.

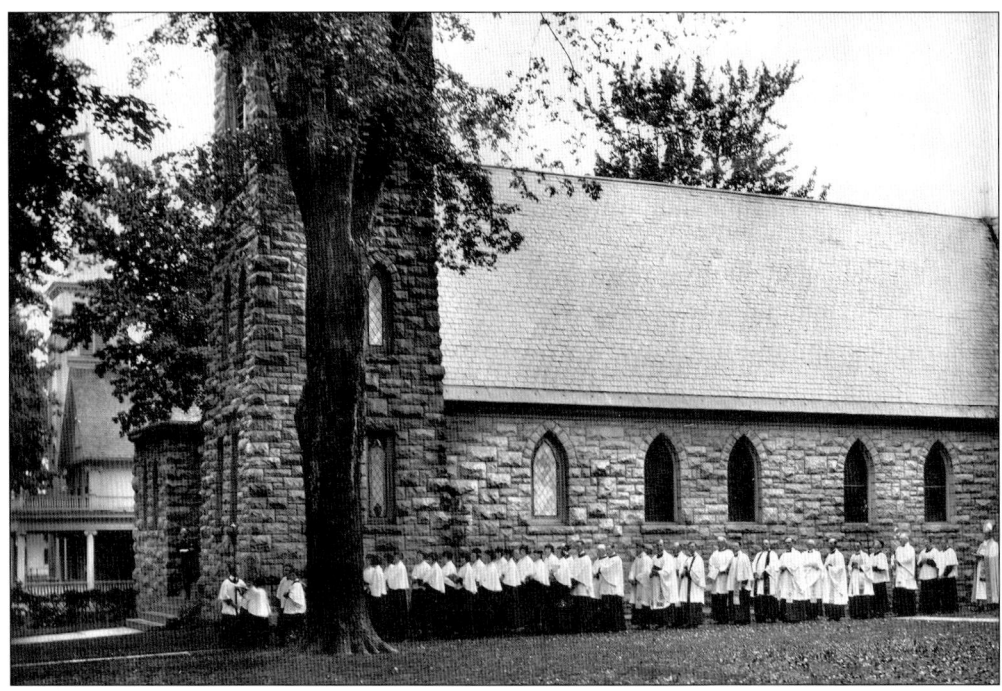

Episcopal Church. In 1836, several distinguished Canton settlers, including Richard Harison, Darius Clark, Harry Foote, and Henry Van Rensselaer, formed the Episcopal Religious Society. The wooden chapel, built in 1841, was later torn down and replaced with the present structure in 1903.

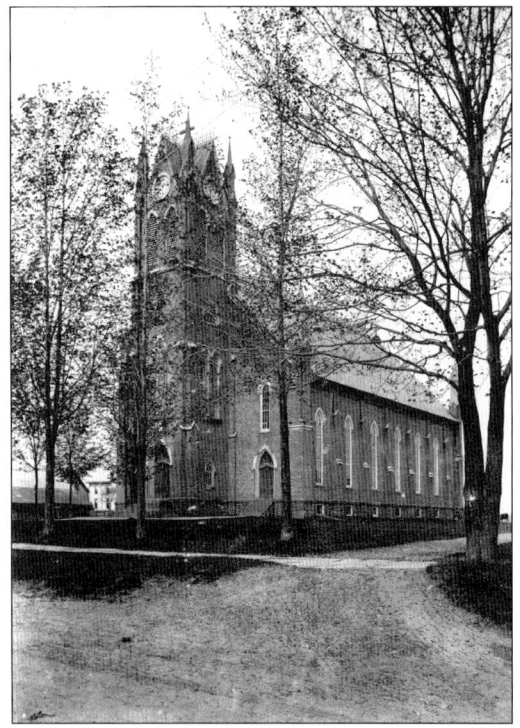

St. Mary's Catholic Church. Canton's first Roman Catholic Society, comprised of Irish immigrants, held mass in a log cabin on the Irish Settlement Road. The original, small-framed church was built in 1853 on the present site of St. Mary's on Court Street, but it burned in 1873. The magnificent St. Mary's Catholic Church of today was built in 1875. Originally, St. Mary's School was located where the Newman Center stands; the present school building was built in 1958.

Six
PUBLIC BUILDINGS

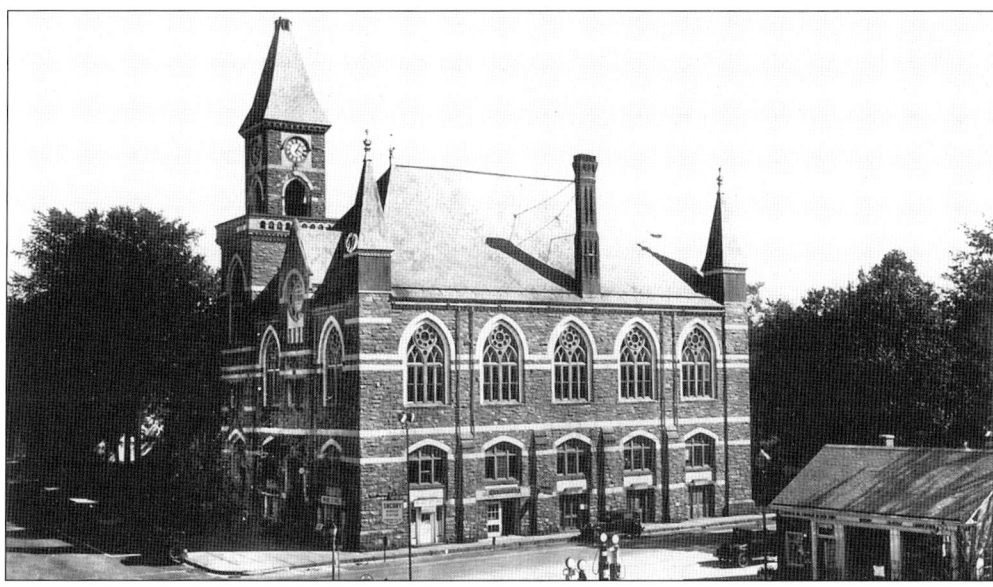

CANTON'S TOWN HALL AND OPERA THEATER. This amazing structure was built in 1877 and 1878 and cost $20,500. It housed local government offices, the post office, Canton Savings and Loan, Mountain Home Telephone Company, and library reading rooms. A few businesses were located on the ground floor including Mr. Downey's Barbershop, a book and stationery shop, dress shop, newsstand, and grocery store. Spirited town meetings and caucuses were held in the Opera House. High school and St. Lawrence University students graduated on the grand stage. During County fair days, Maude Hillman's Theater Company presented plays to a full house of 1,200. Once a year, Gorton's and DeRue Brothers minstrels and the local Merry Monarchs performed on the Opera stage. In the 1860s a group of St. Lawrence students, faculty, and community members marched to the town hall to raise funds for the university. Charles Kelsey Gains, who wrote words and music for the university's alma mater, led the march. $3,500 was raised and the university was saved.

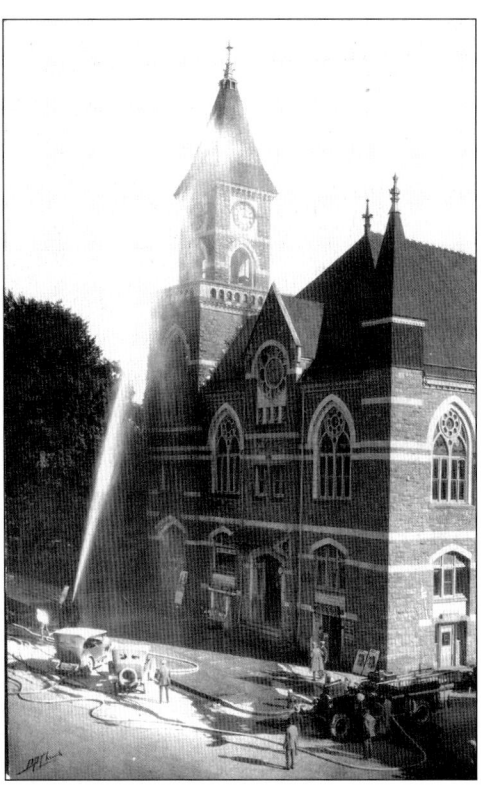

WASHING THE TOWN HALL. The fire department was not rescuing the town hall in this photograph. They were testing their first motor fire pumper, known as "The Old Steward" at the time of delivery in 1923. The men and cars seem small in comparison to the size of the Grand Old Operata Theater and town hall.

TOWN HALL FIRE. The headlines read, "Town Hall and Opera Theater Were Canton's Life." On February 2, 1962, the temperature was minus 20 degrees. As the fire roared, icicles were seen everywhere, covering the building and the courageous firemen. As the tower clock began to toll at 7:00 a.m. on that frigid morning, the clock started to fall with the time still chiming. The bell was salvaged and is on display on the Miner Street side of the new Municipal Building.

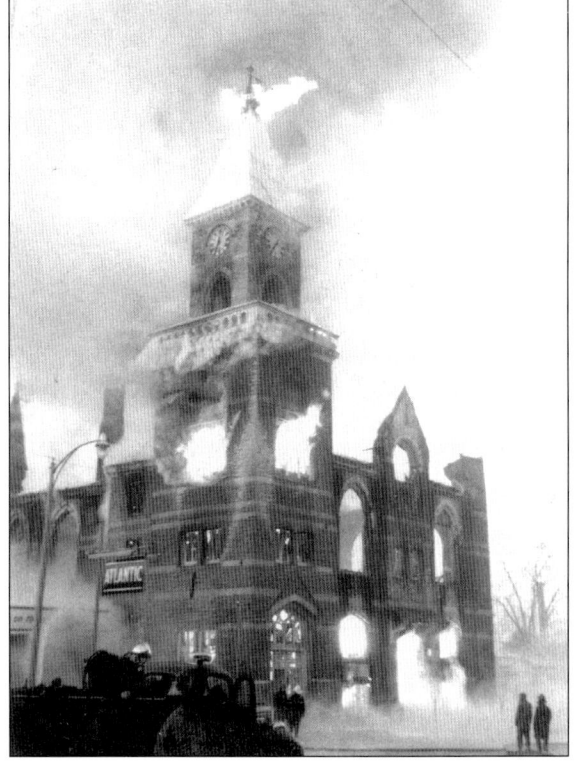

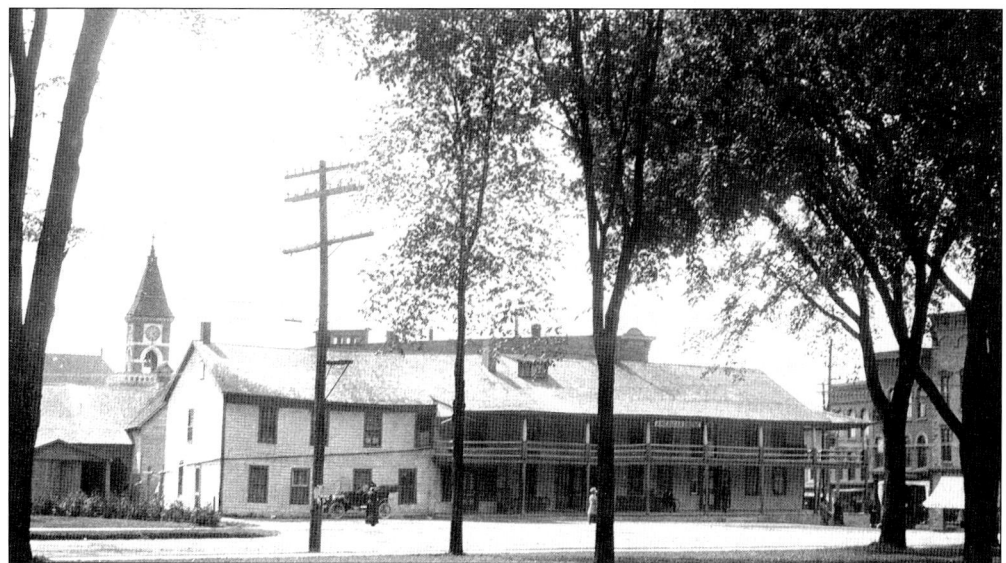

AMERICAN HOUSE. The oldest hotel in the state, the American House, opened to the public January 1, 1825, on the corner of Main and Park Streets, with verandas up and down. This hotel was an early stagecoach stop, and used by the county legislators as their meeting place. Rooms were $2 a night and history (or legend) has it that room number 12 "was in truth a recreation room for tired and lonesome men only. It was understood that time did not hang heavy there unless one was holding too many threes and fours instead of aces and kings." (From *Reminiscences of the Village of Canton*, Carl Witherbee.)

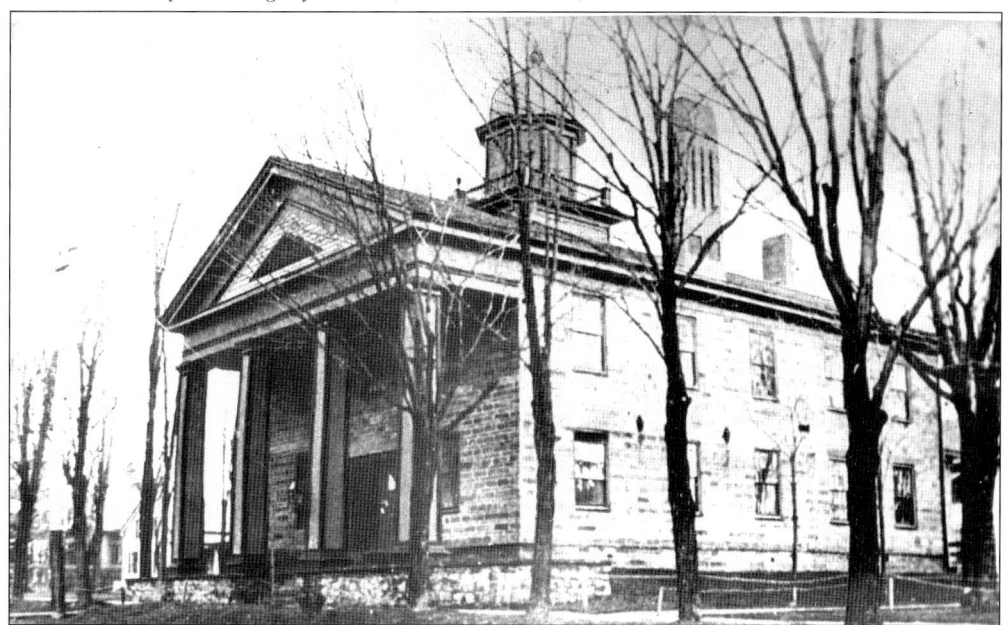

ST. LAWRENCE COUNTY COURTHOUSE. Canton's first county courthouse was built in 1828, after the county seat moved from Ogdensburg. It was a stone building in the classical Grecian style, two stories high, and 40 feet by 44 feet, with four large wooden pillars across the front, and a steeple rising out of the middle of the roof. The building was enlarged in 1852 and served the county until 1893 when it was gutted by fire.

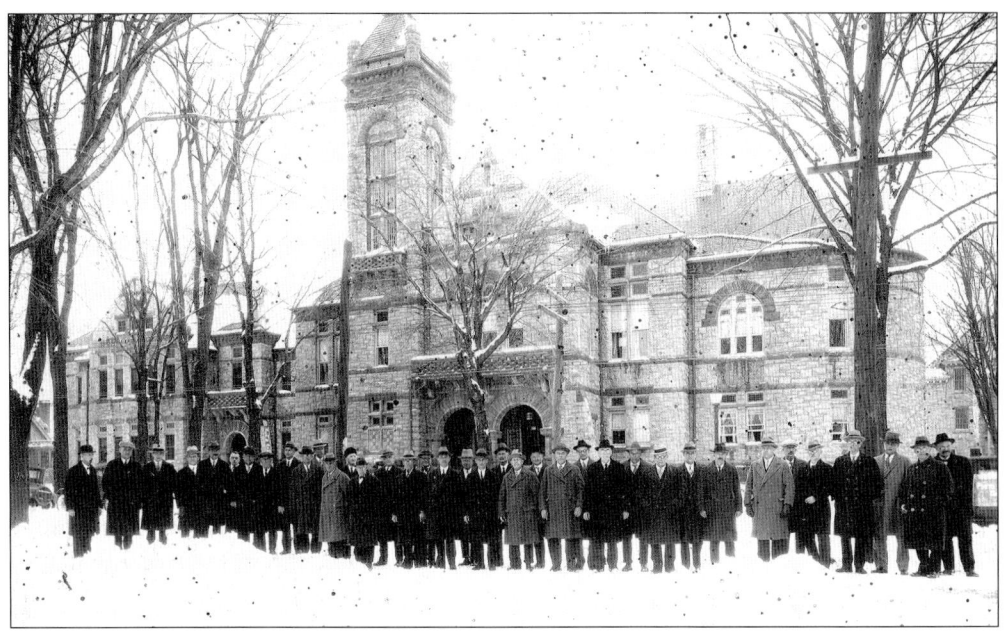

COUNTY'S SECOND COURTHOUSE. This photograph shows the new courthouse, built shortly after the fire by the board of legislators. The foundation, laid 5 feet thick, supported the Gouverneur "blue marble" and Potsdam sandstone walls with a lofty tower. Another fire in 1925 ruined most of the interior of this building, and the courthouse was rebuilt using the walls that remained.

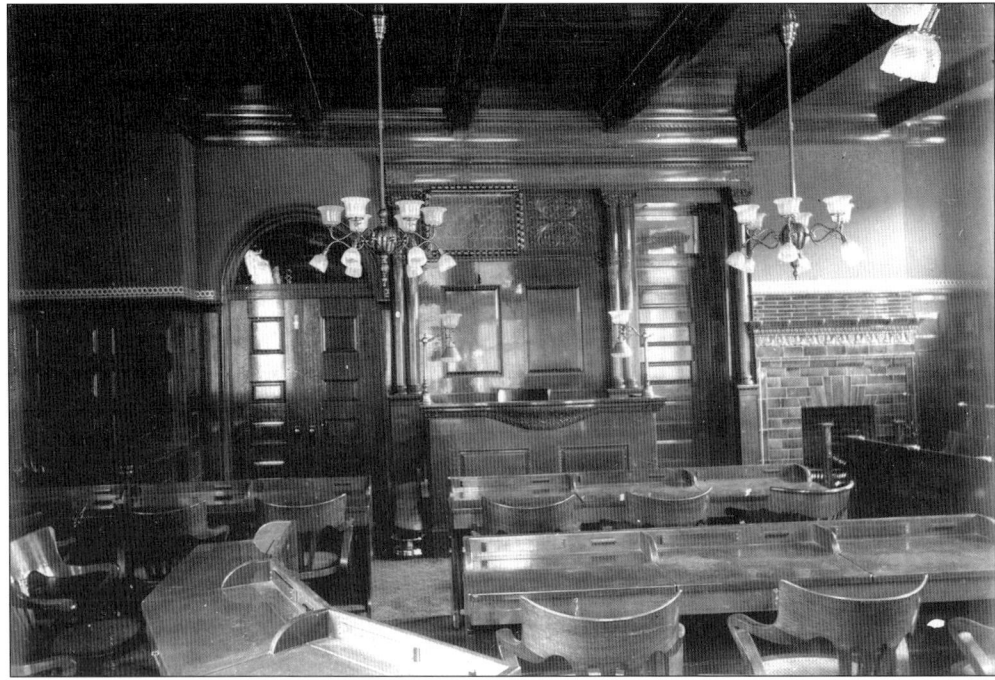

INTERIOR OF COURTHOUSE. A look into the older courtroom before the 1925 fire shows ornamental lanterns, high ceilings, and a fireplace. The board of legislators meets in this courthouse today.

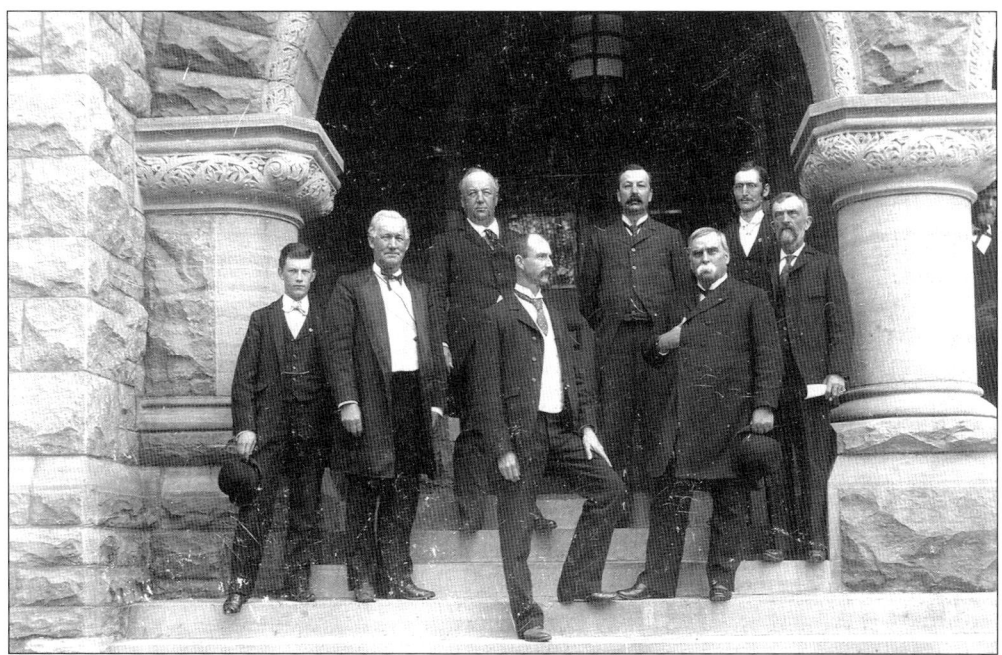

BUILDING COMMITTEE. Much like the building committee of today, in 1893, the committee's task was to formulate new building plans for the courthouse after the fire. Among the men standing on the courthouse steps are the following members: county treasurer R. Porter Johnson, Neuton Aldrich, county clerk W. W. Haile, judge Leslie W. Russell, and attorney Ledyard P. Hale.

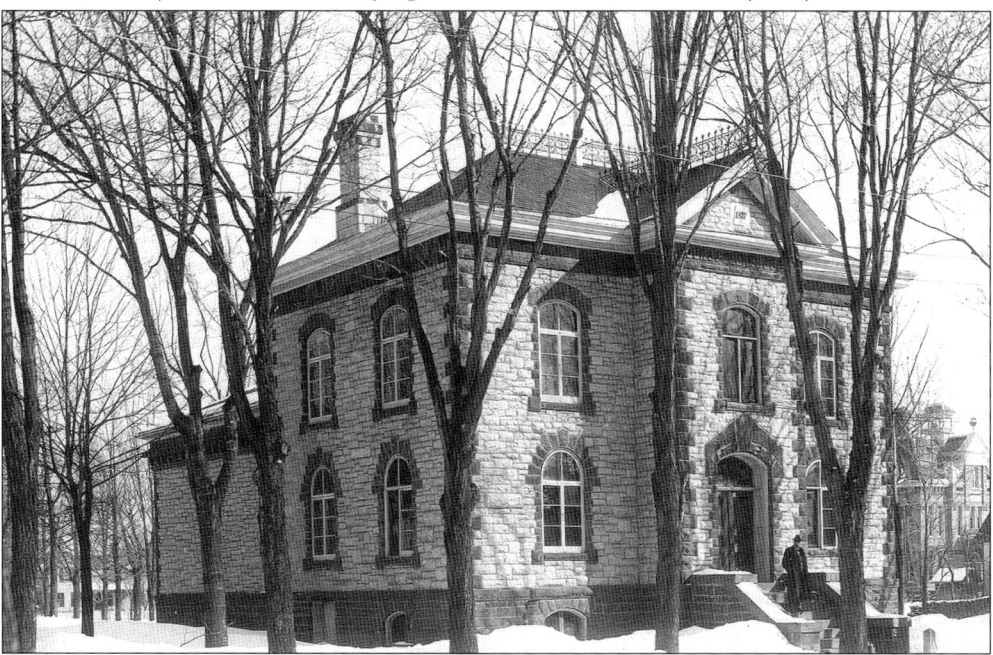

COUNTY CLERK'S BUILDING. The clerk's building on the corner of Judson and Court Streets has never been altered in its outward appearance. In years past, this building housed the board of elections, the farm bureau, the home bureau, and other government offices that needed small office space. The board of elections still has its headquarters in this building.

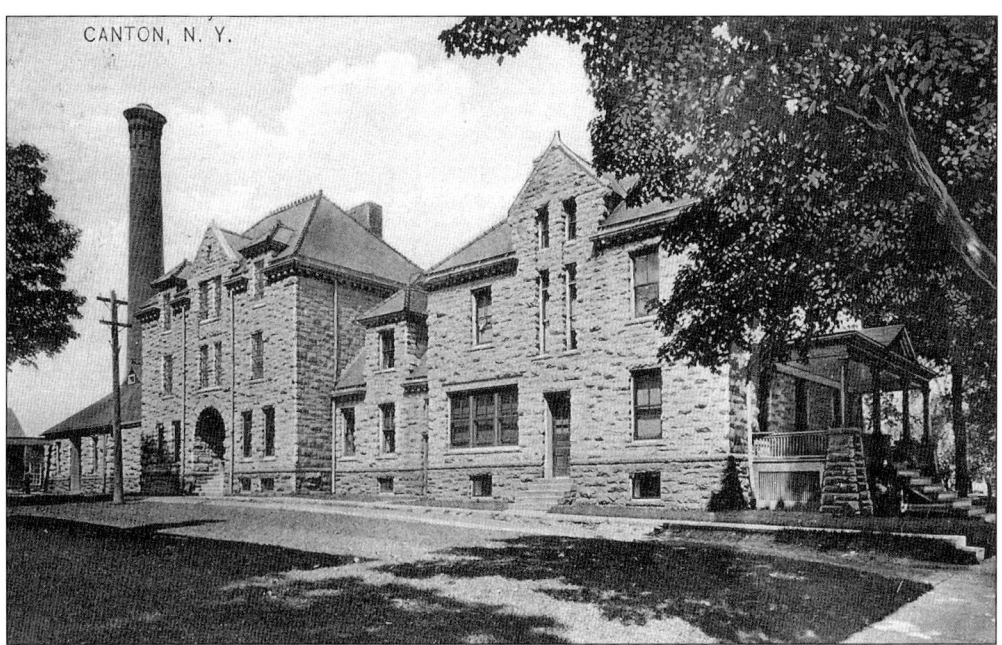

COUNTY JAIL. The first wooden county jail, located behind the courthouse, was replaced in 1889 by a jail and sheriff's complex constructed of Gouverneur marble. In 1927, the jail was again greatly enlarged and improved. Another improvement occurred when public executions in the jail yard stopped being held.

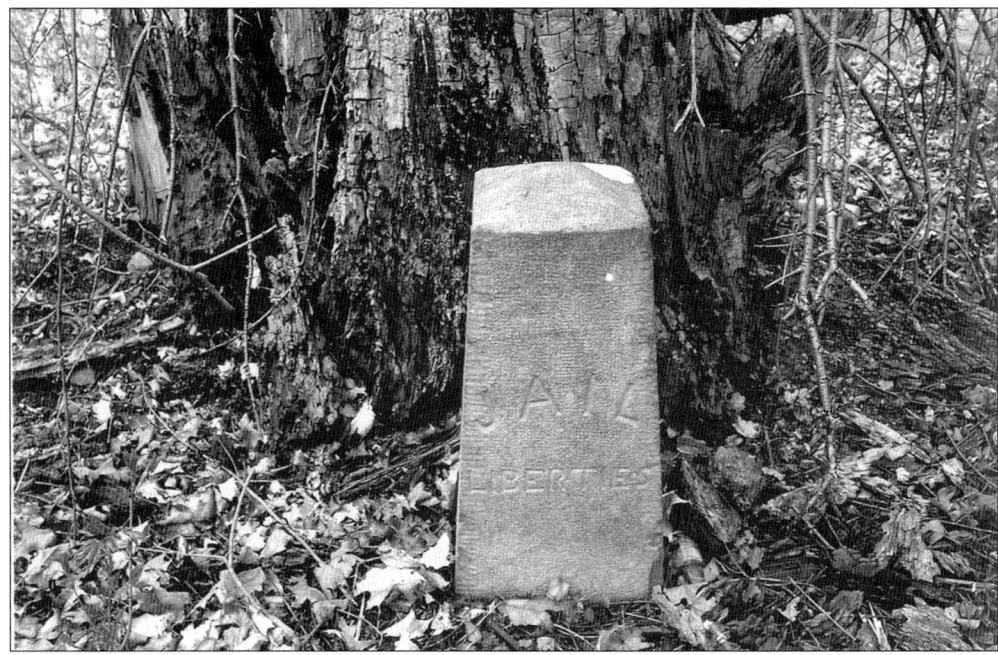

JAIL MARKERS. These stone markers were placed throughout the village in a square mile around the St. Lawrence County Jail. Prisoners were allowed to roam in the village if they were on good behavior status. However, if they were caught outside the markers they were incarcerated for another term. There are still four markers standing within the village.

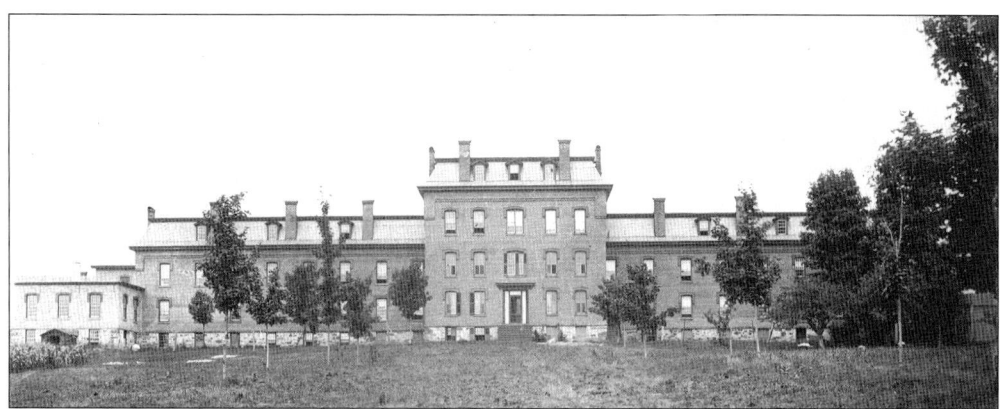

COUNTY ALMS-POOR HOUSE. Canton's first almshouse was located on the Old DeKalb Road. A new home for the county's poor was completed in 1869. At various times throughout the 1900s, it housed the poor and mentally ill, and, interestingly, rooms could be rented at the facility by people who came there by choice to enjoy the beautiful, peaceful setting on the bend of the Grasse River. County social services used the facility from 1970 until it was demolished in 1975.

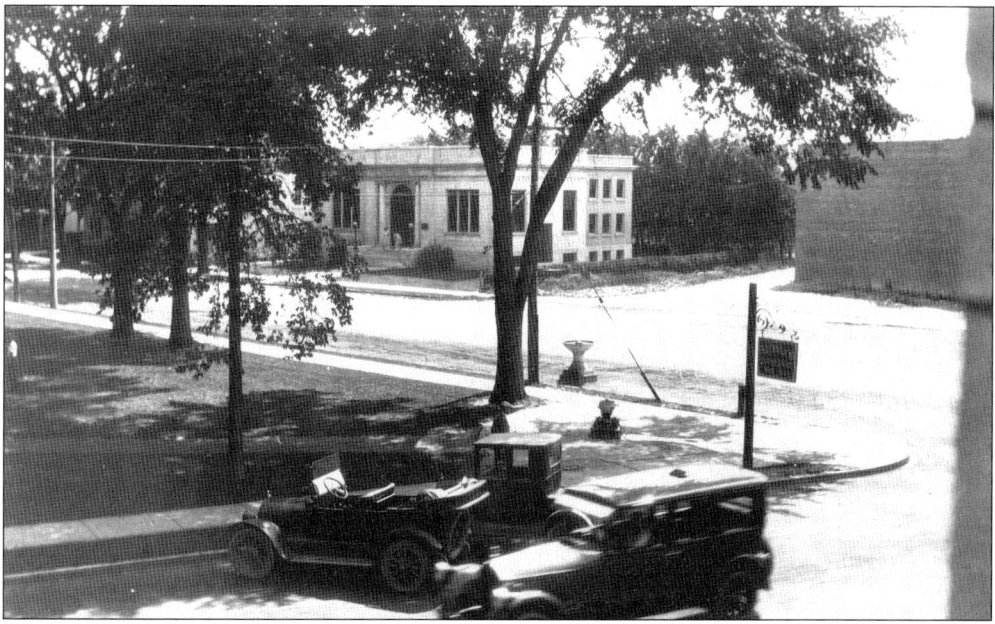

CANTON FREE LIBRARY. In 1894, Charlotte and Elizabeth Kimball, Jessie Russell, and Grace P. Lynde sponsored a public dance held in the Miner Hall to benefit the library. On March 15, 1896, the Women's Library Association was granted a state library charter. Josephine Paige was appointed librarian. In 1907, Emma Prouse Benton donated the Benton Library as a memorial to her husband, Walter. Local philanthropist A. Barton Hepburn gave a $50,000 endowment in support of Canton's library and branch libraries.

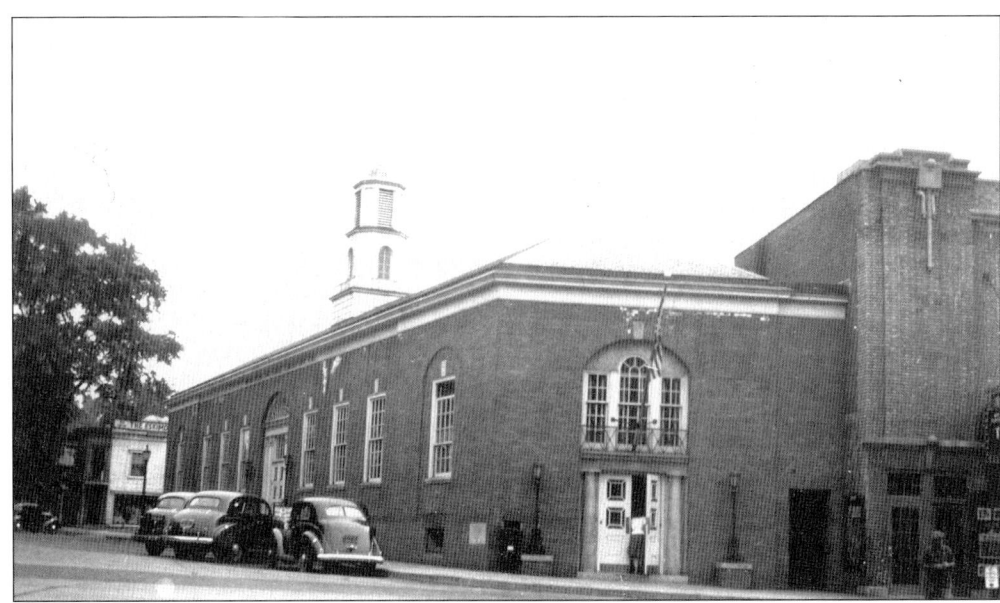

THE POST OFFICE. This post office was constructed in 1936 on the site of the famous old American House. The first post office in Canton was called New Cairo, with Daniel Sayre as postmaster. Several past postmasters still live in Canton, including Richard Lobdell, Michael Maroney, and Patrick Conant. Present postmistress is Mauri Maroney. Charlie Alexander tells stories about delivering mail three times a day, on Christmas Eve night, and to Vetsville.

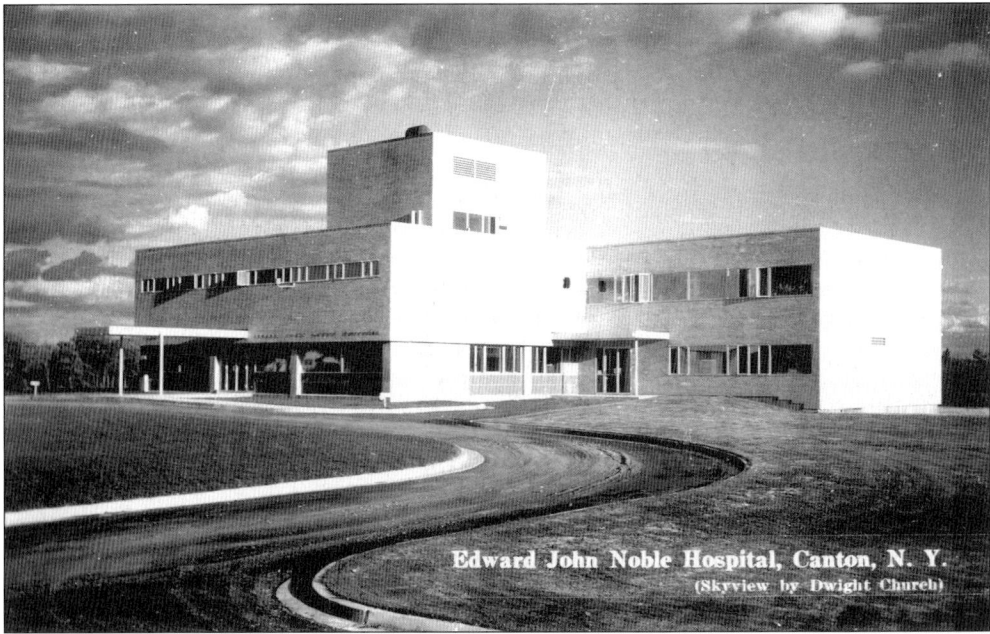

E. J. NOBLE HOSPITAL. The hospital was constructed in the early 1950s with funds provided by Edward John Noble, and it served the community for a number of years with many excellent physicians. It has since become a medical facility, housing doctors' offices, x-ray and physical therapy departments, and North Country Public Radio WSLU-FM.

CANTON'S FIREHOUSES. The first firehouse was a poorly constructed wooden building on Water Street. In 1847, a brick fire engine house was built on Court Street with a 40-foot hose drying tower at the back. In 1881, J. Henry Rushton, water commissioner, oversaw the installation of water mains, sewers, a pumping station, and the purchase of the Silas Wright steam pumper. Richard Robare, George Maine, and Charles R. Cook operated the pumper. The faithful team of horses named Billy and Tom pulled the engine to many fires. This building was replaced in 1927.

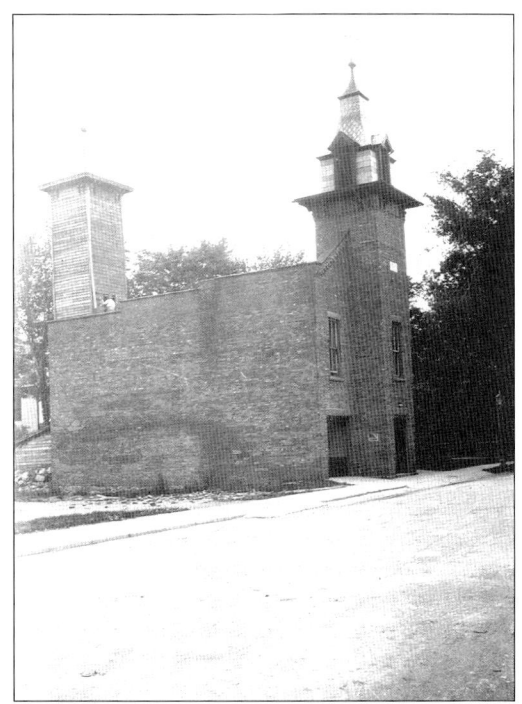

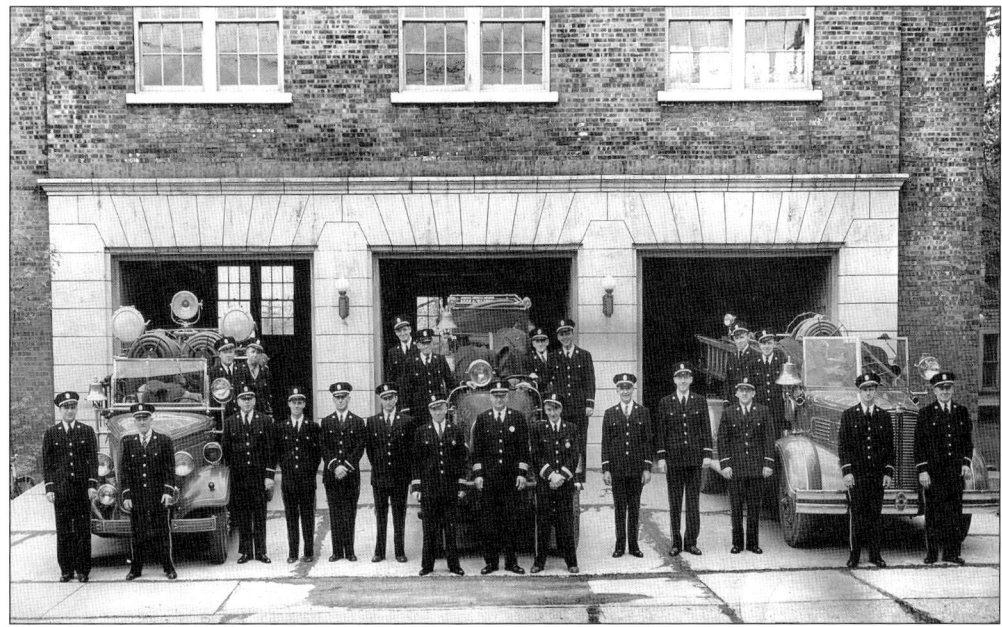

YELLOW BRICK FIREHOUSE, 1946. Shown here are members of the department with their equipment in front of the yellow brick firehouse prior to the Memorial Day Parade in May 1946. The members are, from left to right, Melvin Stover, James Cameron, Audus Todd, Kenneth Burt, Lionel Jubinville, Ira Endersbee, Charles Rexford, Maurice Amo, James Kennedy, Marvin Thompson, 1st Asst. Chief Ceylon Todd, Chief Stanley Barber, 2nd Asst. Chief Robert Elwood, Eldon Howard, Emerson Forbes, Carl Moore, Thomas Patterson, Floyd Firman, Bernard Mousaw, George Robinson, Emerson Bartman and James Welch.

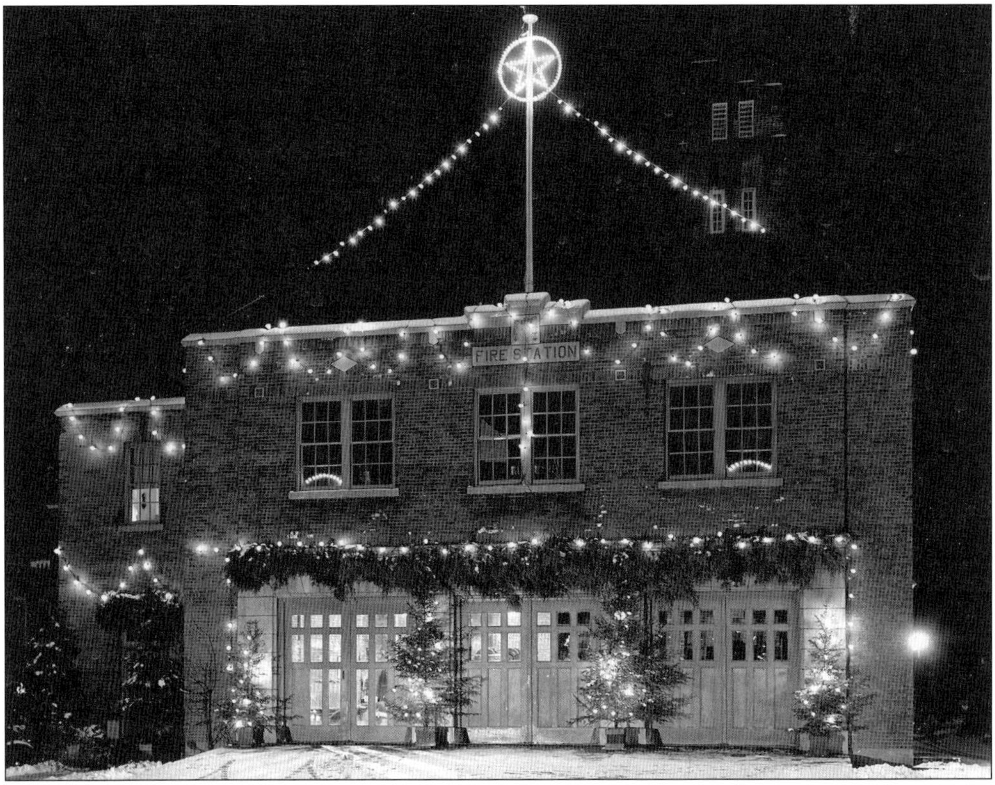

CHRISTMAS CELEBRATION 1947. Here we see the fire station in all its glory before it was remodeled in 1965, from a three- to a five-bay station. This station was completed in 1927 and still stands today, completely remodeled. At one time the town clerk's office was located on the left hand side of this building, and the Village Police were on the top floor.

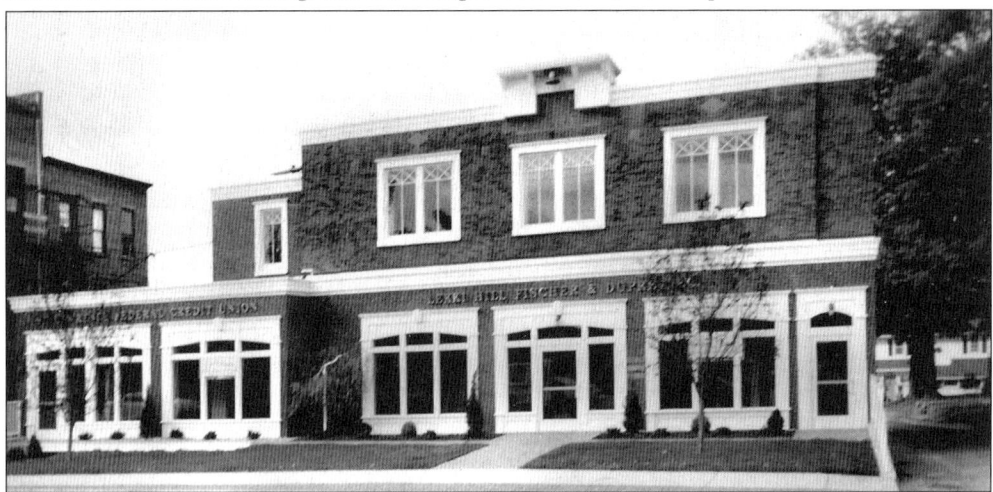

LAW OFFICES OF LEKKI, FISCHER, DUPRE, AND HILL. Pictured here is the same building as the photograph above and a showcase for historic restoration. The project became a political issue at one point on whether to turn this space into a parking lot or save the building. It took cooperation, creative minds, and vision to bring about this office building that serves the community and surrounding area.

Seven
STATELY MANSIONS

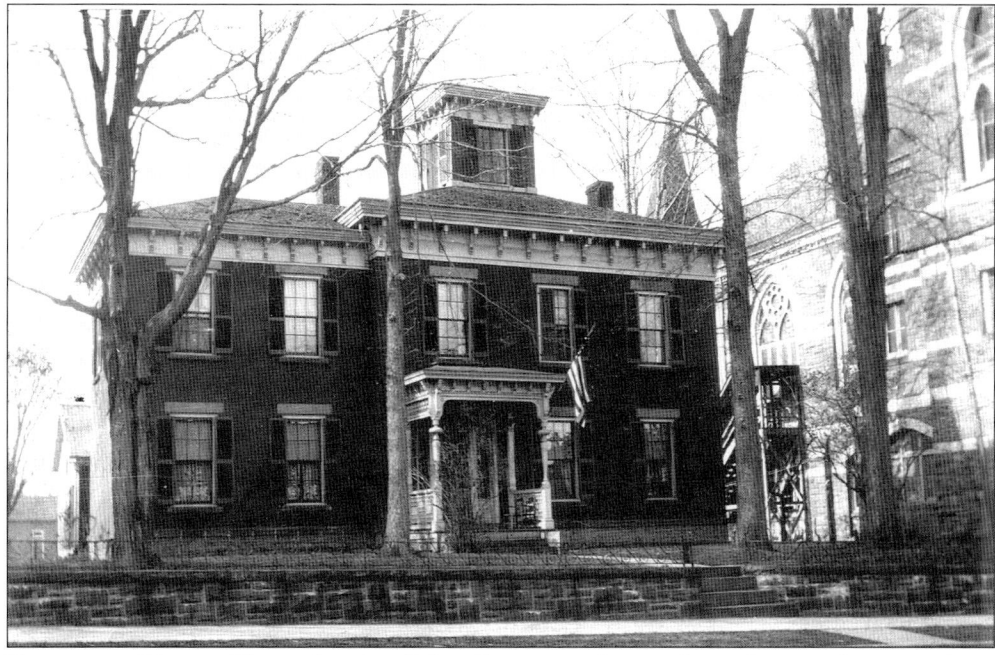

ELLSWORTH HOUSE. The real pride of Main Street was the stately residence and spacious lawn of Joseph B. Ellsworth, located between the town hall and the George Jack Bakery. It was of brick construction, painted red with a veranda and entrance. Green shutters adorned the windows and a cupola graced the roof. A red sandstone wall and foot-high iron-rail fence edged the property. Frederic Remington and his wife, Eva, would often stay with the Ellsworths when they journeyed back to Canton. For many years, an original Remington painting adorned the foyer of the Ellsworth home. Joseph Ellsworth owned the Ellsworth Shoe Store and financially supported J. Henry Rusthon's canoe boat business. This beautiful home was destroyed in 1939, and McDonald's stands in its place.

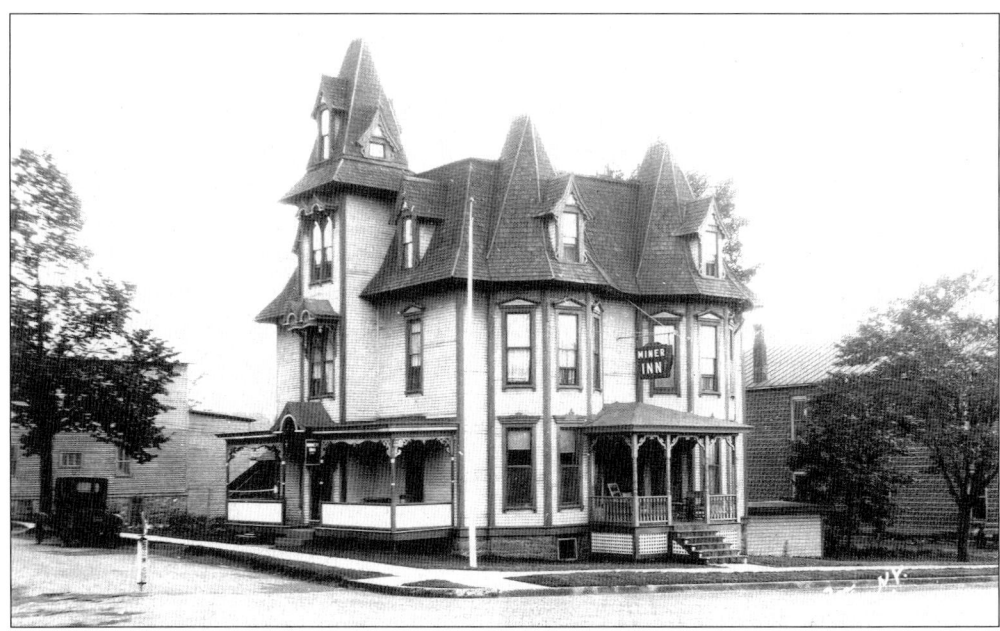

MINER INN. This Victorian home on the corner of Main and Miner Streets was built for Dr. Daniel Campbell. It eventually became an annex for guests from the Hodskin and Harrington Hotels when needed. People in the community spent their honeymoon night at this inn. Horse drawn buses, both sled and wheel, would go the New York Central Railroad and pick up passengers and their luggage for their stay in town.

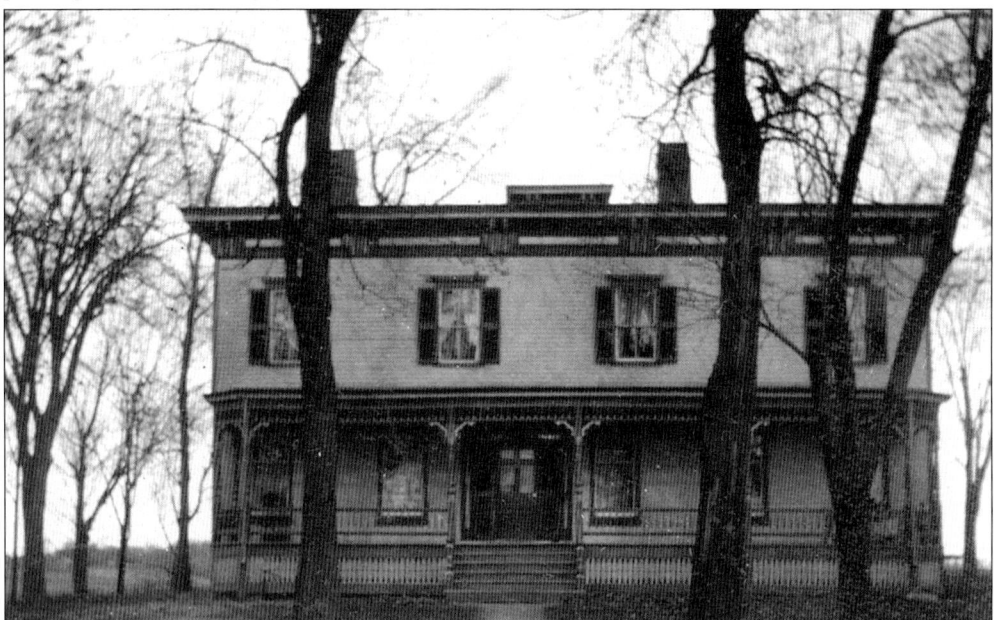

HARISON HOUSE. Richard Harison, a prominent attorney and city treasurer of New York, purchased large tracts of land in northern New York at 8¢ to 12¢ an acre. He built his first home on Judson Street in Canton. It was referred to as a mansion, originally one story high in brick, and entirely surrounded by a pillared piazza. A second story was added later in 1903. It served as the Alpha Tao Omega fraternity house and apartment house. It is now the site of the Howe Apartments.

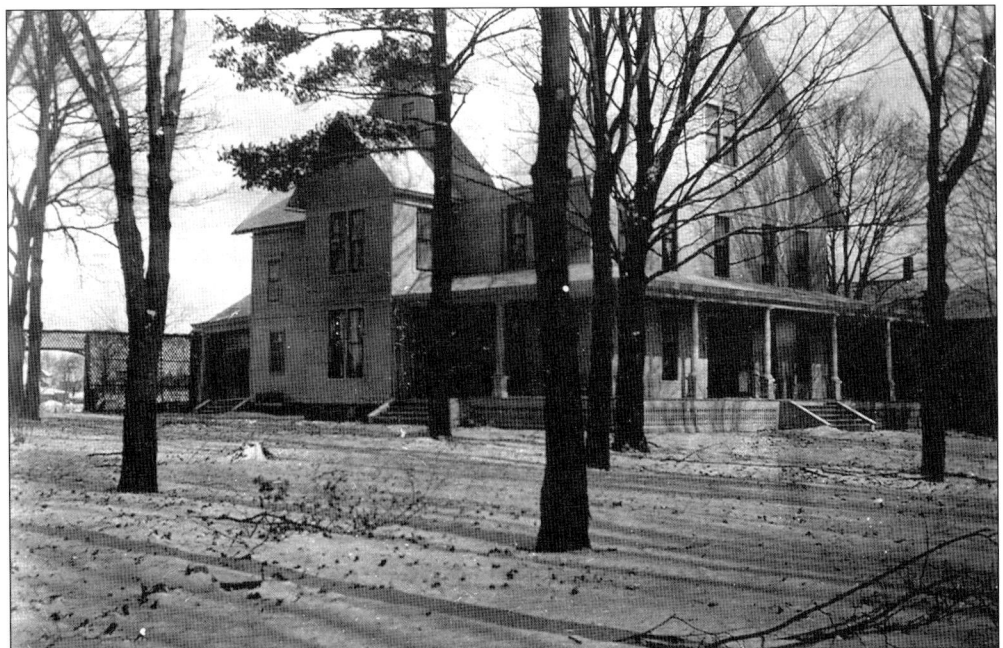

KAPPA KAPPA GAMMA. In 1818, Harison built another mansion across from the farm house (St. Lawrence University's president's house). Two side wings were added and it eventually became the Kappa Kappa Gamma sorority. There was once a hedge in front and a carriage barn at the rear, as well as a land office. (Courtesy of SLU Archives.)

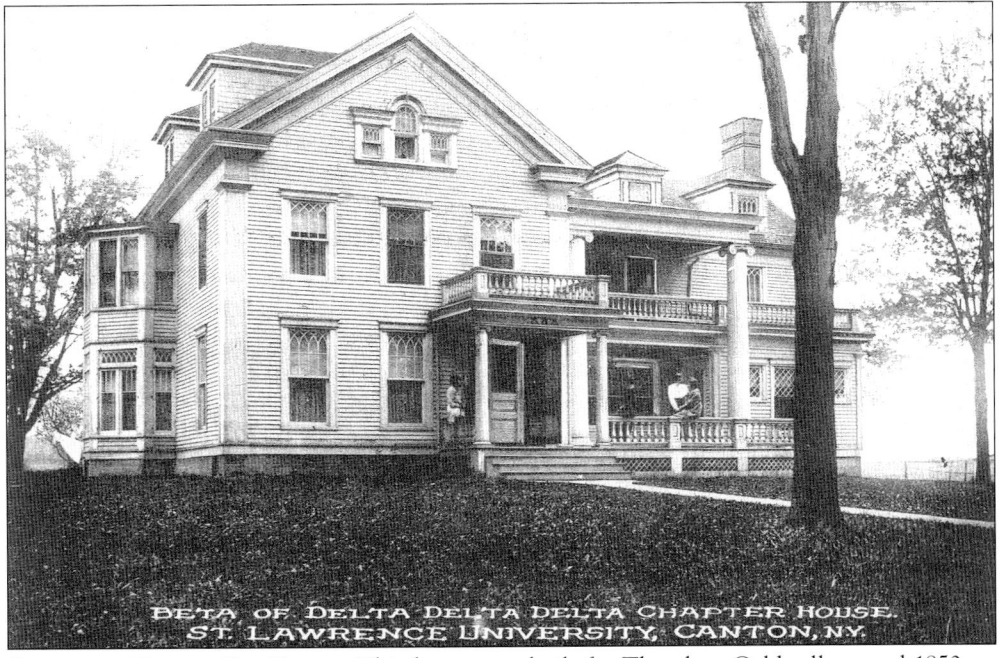

CALDWELL HOUSE, TRI DELTA. This house was built for Theodore Caldwell around 1850 on property purchased from David C. Judson. The house is located on Judson Street and is owned by the Delta Delta Delta sorority chapter. The ATO fraternity was also housed here at one time, having been noted by local author Irving Bacheller.

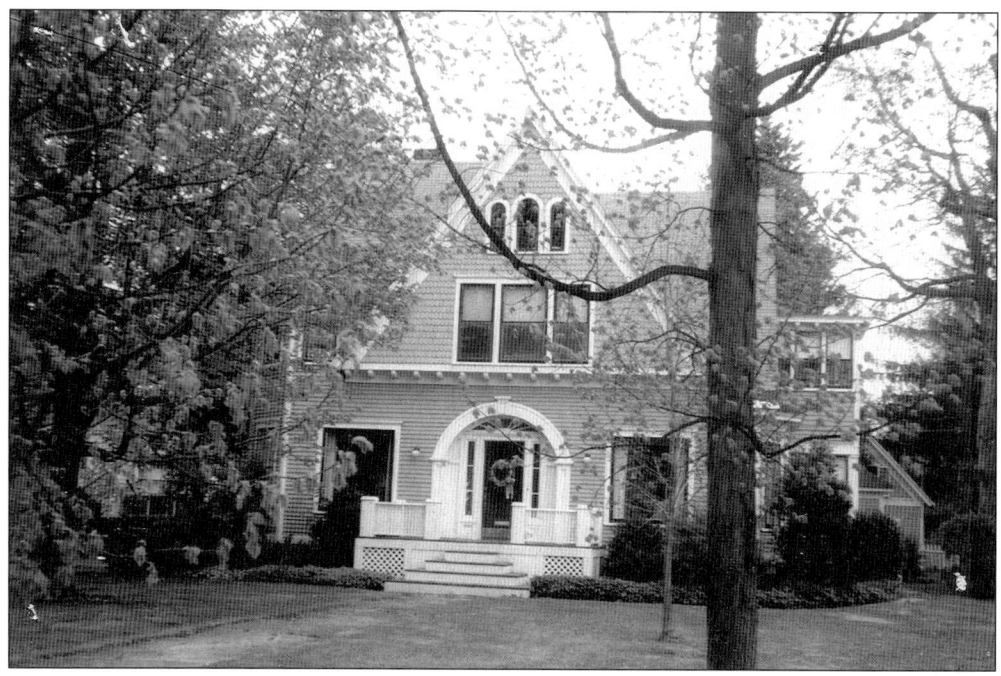

DOLPHUS LYNDE HOUSE. Adjacent to the Kappa Kappa Gamma sorority is the Queen Anne–style house built for Sen. Dolphus Lynde (1878–1884). Queen Anne architecture (1825–1920) was very popular, and featured irregularity, bay windows, and corner towers. Shingled walls vied with classic Greek features. Lynde's daughter Grace inherited the house. This is now the home of Birt and Ann Marie Fitzrandolph Evans.

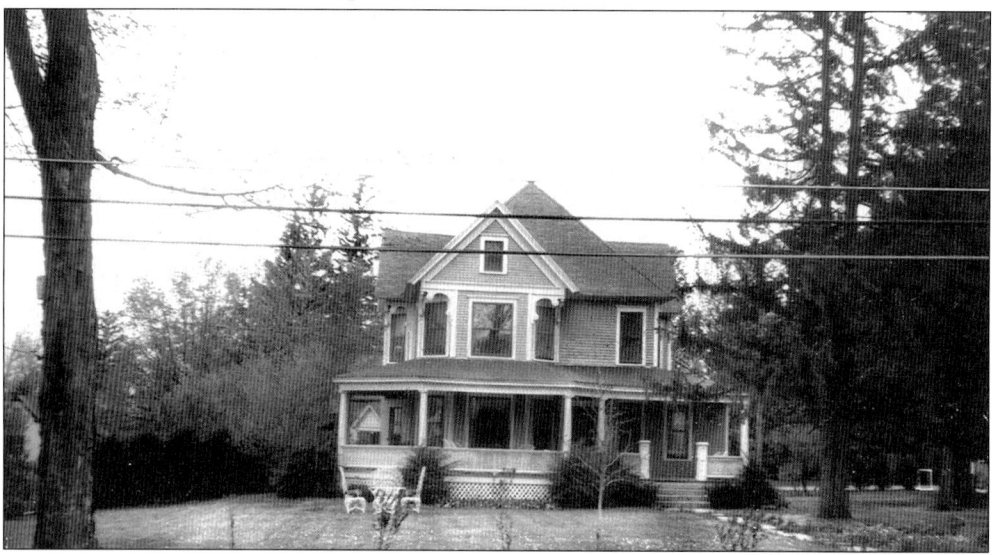

DEAN EDWIN AND MINNIE DOLLAR HULETT HOME. This attractive large house is located on the corner of Harrison and Main Streets. As evidenced here, North Country builders combined various styles during the early years. Edwin Lee Hulett (1870–1942) was dean of the university for more than twenty-five years and his wife Minnie was the college librarian. Dean Hulett's passion was meeting and getting to know all university students, faculty, and North Country residents. The Mazzotta family now resides in this house.

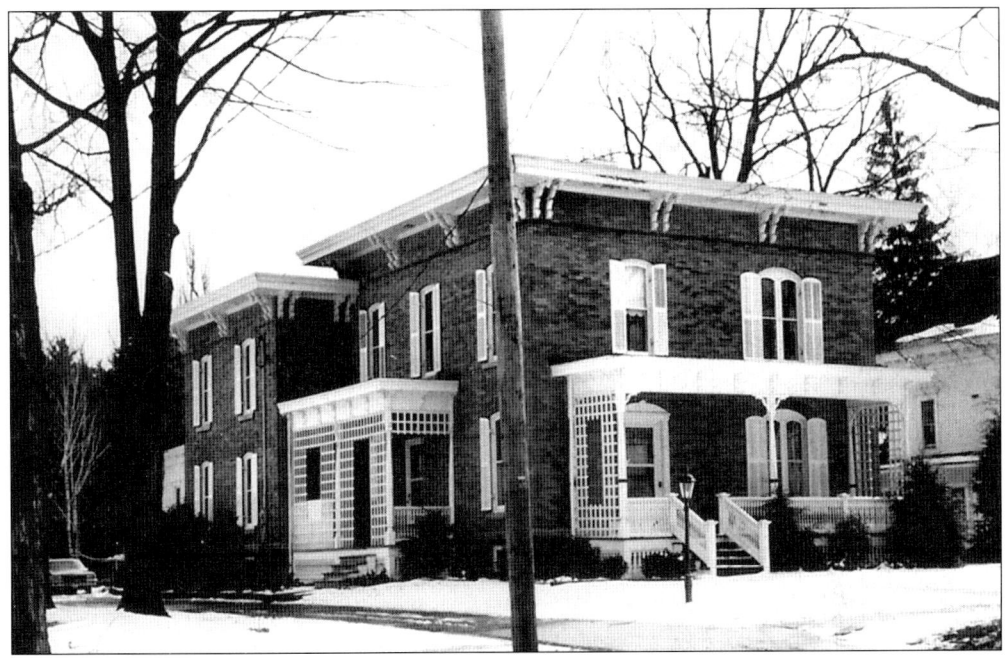

Dr. Noble House. One of the first physicians in Canton, Dr. William Noble, had this charming Italianate-style brick home built at 42 East Main Street. It was also the home of judge Charles Bowers and family. The home has passed down to another Canton doctor, Dr. Robert Nordberg, and his family.

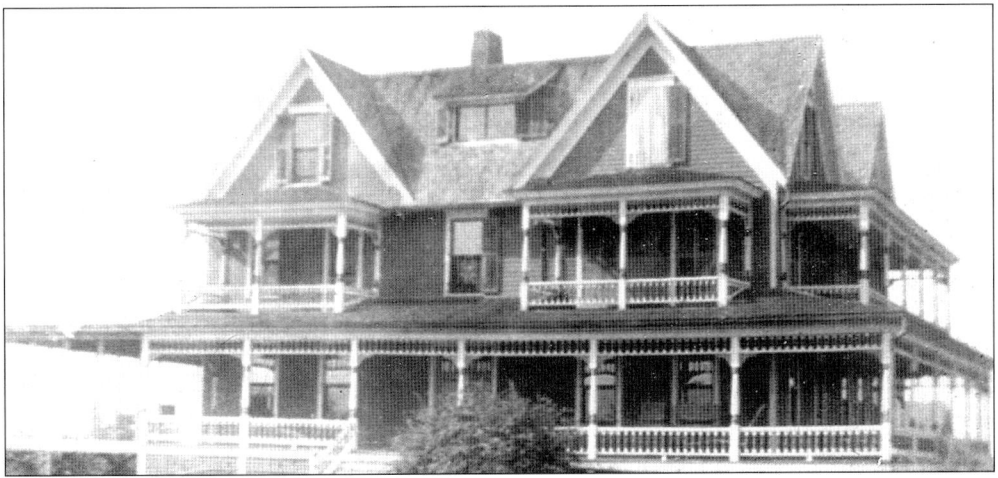

Canton's Famous Mansion. Helen Woods Cowen, conceived the idea of this beautiful structure, which she called Ragnarock, in 1890. The mansion was located a half mile from Route 11, on the road still known as Cowen-Mansion Road. It was Helen's desire to have a summer home near the Canton village to be close to her sister Cammie, wife of St. Lawrence University professor Dr. Charles Gaines. Helen's husband was millionaire John K. Cowen, an attorney and president of the Baltimore and Ohio Railroad. Built on a liberal scale, with nothing spared to make it an attractive place to live and entertain, Ragnarock was a popular entertainment center. Guests were honored to receive an invitation to attend the pink tea parties (punch with whiskey), and wander through the lavish orchards and flower gardens. John Cowen died unexpectedly, leaving Helen with nothing but a railroad car and a pile of debts.

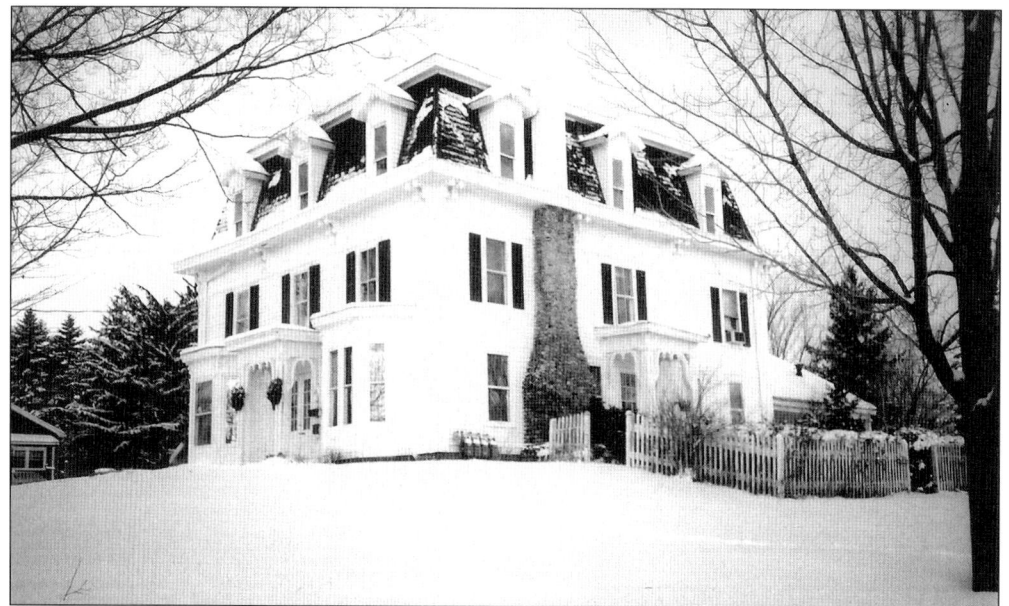

STILLMAN FOOTE HOUSE. Completed in 1804 by Canton's earliest settler, Stillman Foote, this home on 18 West Main Street is the oldest structure in the town of Canton. It was first opened as a tavern by Foote and was eventually sold to Henry Bullis. The peaked roof was replaced with the present mansard roof, porches were added, and six of the seven fireplaces were removed. Presently owned by Christopher Angus, it is used as an apartment house.

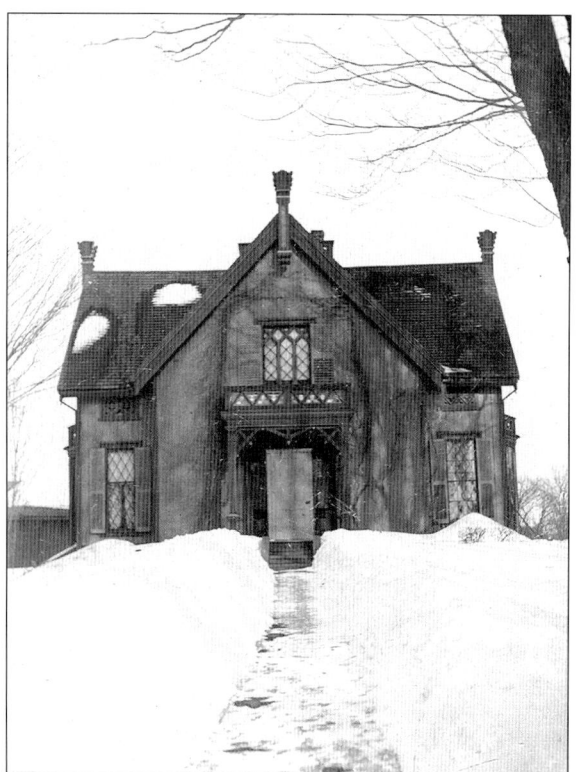

CONKEY HOUSE. This Gothic revival house was a small, elaborate villa built around 1847 by Barzilai Hodskin, one of the founders of St. Lawrence University. Three generations of Conkeys lived in this house on Court Street. It was demolished in 1958 to make room for the St. Lawrence County Courthouse parking lot.

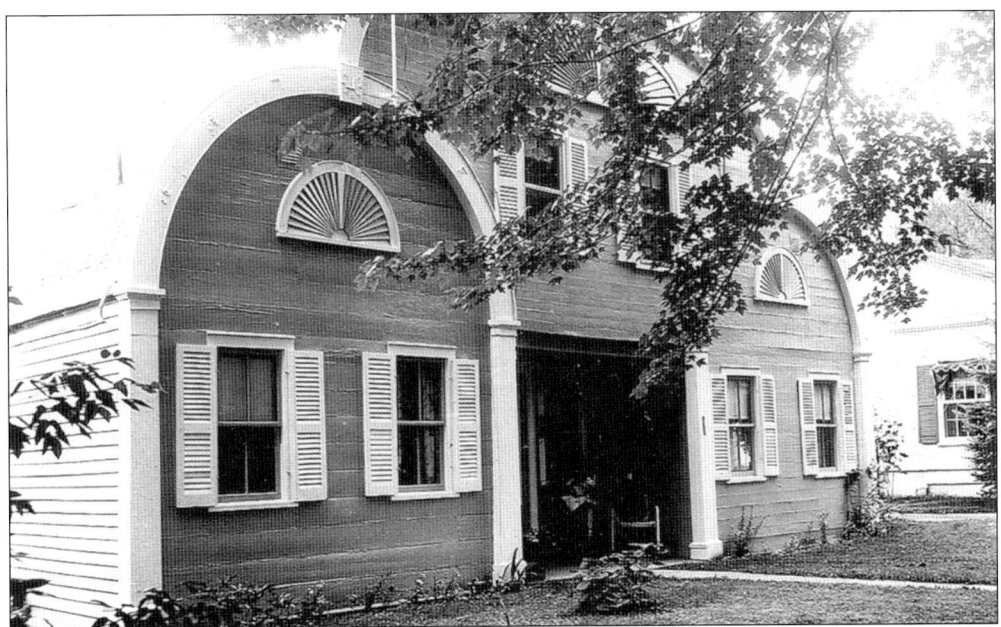

MASONIC HOUSE, ROYAL ARCH HOUSE. Paul Boynton built this unusual house on Pine Street around 1830. The house has three arches and an inscription carved in wooden characters of the Masonic Royal Arch Code. The house had low, plain rooms and a recessed porch. It is rumored to have a secret room where Masons met clandestinely. Boynton was a finely skilled and versatile inventor; he built a pipe organ and the first player organ.

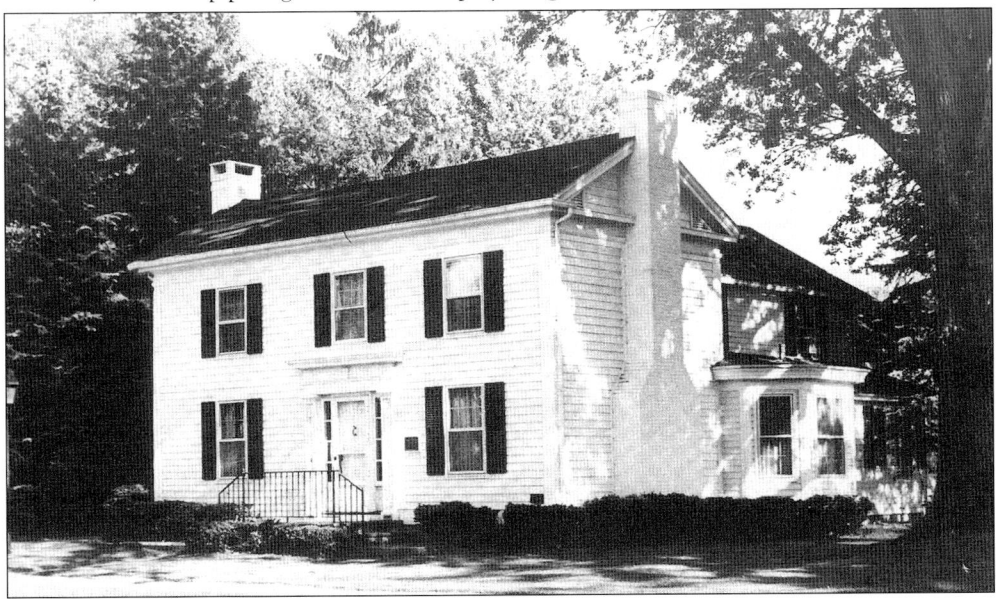

DR. LUCIA HEATON HOME. The lot at 12 East Main Street was once part of Dr. Noble's farm. Theodore B. Marvin purchased the lot in 1841, and built the beautiful house seen here. It served as a Baptist parsonage until 1858. Ira Heaton bought the property for his children who attended college. His daughter Lucia, a St. Lawrence University graduate, became the first woman physician in the county. Additionally, she was well known as a feminist leader and close friend of Susan B. Anthony. (Courtesy of SLU Archives.)

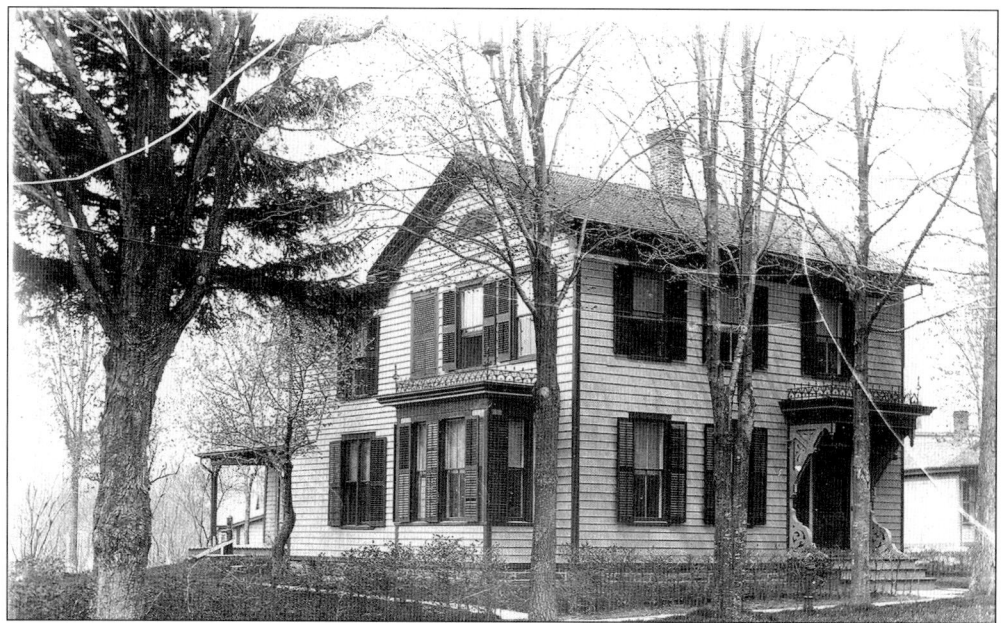

FREDERIC S. REMINGTON'S BIRTHPLACE. Frederic Sackrider Remington was born on October 4, 1862, in this Court Street house. His parents were Clara Sackrider and Seth Pierpont Remington. Frederic, one of the most famous western artists and sculptors, spent a large part of his early childhood in Canton, playing on the Grasse River and St. Lawrence campus. He died on December 26, 1909, and is buried in the Evergreen Cemetery, in Canton.

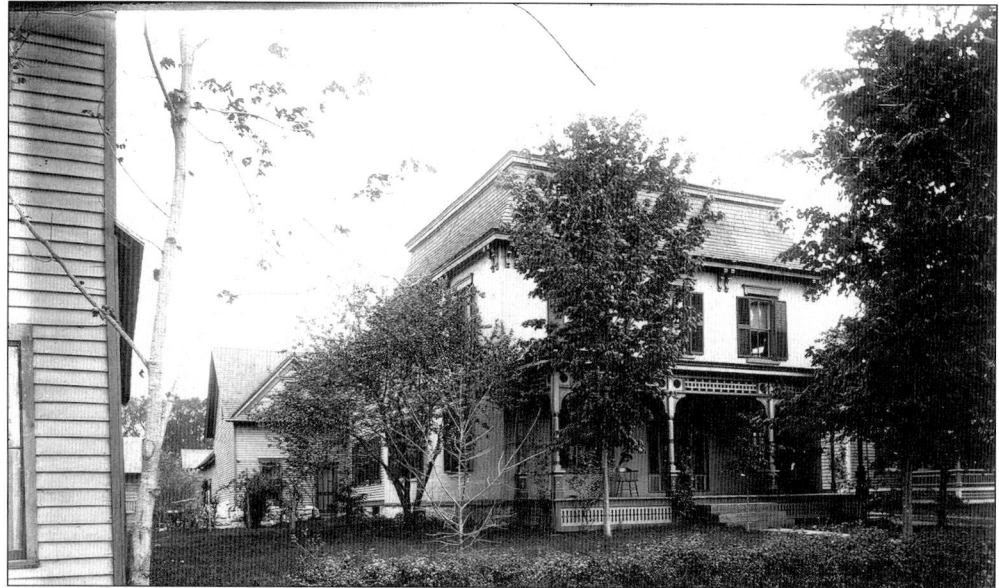

DR. DRURY-DUSKAS HOUSE. Dr. A. C. Fred Drury, one of Canton's first doctors, built this attractive home set back from Main Street, between the Canton Savings Bank and the St. Lawrence County Historical Association. The Duskas family bought the house and raised their seven children here. William ran the Sugar Bowl, and his son Michael became the county judge. The three daughters were given Greek names and the four boys American names. The house was destroyed and the North Country Savings Bank now occupies this spot.

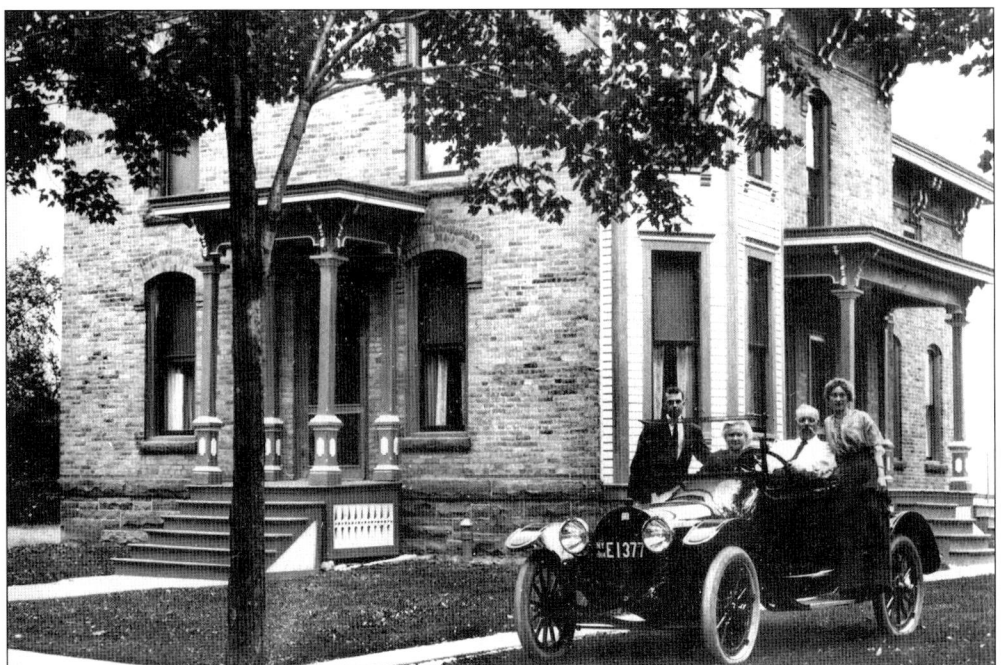

ELMER BARBOUR HOME. Henry Post, an expert local mason, built this Italianate-style brick home in 1880 on Goodrich Street. He sold the house to the Elmer Barbour family in 1921. Seated in the car are Elmer and Maude, Fred is standing on the left and Bessie is on the right. Over the years the home has been owned by the Bowmans, Halls, Spletes, McLanes, and now by the Kosers.

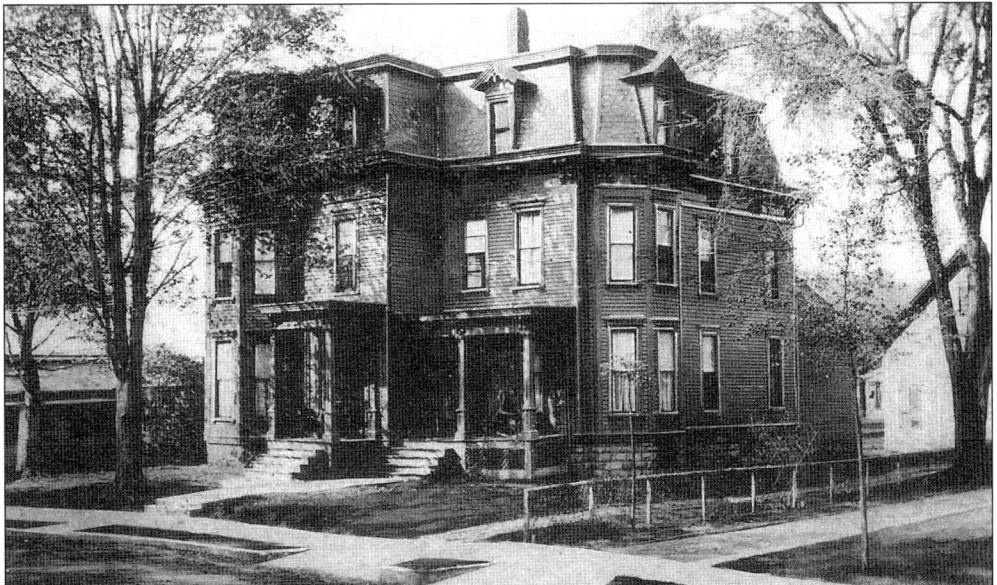

PI BETA PHI SORORITY. This beautiful building was home to the Pi Beta Phi sorority of St. Lawrence University until it burned. It stood where the Pat Collins Real Estate office is located on Park Street. The builder, Heman Matthews, moved a smaller house owned by Dr. Joseph C. Wilson, to make way for this larger home.

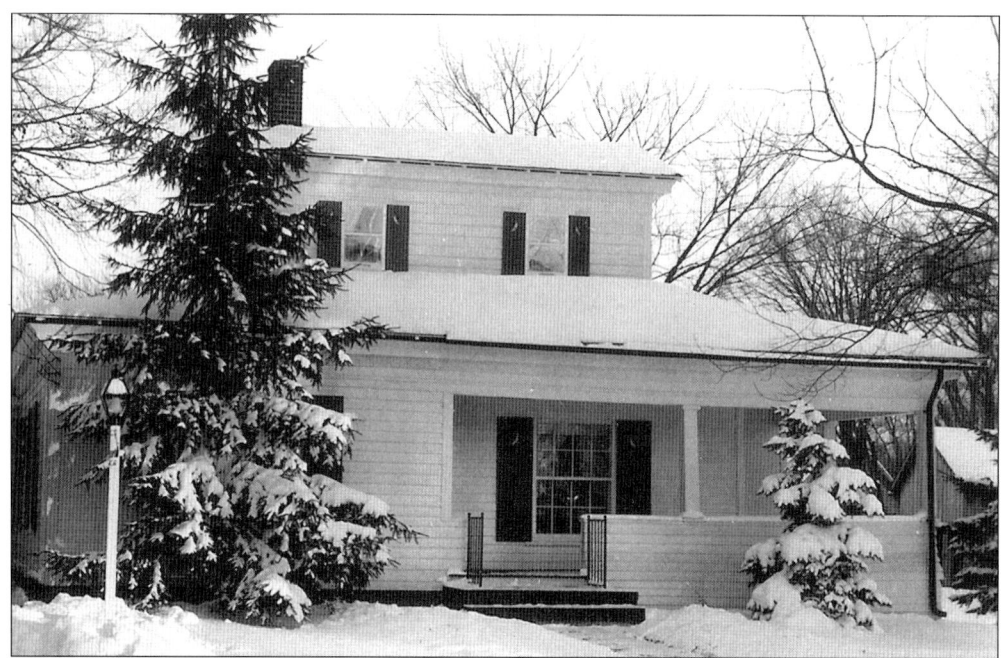

CUP AND SAUCER HOUSE. This unique house on Court Street is believed to have been built by Norman Dayton and was sold to John Barnes. During the Civil War, counterfeit money was printed in this house and the cupola at the top of the house served as a lookout for the Underground Railroad. It is now home to the Lance Rudiger family.

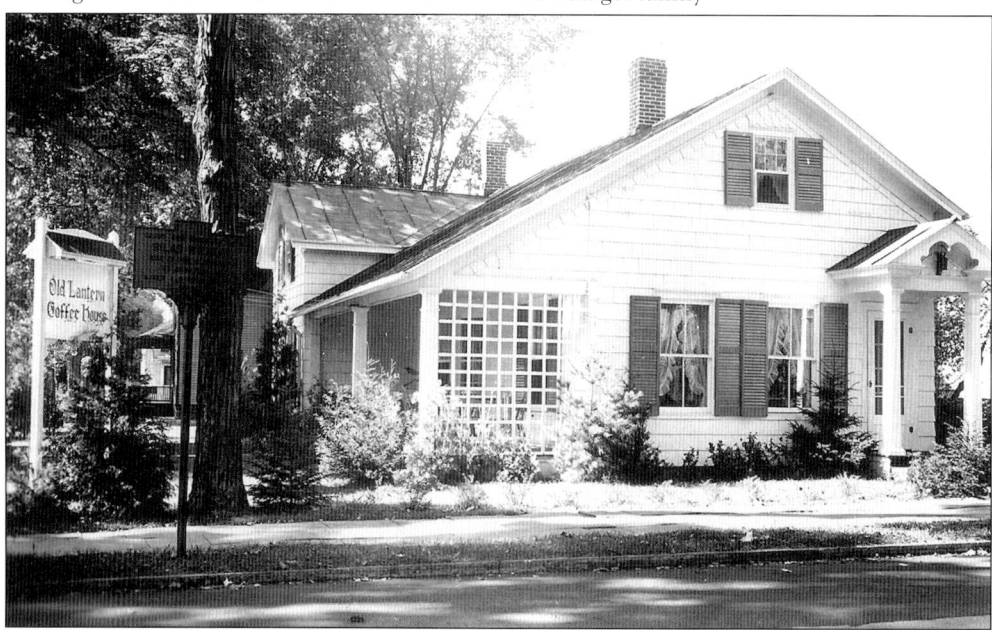

TEA COZY. Also known as the Old Lantern Coffee House, this quaint house was located on Park Street, and belonged to the New York State School of Agriculture. This lot was also part of the Silas Wright estate. Many young women spent three weeks training at the Coffee House in preparation for satisfactory adjustment to family and community life in their chosen occupation. For a number of years this building was also known as the Wool House.

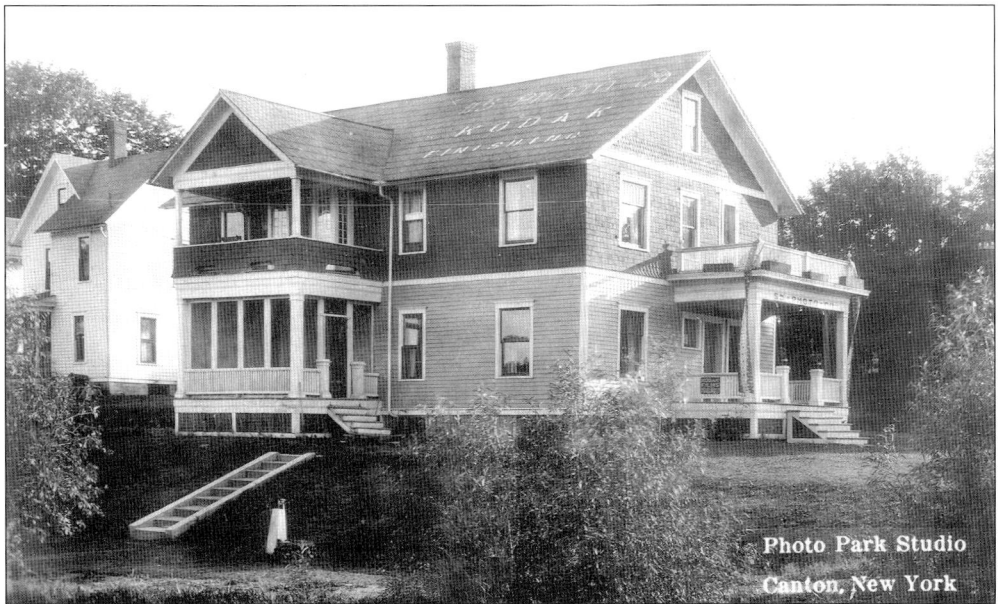

FIVE DOLLAR PHOTO STUDIO. This studio was the home of Dwight P. Church and his family. It was located on the corner of Main and Gouverneur Streets and was demolished in 2003. "Dippy's" collections of photographs ranged from portraits, to families and boating, to aerial photography. People could set their clocks by Dippy Church making his daily runs to the post office. At precisely 4:00 p.m. he ran to the post office, carrying his film to be mailed in his leather pouch.

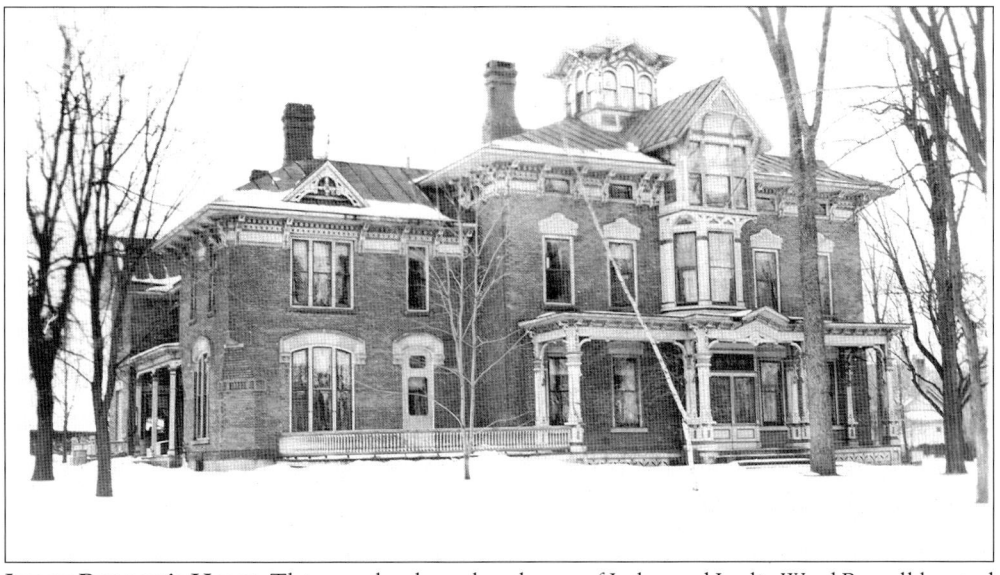

JUDGE RUSSELL'S HOME. This was the showplace home of Judge and Leslie Ward Russell located at the top of University Avenue. Dances were held in the large rooms and Uncle Baldy Livingston played the "Virginia Reel," waltzes, and polkas on the violin. The lot is now home to the Alpha Tau Omega fraternity at St. Lawrence University. (Courtesy of SLU Archives.)

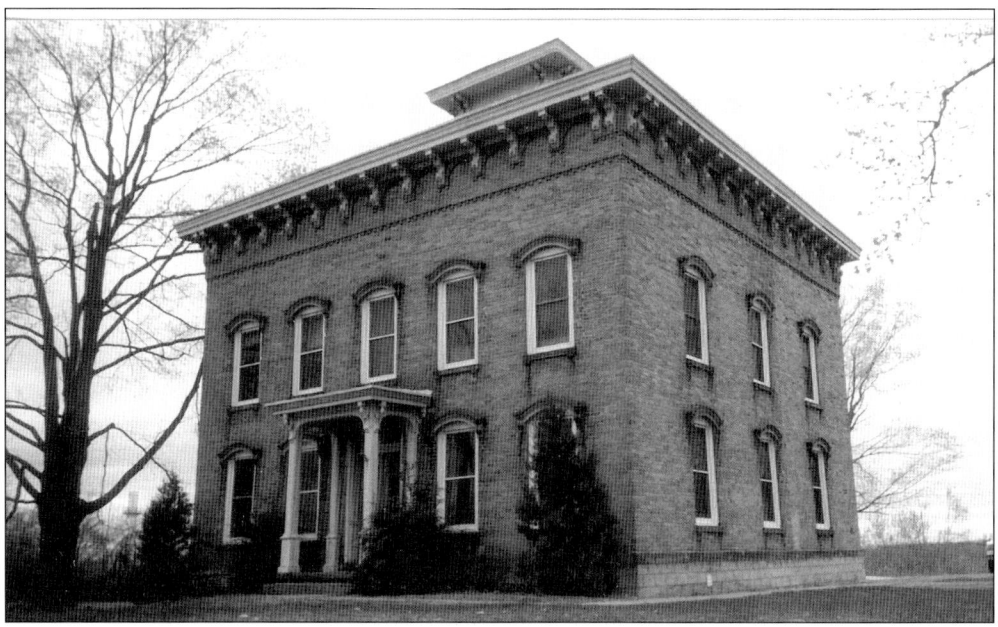

TALLMAN HOUSE. Sitting on the highest point of land overlooking the village of Canton and the sweeping Grasse River, this large brick farmhouse of Frederick T. Tallman was most likely built in the 1860s. The house had 17 rooms, a cupola observatory, a spacious central hallway, and exceptionally fine craftsmanship throughout. Eleven children were born into this family. The building now accommodates professional offices, and is owned by Ted and Phyllis Lawrence.

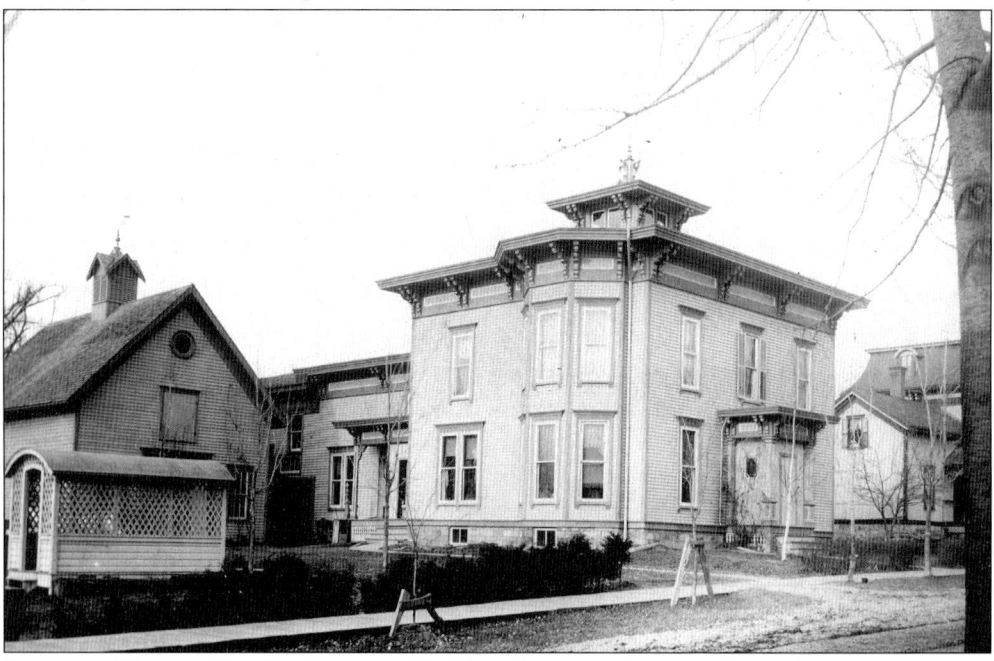

RUSHTON HOUSE. This fine house on Hodskin Street, with its cupola on the top, was once a cottage industry. Leah Rushton would draw and cut out the sails, and J. Henry would design his boats. There was a carriage house located to the left of the house. Leah employed local women to help sew the canvas sails. Sylvia Kingston now owns and has refurbished this house.

Eight
PERSONALITIES

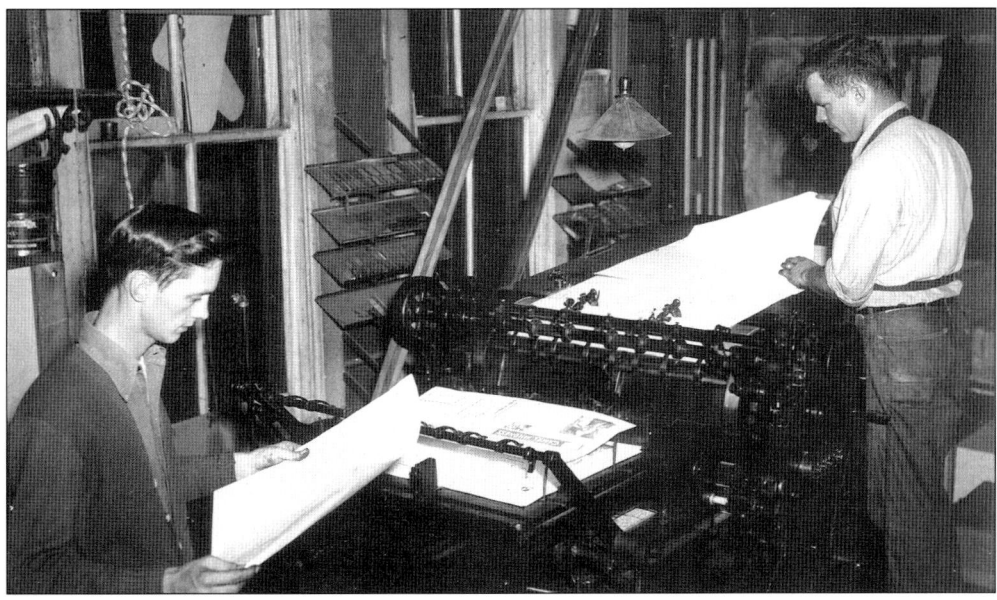

PHILIP D. MCMASTERS (1924–2004). He was a jack-of-all-trades and master of many. Here, McMasters is busy working at the press in the *Commercial Advertiser* office with Denny Bowman, checking out a daily edition of the paper. He worked for his father-in-law, John Finnegan, for a number of years. Phil McMasters was born in, lived all his life in, and is buried in Canton. An avid outdoorsman, an organizer of the Sportsman Club and Rushton canoe races, McMasters had strong moral character, and was proud of his family and home. He grew up on Pleasant Street with his parents, Norman P. and Zona Alta Sprouse McMasters, and two sisters. Norman built The Evergreens Restaurant, a very popular place. Phil and Emma had four children: Katherine, Rouette, Peggy, and Phil Jr., Phil Sr. eventually opened his own printing shop on Buck Street where he provided printing services to local government agencies. Philip McMasters devoted his life to his country while serving in the Navy, to his family, his friends, and his profession. He was also a town councilman for 25 years.

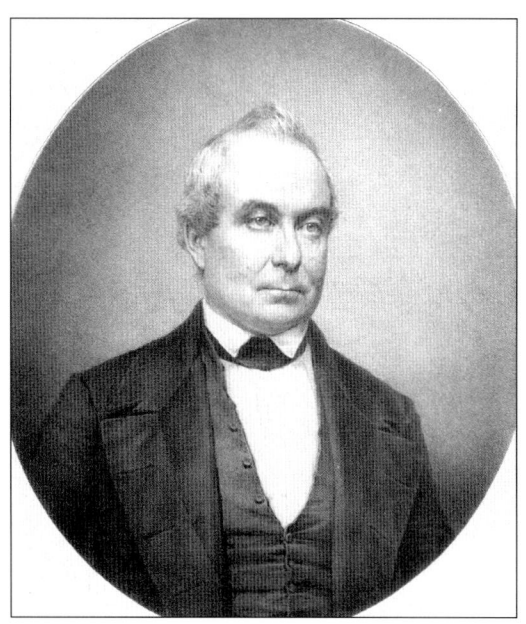

SILAS WRIGHT (1795–1847). Governor Silas Wright grew up in Weybridge, Vermont and attended Middlebury College. In 1819, he became the first lawyer to settle in Canton, and became governor of New York State in 1844. Wright was a close political lieutenant of presidents Andrew Jackson and Martin Van Buren. In 1832, Wright married Clarissa Moody. Silas Wright and Joseph Barnes donated the land for the Village Park and Canton's Presbyterian Church.

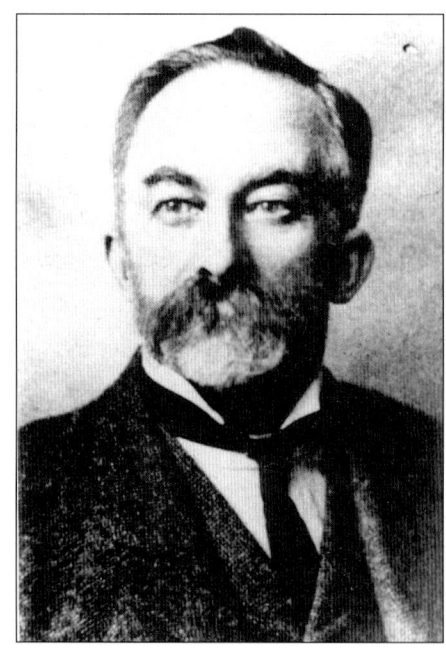

J. HENRY RUSHTON (1843–1906). Born in Edwards, New York, J. Henry Rushton was no bigger than "a pint of cider." He moved to Canton after meeting Joseph Ellsworth and Milton Packard at Cranbury Lake. After building several large, heavy, cedar lapstreak canoes, he was commissioned to build a smaller boat for Adirondack guide George Washington Sears, known as "Nessmuck." The 18-pound Sairy Gamp was displayed at the Chicago World's Fair in 1893. Rushton served on school boards and held village offices. He was instrumental in the founding of Stillwater Hunting Camp and belonged to the American Canoe Association.

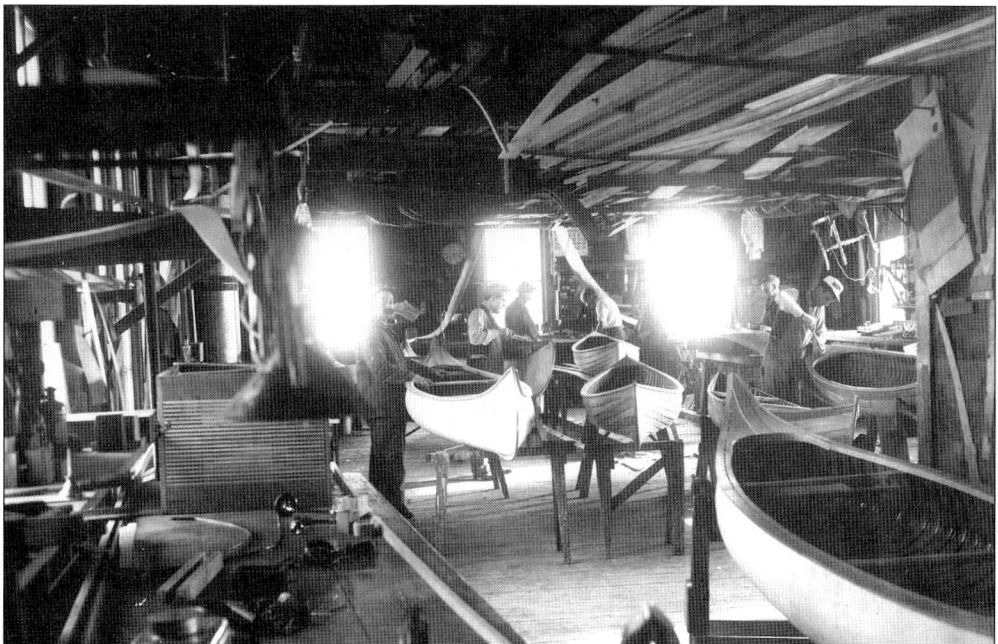

RUSHTON'S FACTORY AND MEN. Shown here is the finishing room of the Rushton factory, located on the corner of State Street and Riverside Drive. The Rushton boat shop employed between 20 and 30 men, depending upon the level of demand for his canoes. Nelson Brown served as Rushton's foreman until the shop closed in 1917.

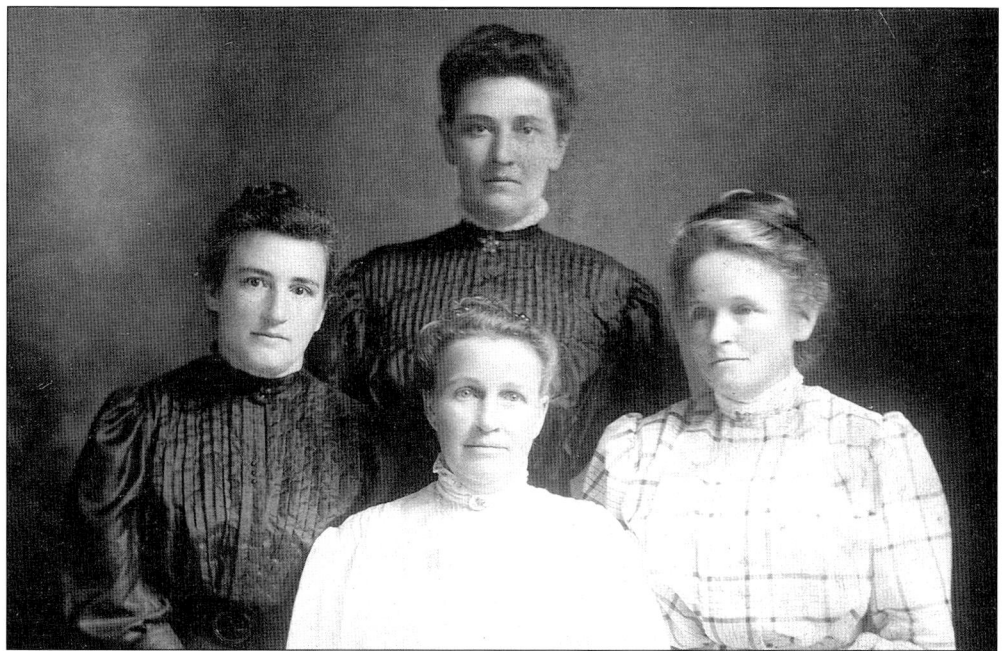

RUSHTON WOMEN. These beautiful women, Margaret, Nellie, Leah, and Carrie, were wives of the Rushton boys. Nellie Rushton was Frances Van Horn's grandmother. J. Henry married Leah Pflaum in 1883. Leah drew the patterns for making the canvas sails on the wooden floor in the upstairs back room. She hired local women to work for her in her own cottage industry.

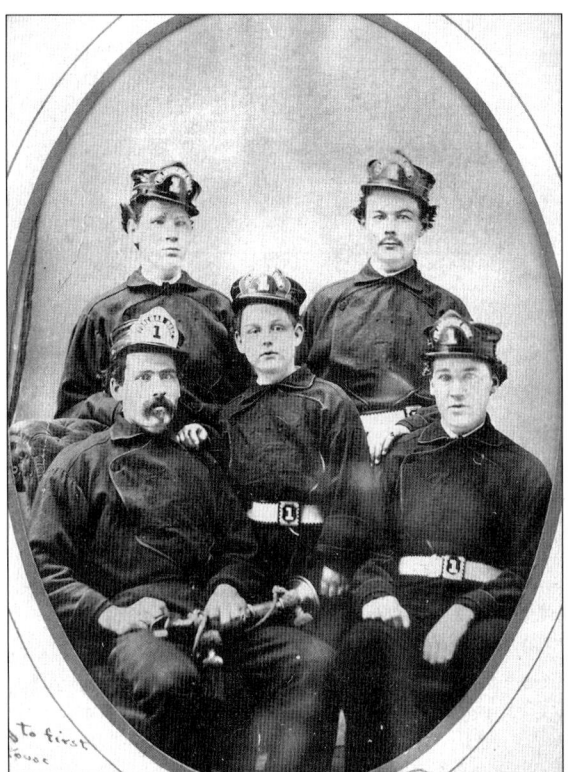

FREDERIC S. REMINGTON (1861–1909). Pictured here in the center, Frederic Remington became one of the country's most notable western artists and sculptors. As a boy, young Freddie was the mascot for the local fire department and often rode on the engine to the fires. After leaving Canton, he always found time to visit his birthplace. He married Eva Caten after meeting her at the county fair.

A. BARTON HEPBURN (1846–1922). Alonzo Barton Hepburn was born in the small hamlet of Colton. He grew into a self-reliant, industrious boy. He attended Middlebury College and later established seven libraries in small rural communities, including his hometown. He served as a state legislator and state superintendent of banking. Hepburn was involved in Canton's early logging operations. He married Emily Eaton. Hepburn is buried next to his trusted friend, Frederic S. Remington, in the Evergreen Cemetery in Canton. (Courtesy of SLU Archives.)

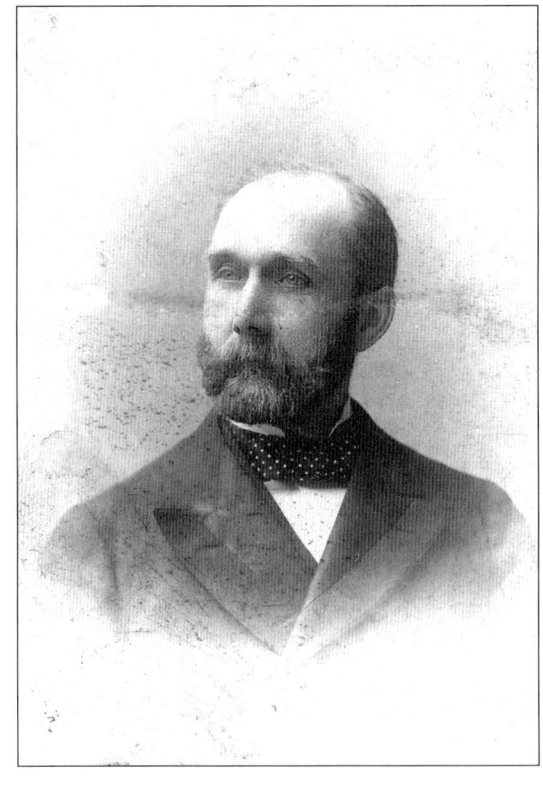

DR. LUCIA HEATON (1856–1937). This notable personality was born into one of the earliest Canton settlement families. Lucia Heaton attended local schools and St. Lawrence University. Dr. Heaton became the first woman doctor in the county, served on the Canton school board, and was quite involved in the Women's Temperance Movement. She was a good friend of Susan B. Anthony. Dr. Heaton participated in welcoming Madame Curie to the St. Lawrence University campus in the 1930s. (Courtesy of SLU Archives.)

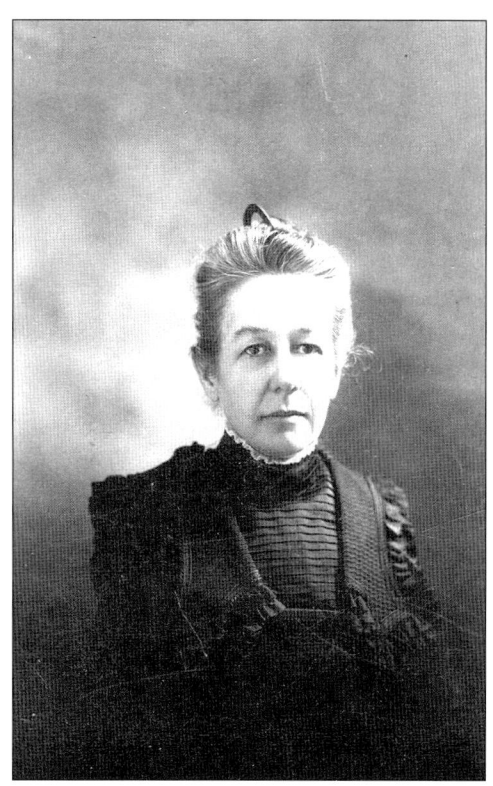

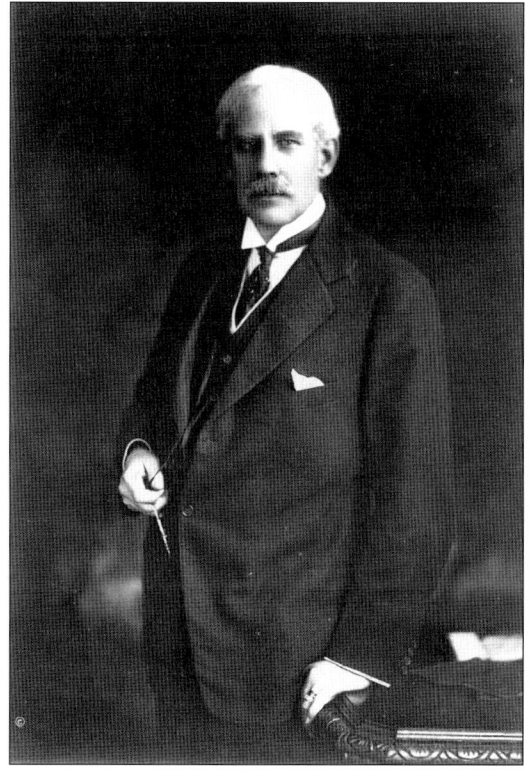

IRVING BACHELLER (1859–1950). A distinguished figure of a man, and a North Country native, Bacheller was an author and syndicated columnist. He grew up in Pierrepont, but his family moved into the village so he could attend college. Bacheller became well known for his North Country journals, and several published books. He donated the chimes that toll each evening in the chapel at St. Lawrence, in memory of his wife, Ann. (Courtesy of SLU Archives.)

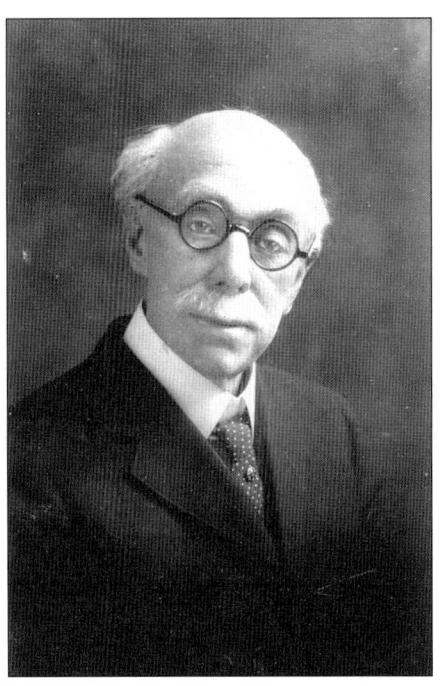

DR. JAMES M. PAYSON (1848–1941). Dr. James M. Payson was born in South Freedom, Maine. He came to Canton in 1872, and graduated from the Theological School in 1874. He also served as a Universalist pastor. Dr. Payson was one of the primary founders of the State School of Agriculture at Canton. He also served as president of Canton's board of education. Dr. Payson and Flora Bassett Payson lived at 53 Court Street, now the Theta Gamma fraternity house at SUNY Canton.

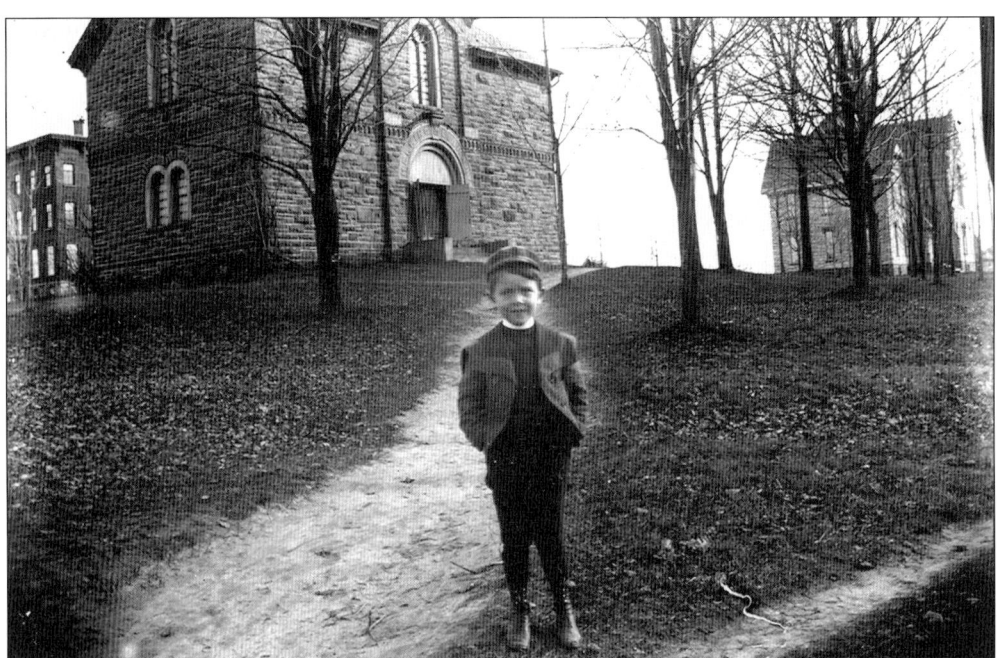

G. ATWOOD MANLEY (1893–1989). Pictured here at five years old on the St. Lawrence University campus, Atwood Manley was the third generation in his family to be an editor at the *St. Lawrence Plaindealer* after his father, Williston, and grandfather, Gilbert. He was an avid canoeist, historian, author, and politician. He was a man who embodied small-town values and traditions. Atwood graduated from St. Lawrence, and lived in a grand home on Judson Street with his wife, Alice. (Courtesy of SLU Archives.)

DWIGHT P. CHURCH (1891–1974): Dwight Church was a noted photographer, pilot, canoeist, and an interesting personality. "Dippy" spent many hours flying and taking aerial photographs. His daughter Bonnie helped fly the plane, while her father snapped pictures, reportedly sometimes on the wing of his plane. His photograph shop was within his house, on the corner of Main and Gouverneur Streets.

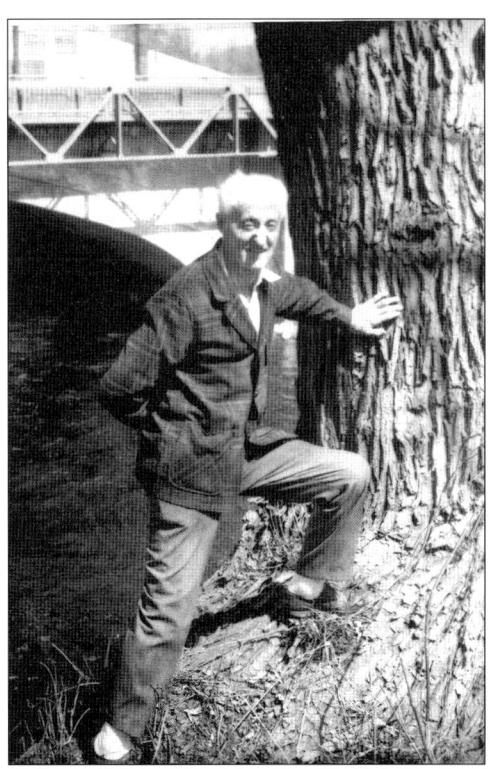

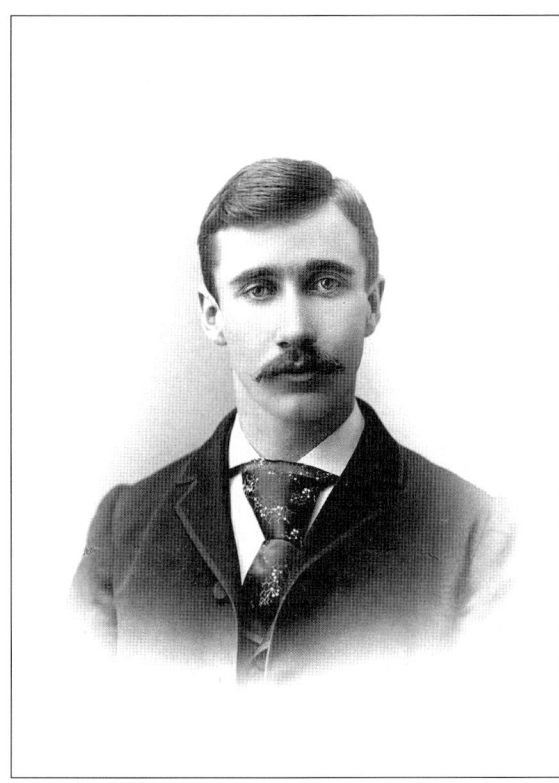

JOHN FINNEGAN (1870–1958). Canton's acknowledged citizen was John Finnegan who wrote, "Looking Through A Main Street Window," a weekly column in the *Commercial Advertiser*. Born in a log cabin on the Jingleville Road, Finnegan attended the Canton Union School and graduated from St. Lawrence University in 1893. He entered into the commercial advertiser business as a partner with J. D. Tracy. Finnegan became editor and publisher, and penned his weekly column while watching life pass by on Main Street. (Courtesy of SLU Archives.)

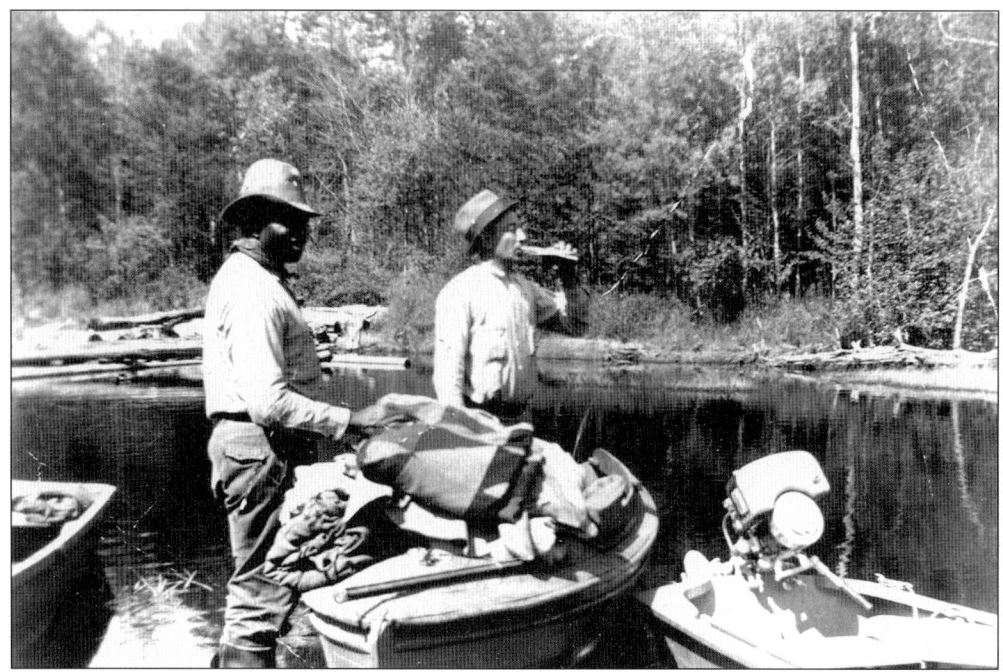

JAKE (FRANK) TOMPKINS (1885–1955). Jake settled in Morley with his parents, Walker and Nancy Tompkins. His parents were members of the Underground Railroad movement during the Civil War. Jake, his father, and brother Delbert worked in the logging mill until the mills shut down. He is shown here on the left with Bill Infantine, enjoying one of his favorite pastimes— fishing at Brandy Brook. He ran a barbershop for many years, where card games were a favorite pastime.

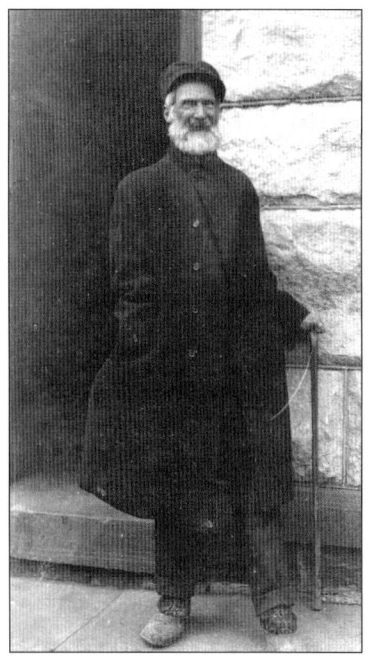

EDDIE PERRY (1863–1929). Edward W. Perry Jr. was a most unusual Canton character. Eddie was afflicted with St. Vitas Dance disease, an illness that causes tremors, but had a unique talent for painting and gardening. Daily he sat across from the town hall, painting and selling his work; especially postcards. His most famous painting is of Jimmy Murray, a mason with his corncob pipe. Reportedly, this likeness hung in many local and state saloons plus thousands across the country.

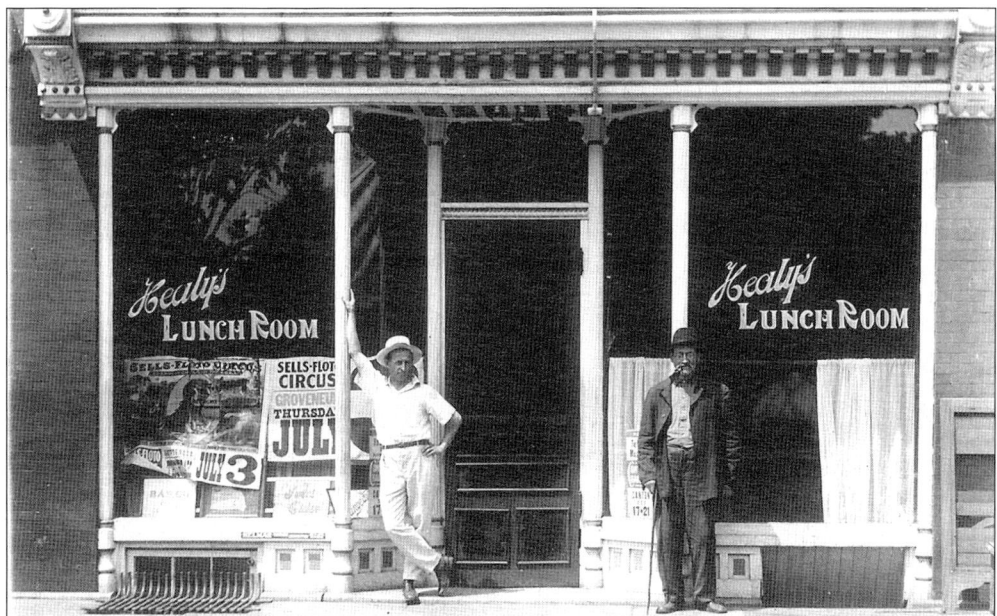

PHILIP H. VAN HORNE, SR. (1844–1931). Shown on the right in front of Healey's Lunch Shop on lower Main Street, is Philip Van Horne Sr. Van Horne was one of Rushton's prized carpenters. A Civil War Veteran, he lived in the D. P. Church house at one time. His grandson Otis, a retired instructor at SUNY Canton, lives in the village with his wife, Frances McCormick Van Horne. Fran is the granddaughter of Molly Rushton.

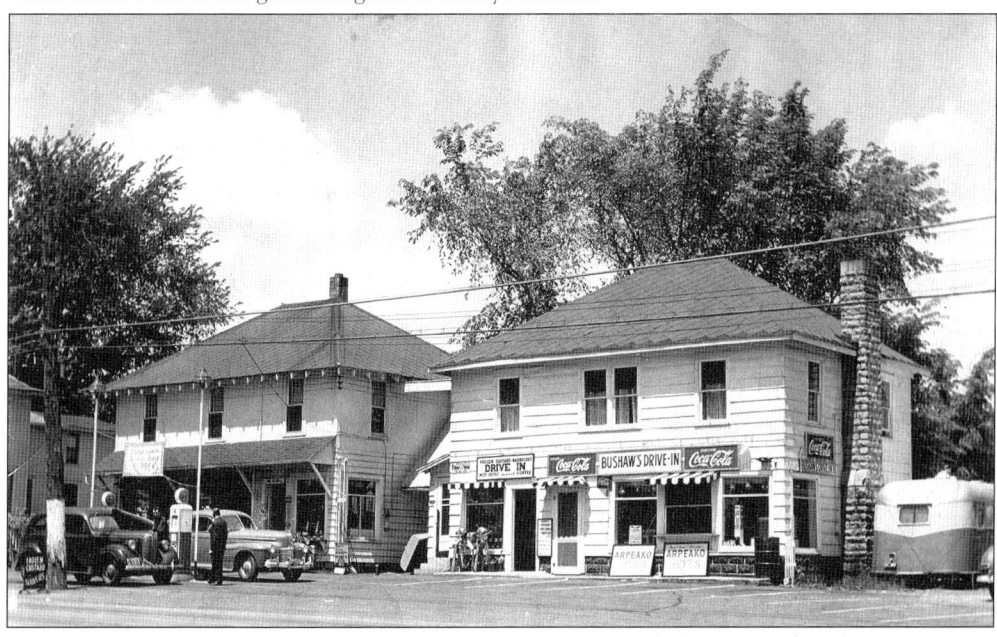

BUSHAW'S. John and Della Perry Bushaw and their daughter Thelma, owned Bushaw's Drive-In. It was located on Route 11, where the Sunoco convenience store is now located. This drive-in was the first place in town to have a frozen ice-cream machine, and Arpeako Hots. The shop next door was Bushaw's sporting goods store. These were the days when mom-and-pop stores were usually passed down to their children.

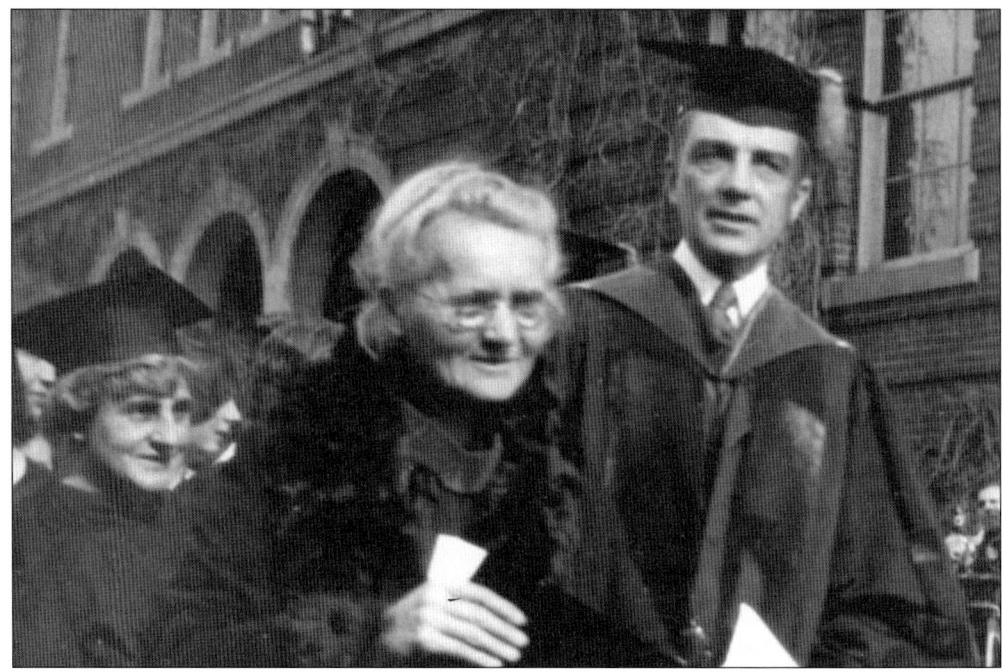

MADAME CURIE'S VISIT. Madame Curie, co-discoverer of radium, is known as one of the world's greatest scientists. Making only two trips to the United States, on October 26, 1929, she came to Canton for the dedication of the Hepburn Chemistry Laboratory at St. Lawrence. Owen D. Young, seen here by her side, arranged the visit. It was a three-day event with over 10,000 people in attendance. Madame Curie stayed at the St. Lawrence University president's house on Main Street. Her reception dinner was held at the Hotel Harrington. (Courtesy of SLU Archives.)

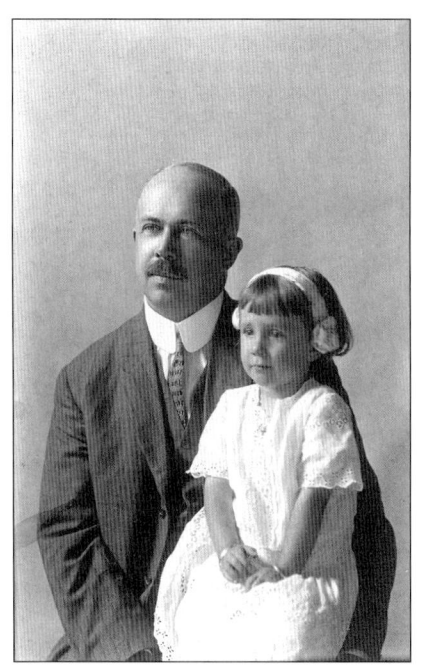

HENRY DEVALCOURT KIP (1830–1909). Henry Kip is shown here with his daughter, Welthea. He was a North Country artist and man of many carpentry skills and artistic talents. He was the son of a blacksmith and father of artist Benjamin Kip. The elder Kip was a painter, decorator of wagons, and even made a violin. He painted frescoes on the interior walls of churches and other public buildings in Canton. Henry kept several journals on local oral traditions and on contemporary newspaper accounts. The Kips lived in the family house on Chapel Street for 110 years.

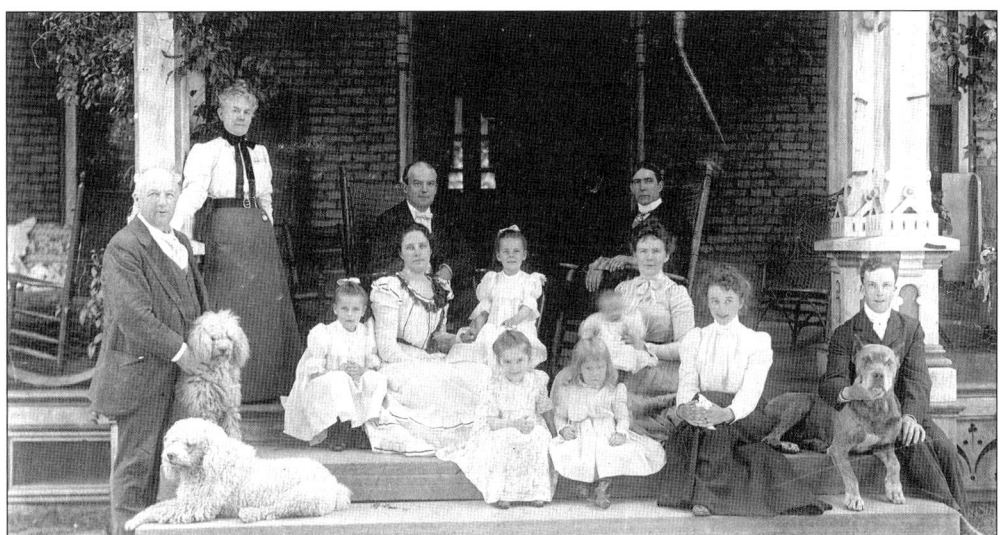

JUDGE LESLIE W. RUSSELL (1840–1903). Pictured here with his family, Judge Russell was the son of a very politically active family. Though he never attended college, he possessed a strong, vigorous, and intuitive mind. Judge Russell served as a county district attorney, was a St. Lawrence law professor, town supervisor, and county judge, and was elected to the New York City supreme court bench in 1892. Judge Russell, with William H. Sawyer, and Ledyard P. Hale, were respected for their extensive legal knowledge, courtesy, and eloquence. Many students from the university and Canton Academy would attend important trials. It is said of this remarkable group that Russell was the "King."

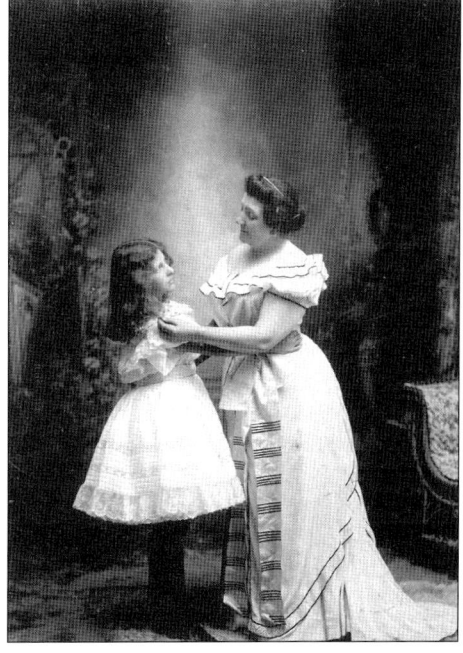

HELEN COWEN AND SARAH. This rare photograph shows Helen Cowen and her daughter Sarah as a young child. Sarah was in her twenties before the building of Ragnarock, and rarely, if ever, visited the mansion. Upon her father's death, she became a very wealthy young woman, but due to her frivolous habits, squandered her money away within a few months. (Courtesy of SLU Archives.)

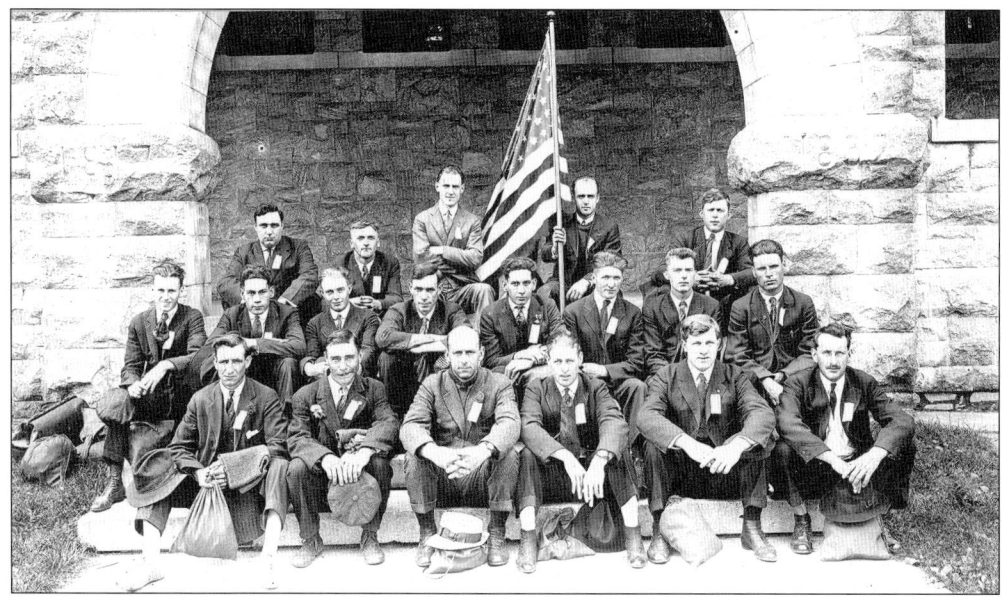

WORLD WAR I DRAFTEES. This is a picture of a group of St. Lawrence County men sitting in front of the county building. They had been drafted during World War I. The man in the middle is Beulah Crossman White's father, Fritz Crossman, from Russell.

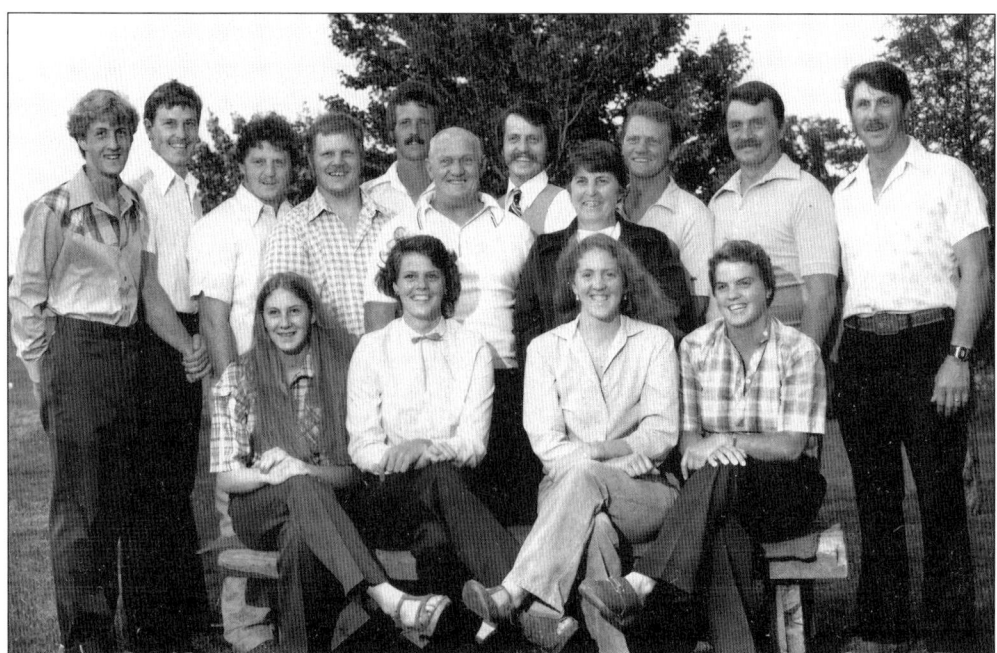

THE LOCY FAMILY. Shown here at a family gathering, Robert and Loana Locy raised 14 children on their family farm. They are, from left to right, (first row) Rene, Marta, Roxanne, and Katherine; (second row) Robert and Loana; (third row) Paul, Joe, Aloysius, Mike, William, James, Christopher, and Robert Jr. Missing from the photograph is Patrick.

Nine
VILLAGES AND HAMLETS

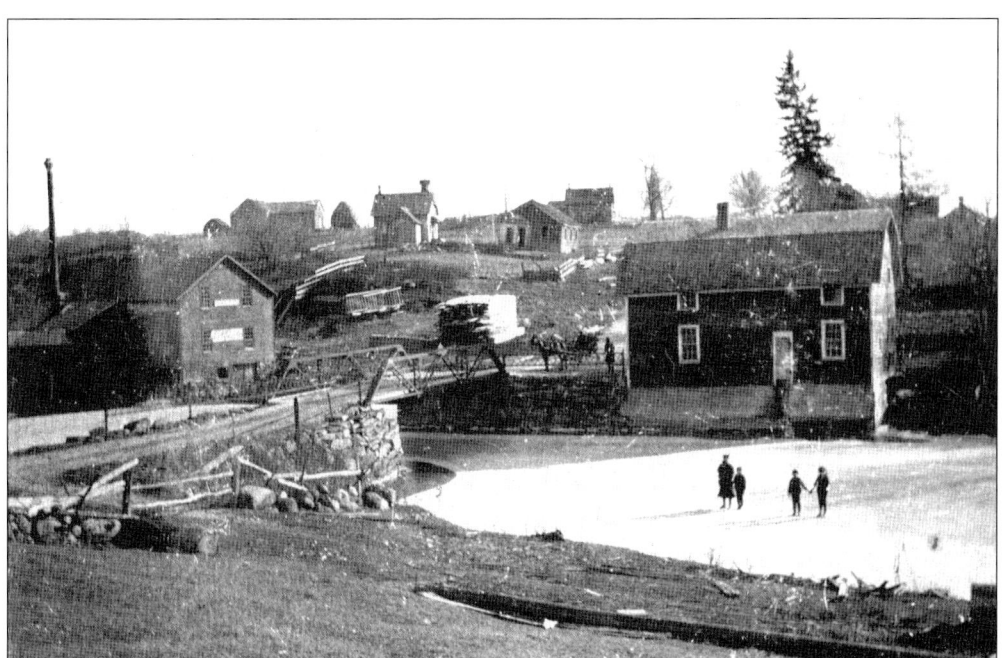

BRICK CHAPEL SETTLEMENT. The tiny hamlet of Brick Chapel was one of the first settlements in the town of Canton. It boasted two cheese factories, a sawmill, a blacksmith shop, a school, and a beautiful church set high on the hill overlooking the rest of the hamlet.

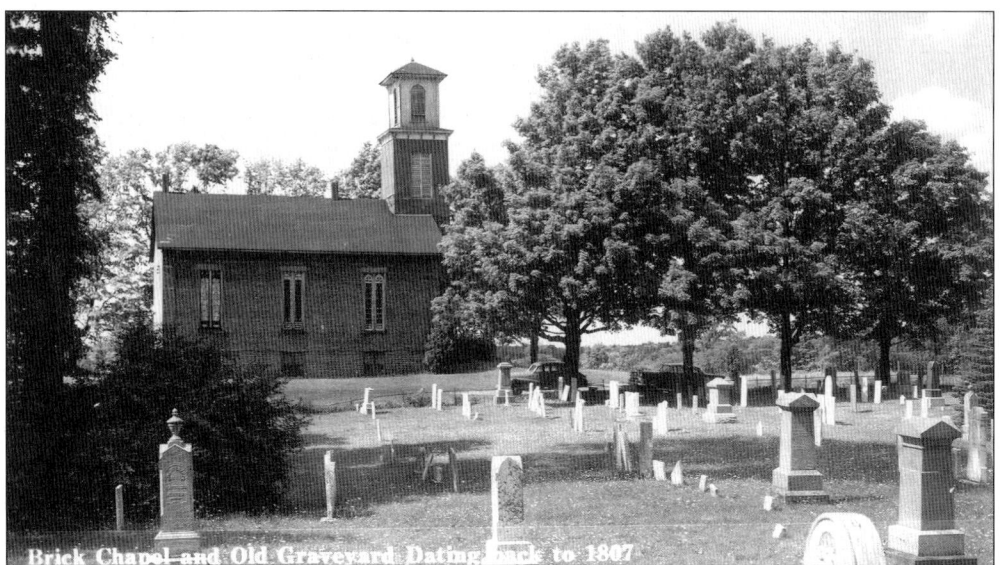

THE FIRST CHURCH BUILDING ERECTED IN CANTON. As early as 1807, religious society prayer meetings were held in the western part of the town. By 1815, the first board of trustees was organized, and in 1823, measures were adopted to construct a church edifice. This resulted in the building of a brick chapel at South Canton. John Richardson donated the land to the society "for church and cemetery purposes." Brick Chapel, as the area is still known, was built after subscriptions totaling $868.25 were gathered in the form of cash, meat cattle, grain, and building materials. The church congregation is still very active.

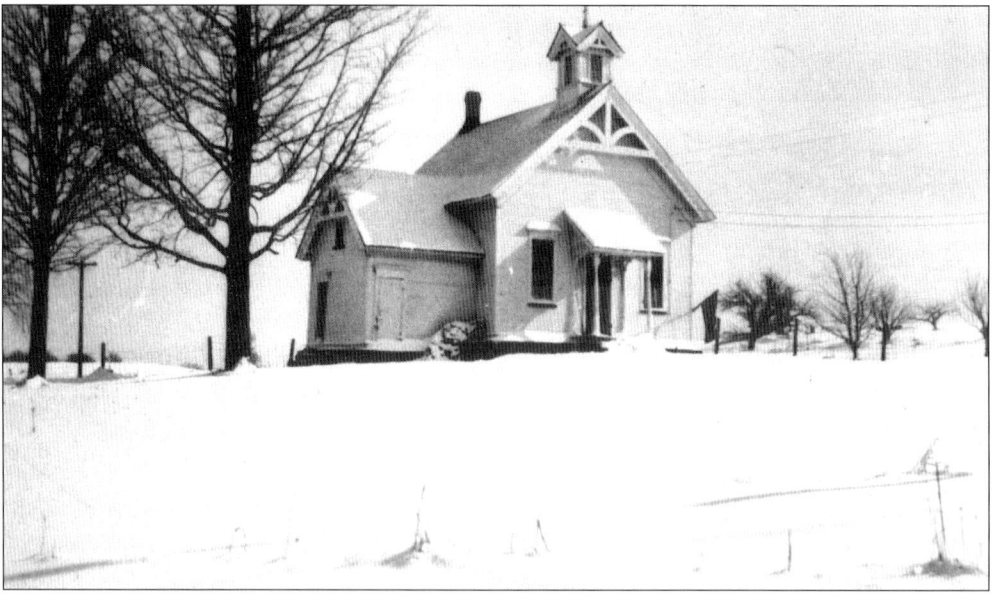

BRICK CHAPEL SCHOOL. The people who settled in the countryside around Canton valued education for their children. Almost as soon as homes and barns were constructed, a one-room school appeared. This photograph, taken in the late 1800s, shows Brick Chapel School, in the tiny hamlet of Brick Chapel. This one-room school was the first square-built schoolhouse in the township. A classic school bell hung in the tower, and could be heard for miles, reminding dawdlers to walk a little faster.

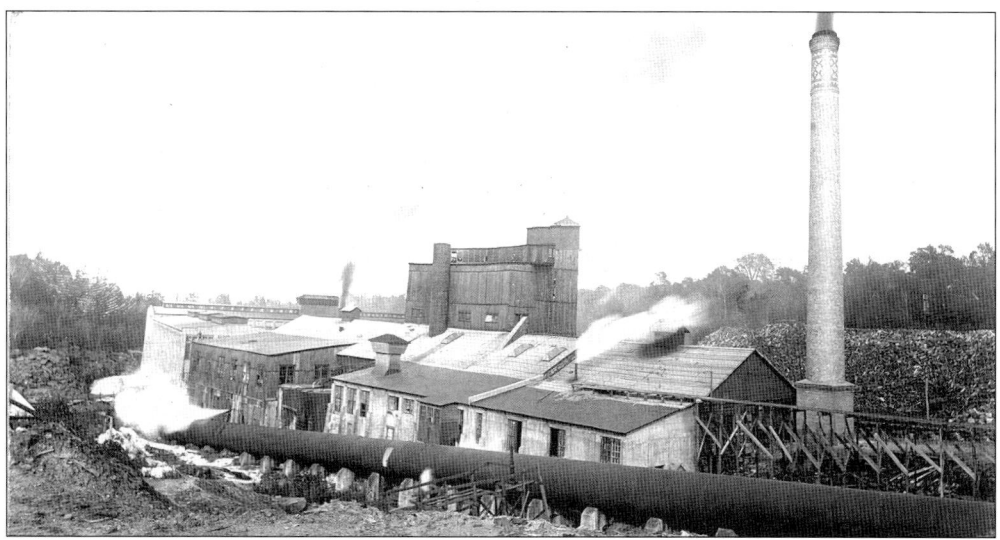

THE HAMLET OF PYRITES. Near the southern part of the town of Canton at the foot of Hill Falls, lies the hamlet of Pyrites. Stillman Foote, a founding father of Canton, discovered this area on the Grasse River and began manufacturing alum and copper as early as 1832. The operation proved fruitless, and he abandoned it four years later. In the early 1890s, the process for burning iron pyrite to make sulfuric acid was invented. Found in abundance in the area, iron pyrite was used in the pulp-making industry. Several men, including Frank Augsbury Sr. started the DeGrasse Paper Company, which proved to be a very successful venture.

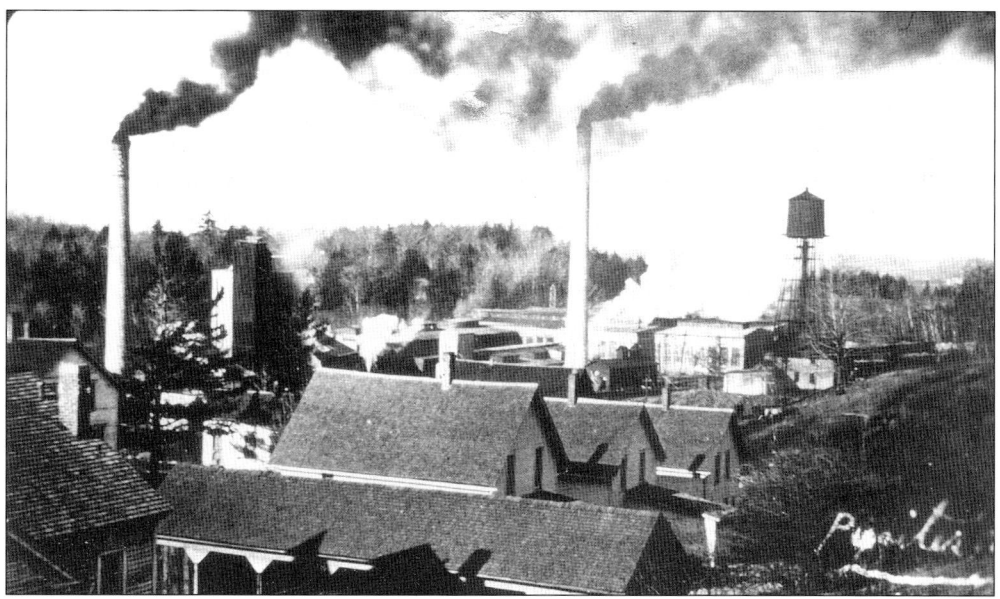

RISE AND FALL OF THE PYRITES PAPERMILL. Pyrites became a boomtown, with stores, hotels, and other businesses in abundance. Over 180 building lots provided housing on the blocks surrounding the mill. Immigrants made their way north from New York City with a promise of good wages and lodging for workers and families. The stock market crash of 1929 hurt business considerably, and the paper mill closed the next year. Pyrites became little more than a ghost town, leaving behind mill houses, boarded-up storefronts, and the ruins of a paper mill.

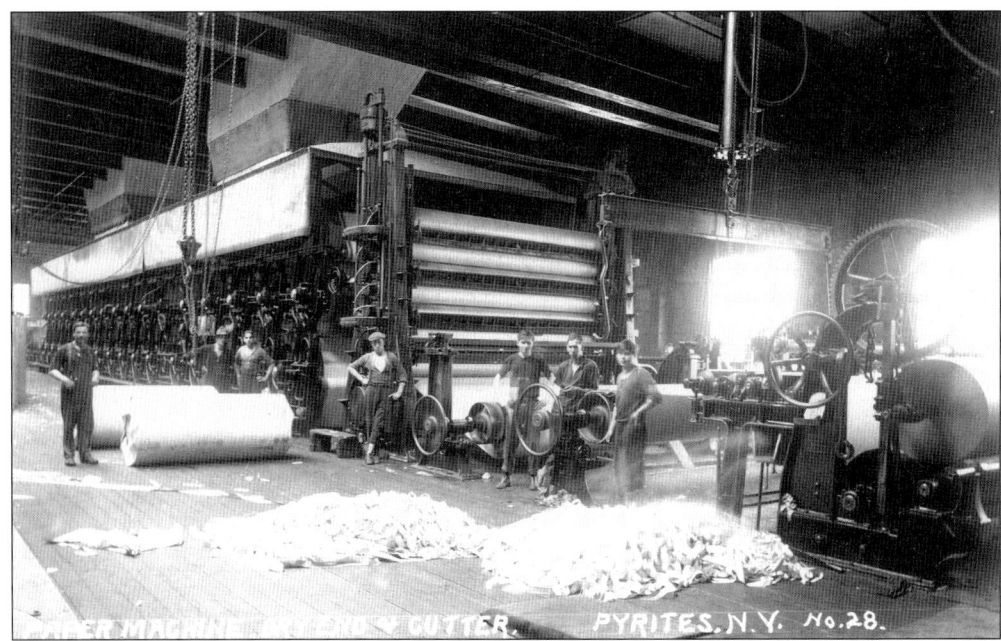

PYRITES PAPER MACHINE DRY END AND CUTTER. The DeGrasse Paper Company in Pyrites manufactured paper from the early 1890s until 1919 when it was sold to New York World Newspapers, and later, to the International Paper Company. It continued to manufacture paper until July 26, 1930. The company employed 500 workers and made 200 tons of newsprint daily.

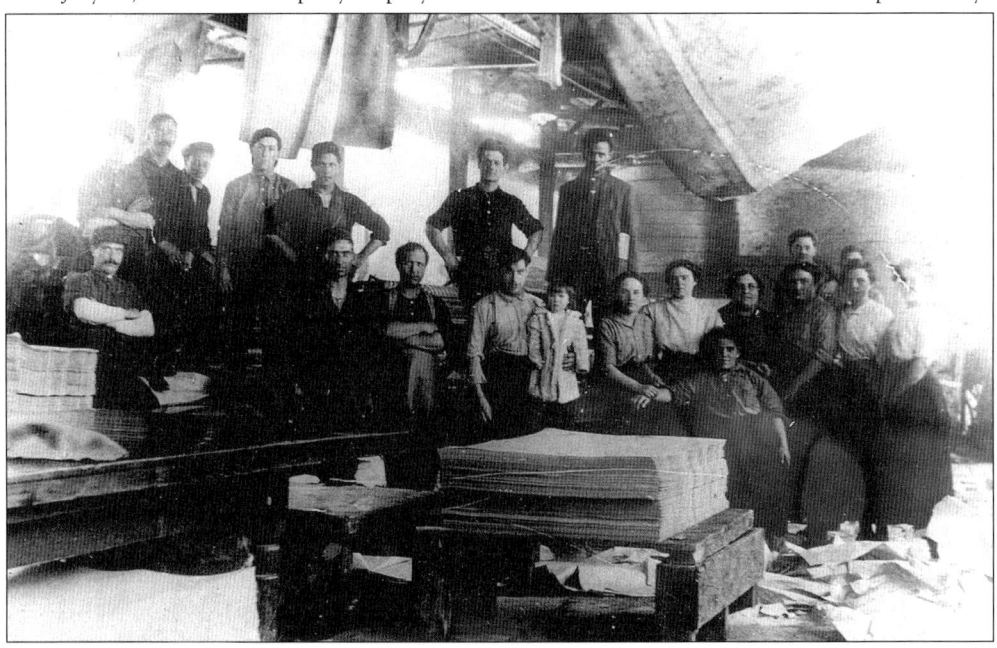

FINISHING ROOM HELP. Women as well as men were employed in the paper mill. This may be a finishing room where women finished the process of packing and readying the paper for railroad shipment. During its heyday, the Pyrites workers helped support Canton's economy with its $15,000 weekly payroll. When the new road from Canton to Pyrites opened, much of the workers' money was spent in the county seat.

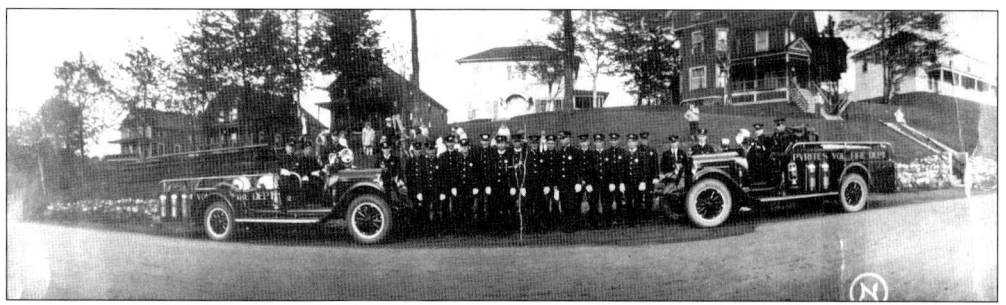

PYRITES FIRE DEPARTMENT. As the mill grew between 1902 and 1930, the population of Pyrites increased to 1,500. The need for an organized fire department was obvious. Organized in 1919, the 20-member department was at first run by the mill. In the early days, the fire department had two horse carts with 550 feet of hose, and a hook and ladder wagon with 500 feet of hose. This 1928 photograph is of the Lone Wolf motorized truck. Residents of Pyrites took particular pride in their fire department. This is still true today.

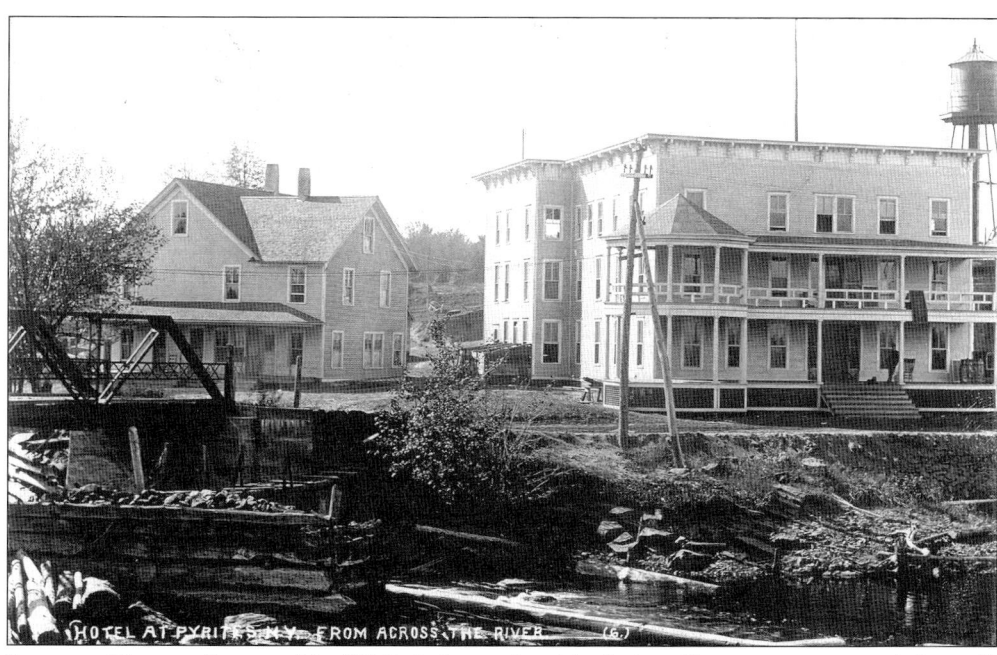

SEVERAL HOTELS SPRANG UP. While industry flourished, the village grew up around the mill. Several hotels sprang up to accommodate the men working on the construction of the new mill. The first hotel was the Rushton House, built in 1892. Seen here is the Locklin Hotel, built shortly thereafter. Murray Hall, later known as Union Hall, held most of the social occasions such as the annual Papermakers' Ball, which occurred on Easter Monday evening each year.

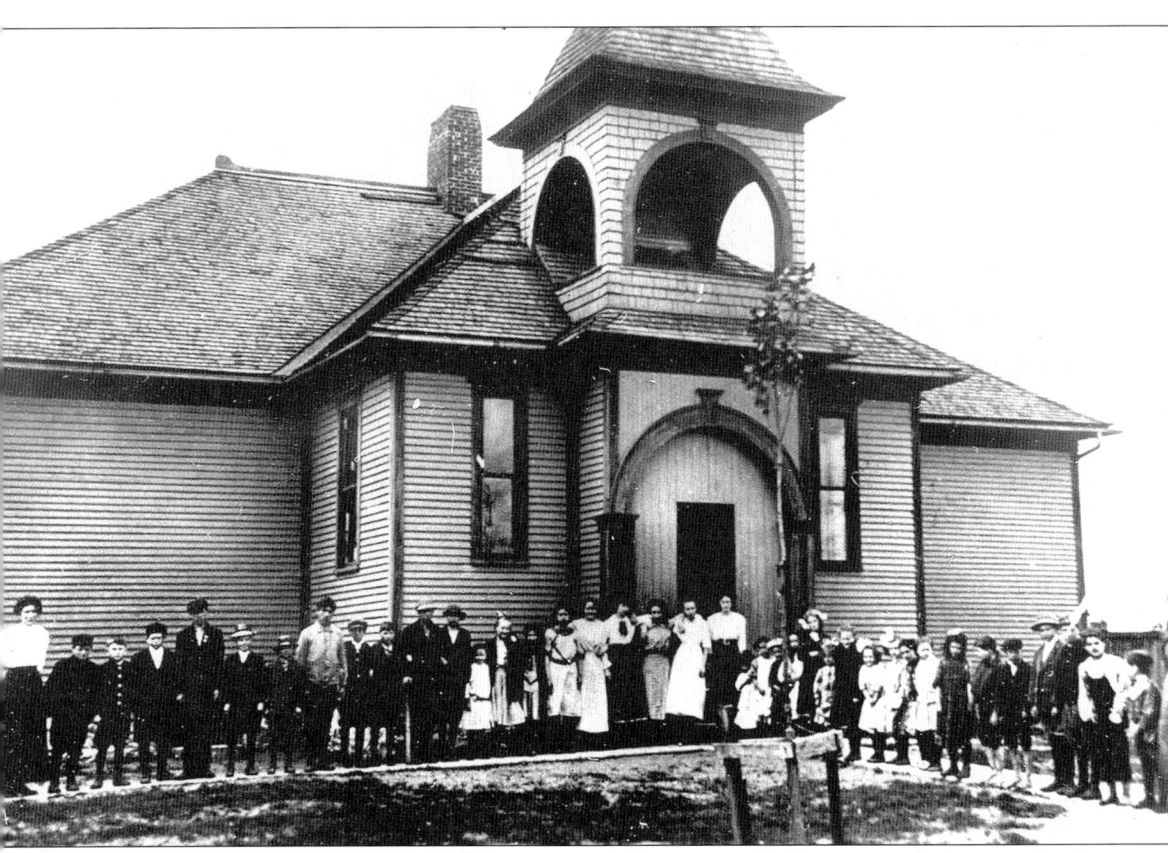

THE PYRITES SCHOOLS. With the success of the papermill, Pyrites needed new schools. A. W. Crane donated a building site, and the Pyrites Union Free School was organized in 1915. Townline and Cousintown Schools were established soon thereafter. In 1921, $50,000 was set aside for a new high school. Following the closing of the papermill, population dwindled, which forced the high school to close in 1938. Pyrites residents were unhappy with its closing, but managed to keep the elementary school open until 1968.

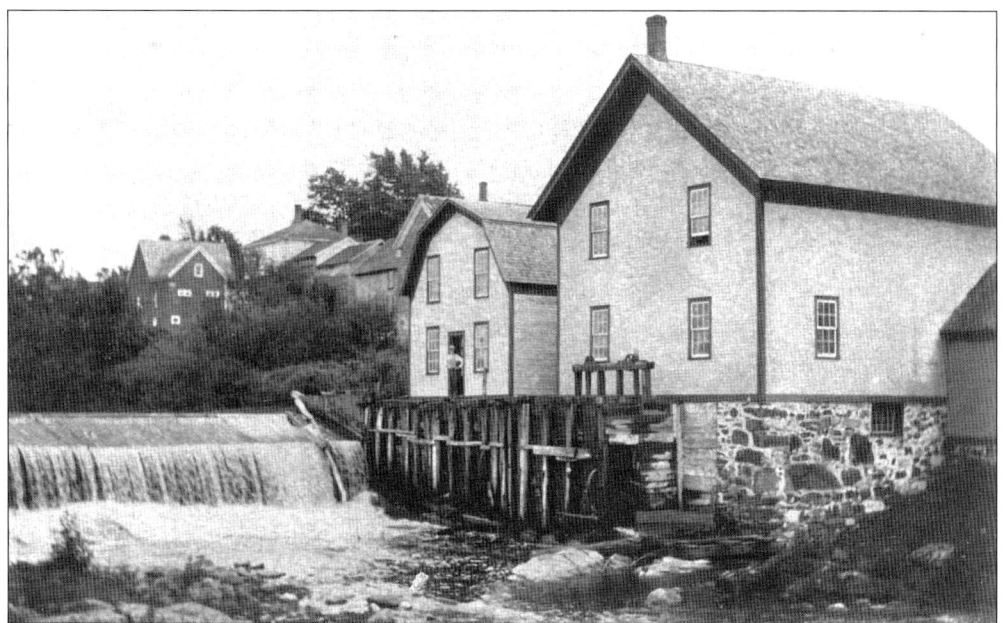

THE EARLY SETTLEMENT OF CRARY MILLS. Around 1813, Joseph Harvey and his wife Hannah, along with a few other Vermont families, braved the wilds of the Chateguay trail as they made their way to northern New York. Several homes were constructed, and Edward Crary built the first mill. In 1835, he built a gristmill on Grannis Brook, and later added a sawmill nearby. For several years, the hamlet was known as Crary's Mills.

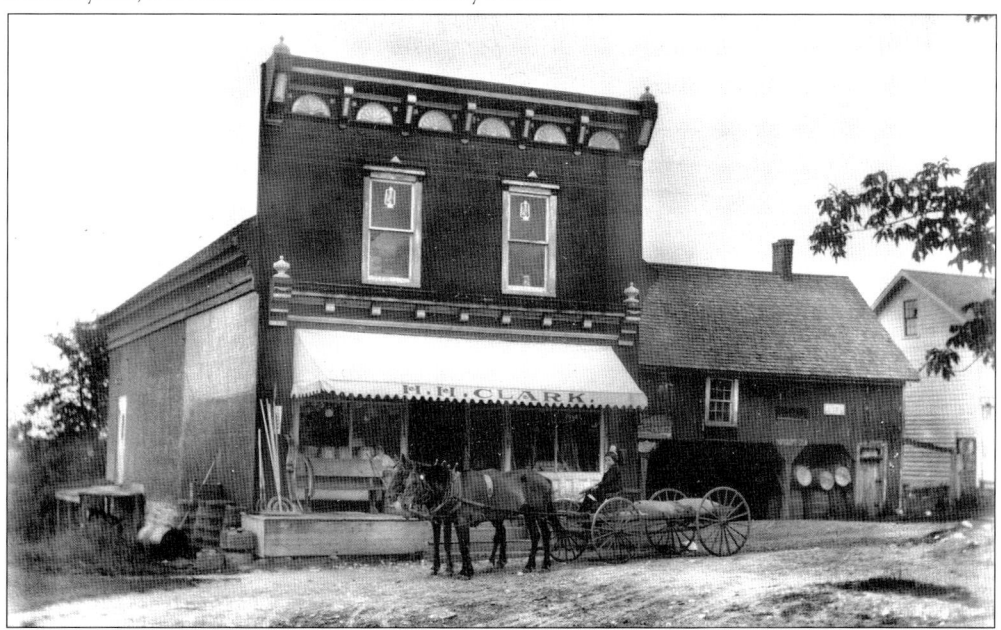

CRARY'S MILLS, A THRIVING COMMUNITY. Pictured here, we see the H. H. Clark General Store, around 1900. In the late 1880s, many small enterprises flourished in Crary's Mills: a cobbler's shop, tannery, blacksmith shop, carriage shop, wheelwright shop, millinery store, butter factory, and several general merchandise stores. Around 1900, the United States Postal Service dropped apostrophes on community names, and the settlement became Crary Mills.

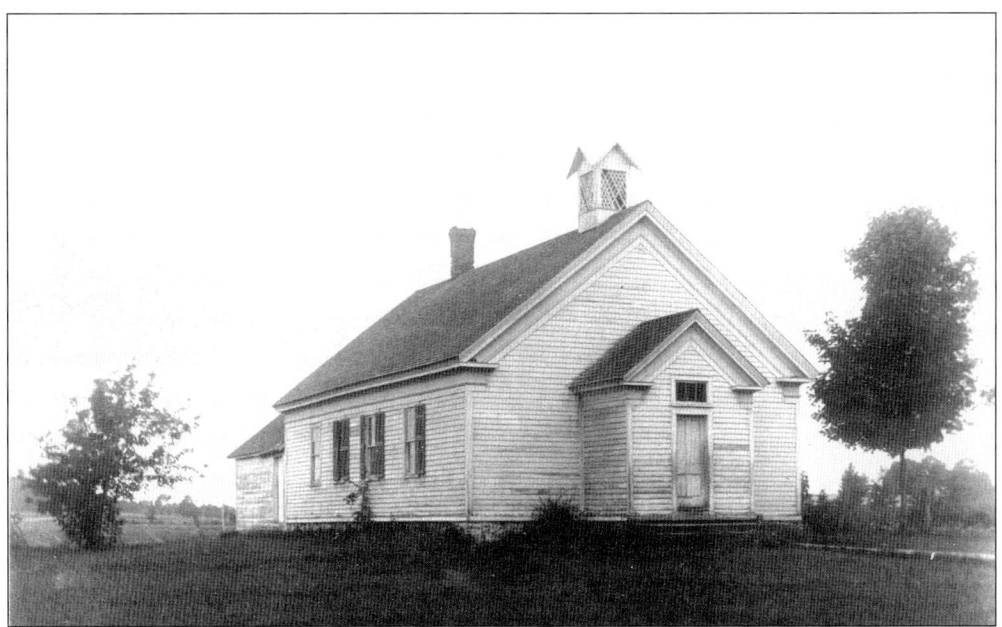

CRARY MILLS SCHOOL. This is a picture of the Crary Mills School, located in the town of Potsdam. Two years after J. Manley (Mac) McKenney took over as elementary supervisor of all Canton schools, there was debate over the future of this school. In 1952, after much discussion among Mac, Melissa Carroll (née Potsdam), and district superintendent Clarence Armstrong, the decision was made. The Crary Mills School would join the Canton district.

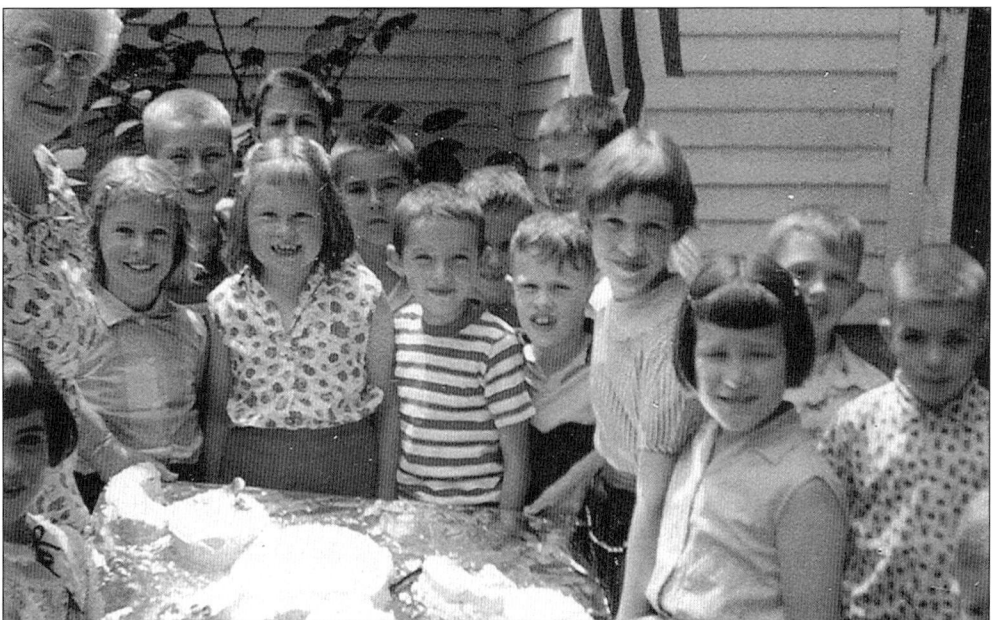

LAST DAY OF SCHOOL, 1960. The last day of the school year in the country was just as exciting for pupils then as it is today. Often children displayed their work and performed skits and recitations to show their parents what they had done all year. In this picture, Marion Hale Hitchcock, the last teacher at Crary Mills is shown with her students. One of the mothers made the cake.

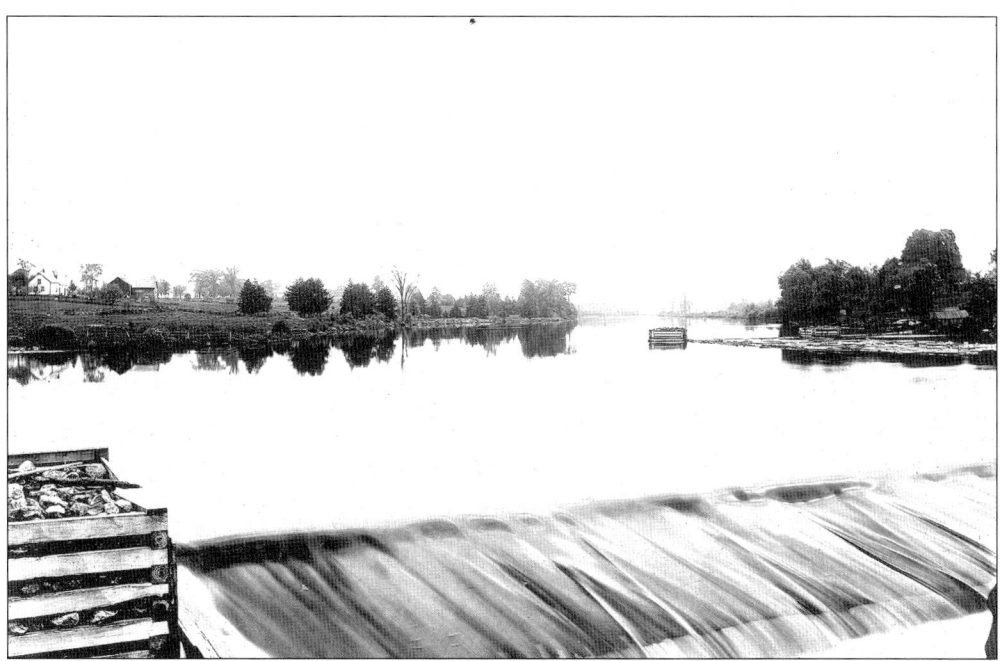

THE HAMLET OF MORLEY. In 1810, a group of settlers, led by Stillman Foote, started a small community near the north part of the town. At first named Long Rapids, this hamlet lays on the Grasse River, about six miles downstream from the Canton village. Foote built a dam and a sawmill.

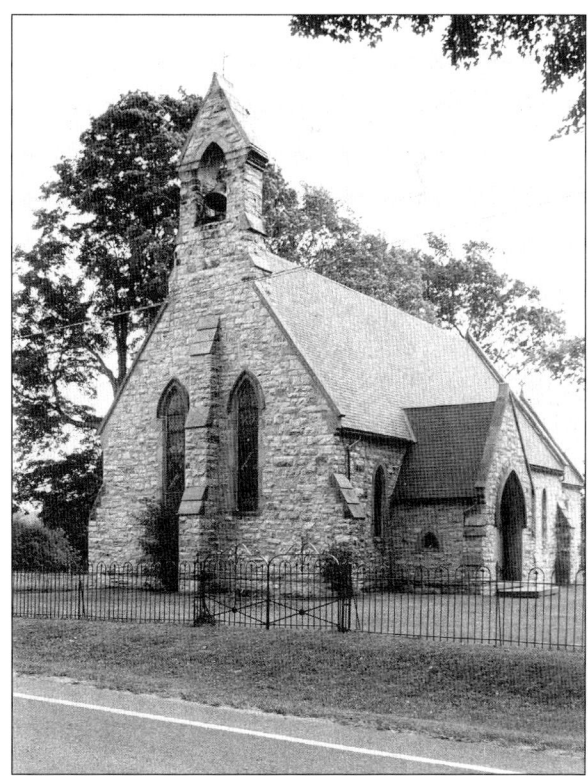

TRINITY CHAPEL IN MORLEY. This handsome church was built on land donated by Thomas Harison, with a $15,000 gift from the sale of his prize bull. The chapel is reported to be a replica of a 13th-century English Gothic church where the Harisons worshipped before emigrating to America. Construction work was completed in 1871.

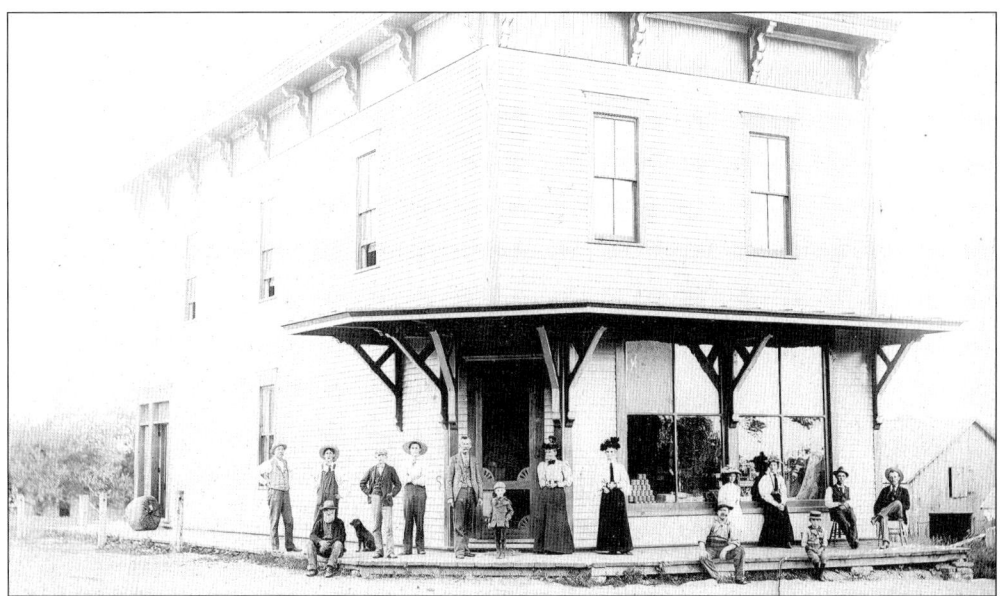

SPAULDING STORE IN MORLEY. The Spauldings, who ran this store in the late 1800s, were a brother and sister team, both unmarried. In the 1930s and 1940s, Aggie Lincoln and her stepson ran the store. A tiny woman, Aggie was a "grandmother" to most of Morley's youngsters. Children would stroll into the store for candy, most often a gift from Aggie. Saturday nights found cigar-smoking farmers around the wood stove in the back, and their wives up front, collecting the gossip of the week. The building stands today.

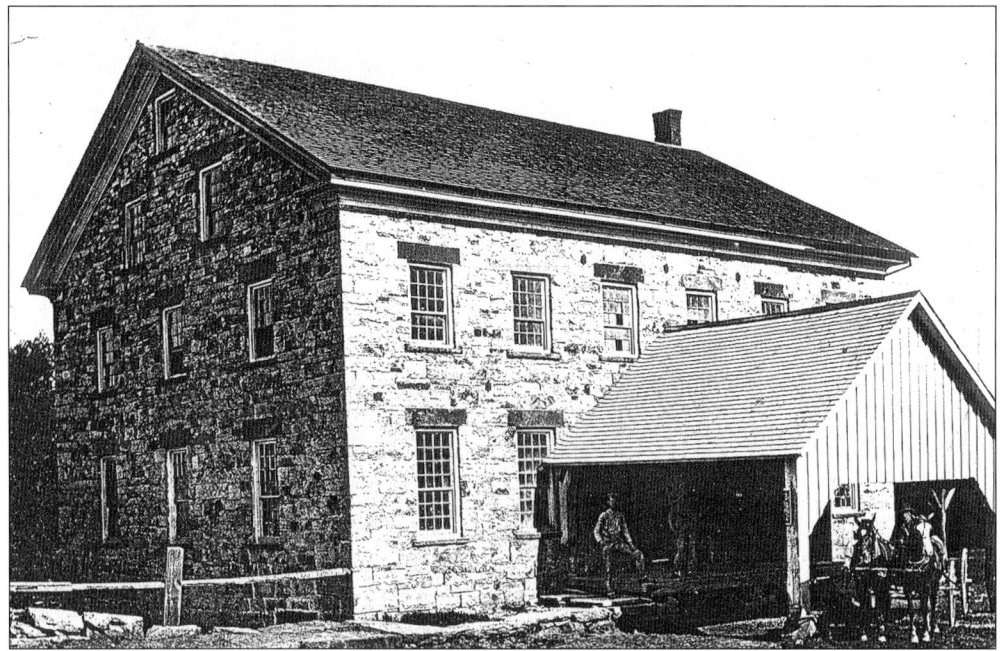

THE OLD GRIST MILL. Thomas Ludlow Harison built this mill in 1840, and Rufus K. Jackson managed it for several years. In the photograph, Billy Newby waits patiently for his corn or oats to be ground. The old gristmill is still standing, and is being refurbished by a group known as the Heritage Grist Mill Association. (Courtesy of SLCHA.)

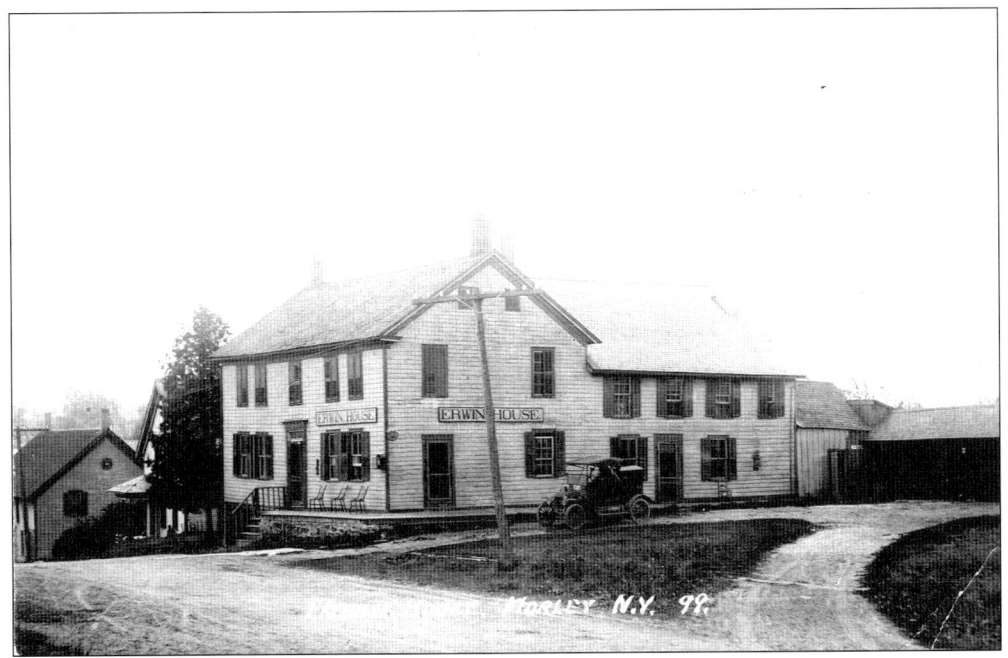

ERWIN HOUSE, MORLEY, NEW YORK. This hotel stood diagonally across from Morley's library. Roy Sands ran it for a time, but then moved on to his hotel in Rensselaer Falls. After a night of drinking at the bar, most out-of-town travelers stowed their horses in the hotel's sheds, and rented a room for the night.

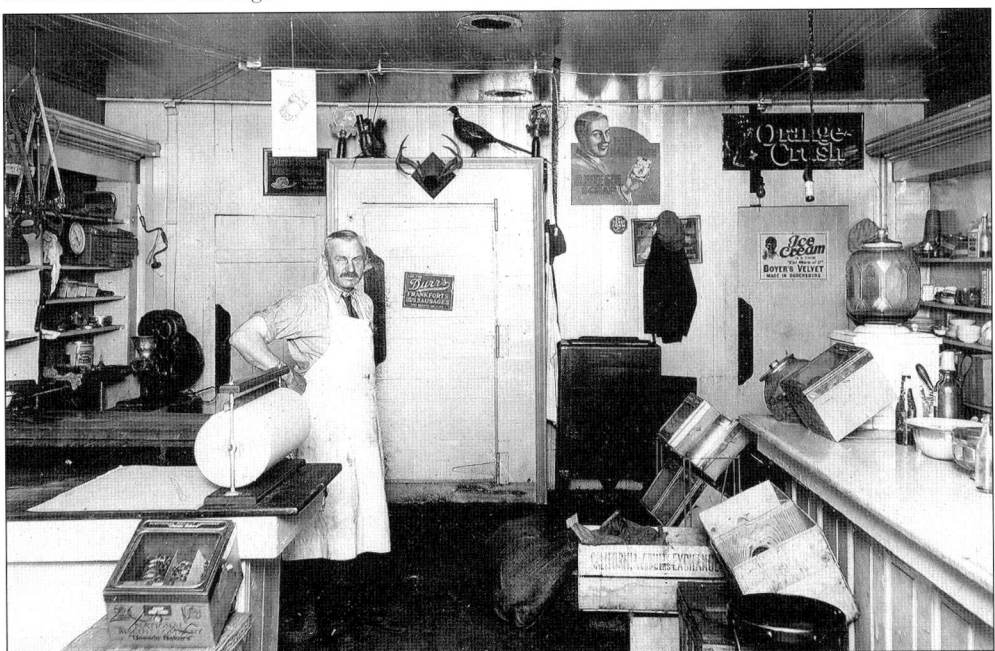

MEAT MARKET IN MORLEY. In the days when horse and buggy was the only transportation into the Canton village over rough roads, every hamlet had its own meat market. Pictured here is the Meat Market in Morley, run by Ed Lincoln and his son Clarence. This market was located across the street from the Spaulding Store.

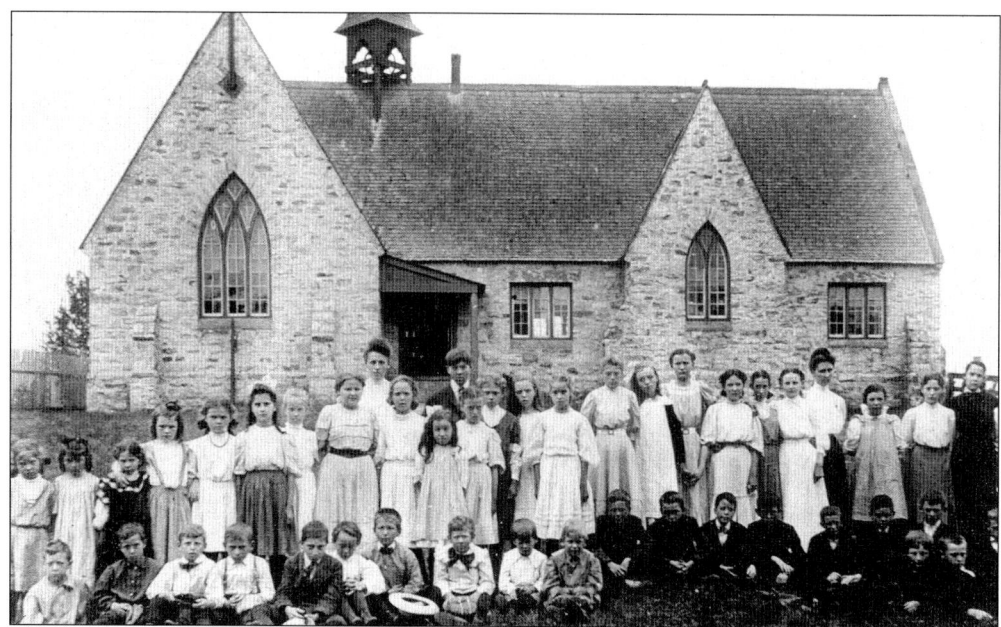

PHOTOGRAPH OF THE MORLEY SCHOOL, 1895. The larger hamlets built schools to serve their children from first grade through high school. In 1857, this school was built of local sandstone at a cost of $1,067. The school closed in June 1966, when centralization moved the students and teachers to the elementary and grammar schools in the village of Canton. Fire nearly destroyed the Morley School in 1969. Only a shell remains as a reminder of days gone by.

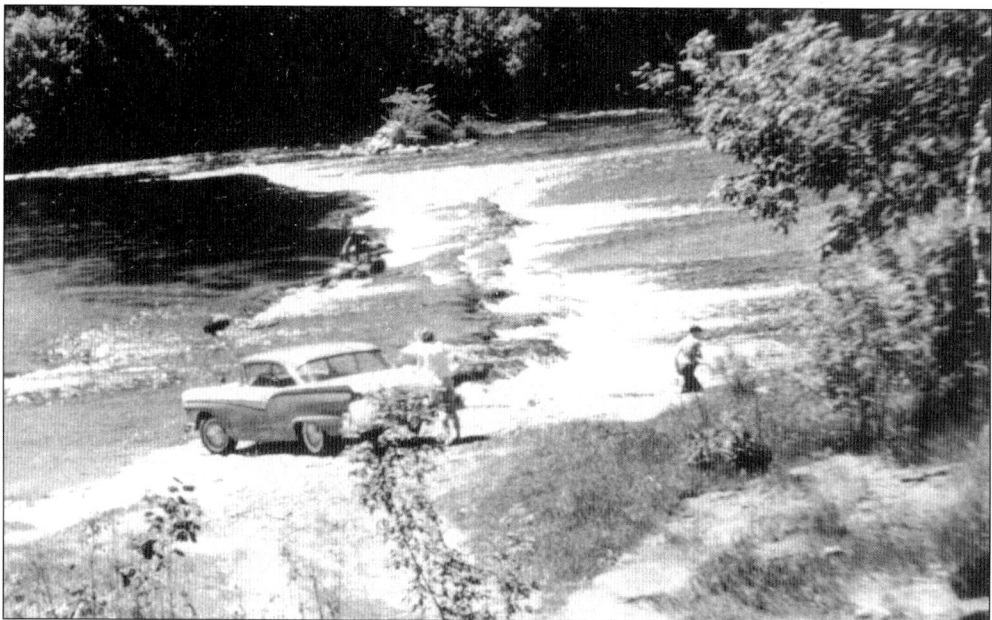

RENSSELAER FALLS, THE OTHER VILLAGE IN THE TOWN OF CANTON. The first name given to the settlement of Rensselaer Falls was Taitville, then Canton Falls. Finally, on December 19, 1851, the postal service forced the community to make up its mind on a name. The village chose Rensselaer Falls. This photograph shows a favorite swimming hole for generations of Falls folks. (Courtesy of Kyle and Sally Hartman.)

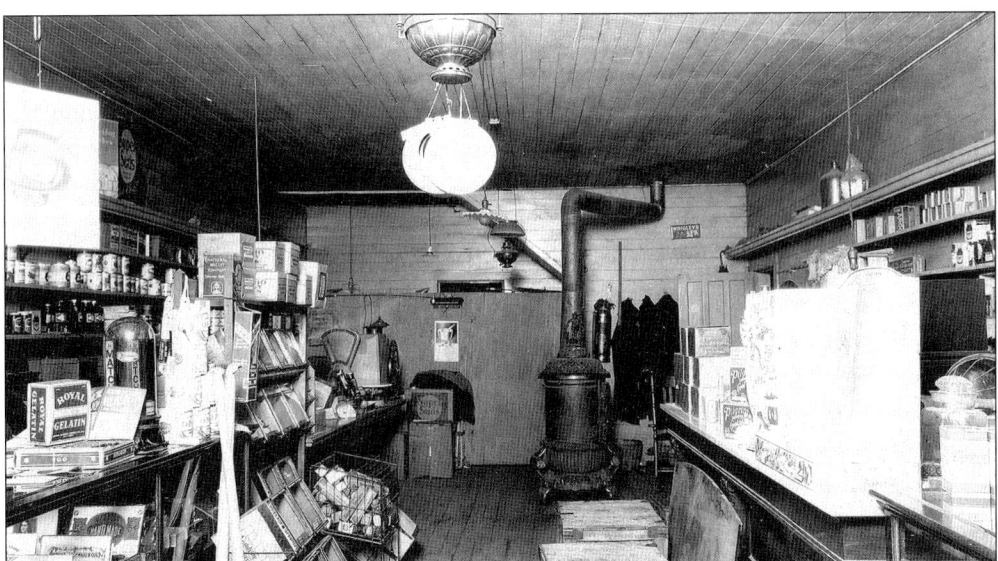

INTERIOR OF THE C. W. WAINWRIGHT STORE. This store escaped the wrath of several fires, which destroyed many Rensselaer Falls businesses. The building still stands. Following the death of C. W., Jeanette Wainwright continued to operate the store, and lived in the back with her son Herb, his wife Jessie and their daughter Linda. When guests stayed over, Linda remembers being scared while sleeping in the casket room. Recently sold to Jacqueline Lane, the store will soon have a new look. (Courtesy of Jessie Wainwright.)

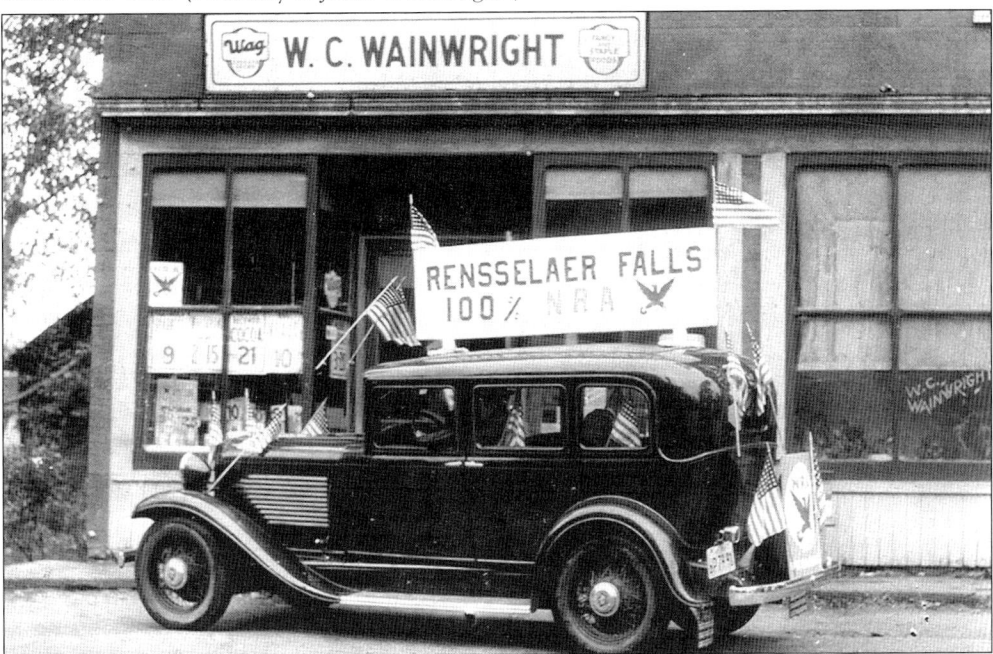

UNDERTAKER FACED DEATH AT CROSSING. Chester W. Wainwright, proprietor of the Rensselaer Falls store above and the funeral parlor next door, narrowly escaped death while crossing the railroad tracks. A freight train crashed into Wainwright's Overland Touring car, and demolished the entire rear of the vehicle. Luckily, he was able to slip out of the car uninjured. He was on his way to a funeral. (Courtesy of Jessie Wainwright.)

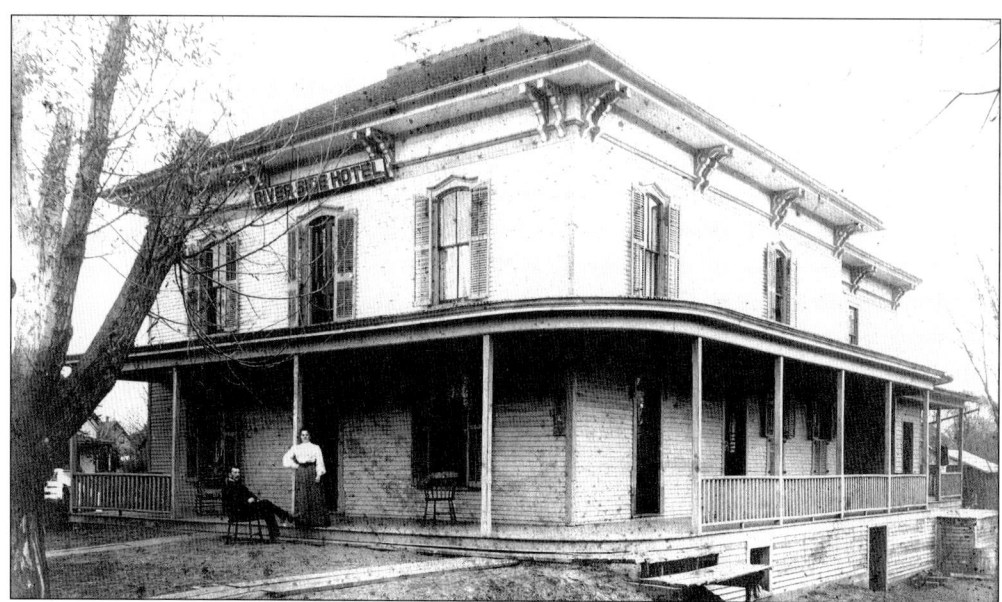

RIVERSIDE HOTEL. This hotel was originally a home built by M. W. Spaulding. The Riverside Hotel spent most of its years as an inn. Webster Wainwright bought it around 1900, and turned it into a hotel. From the architectural style, with its hip roof, and bracketed cornice, the building was reminiscent of a simplified Italianate villa, popular in the era of the 1870s. The Riverside's long life as an inn ended on February 8, 1984, when fire destroyed the historic establishment. (Courtesy of Jessie Wainwright.)

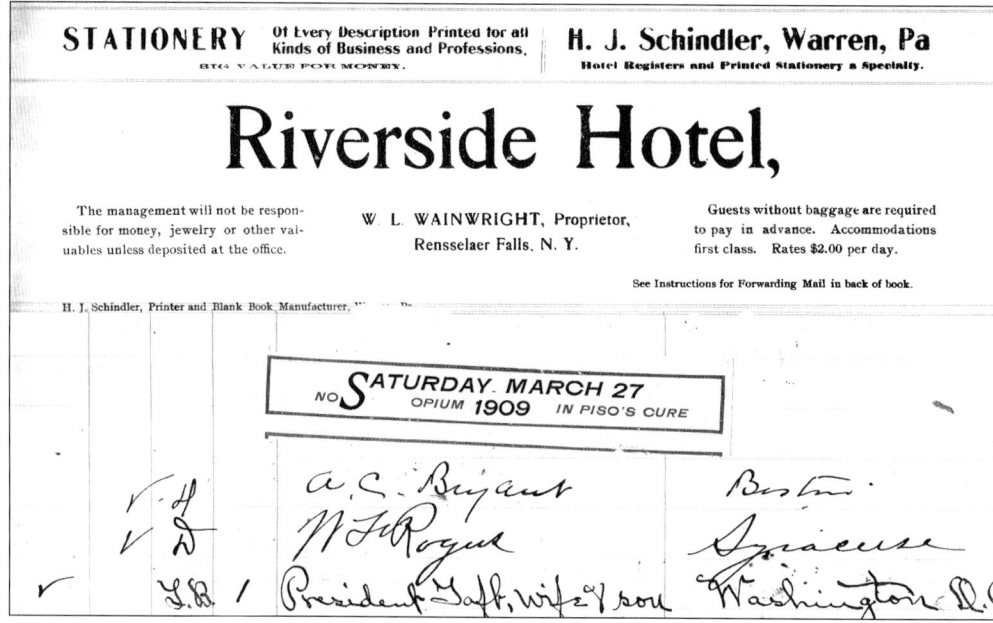

THE PRESIDENT SLEPT HERE. Pictured here, is one page of the Riverside Hotel's ledger. On March 27, 1909, Pres. William H. Taft, his wife, and son signed the ledger and spent the night at the hotel. Some time later, Mr. and Mrs. Webster L. Wainwright, proprietors of the inn, traveled to Washington, D.C., and received cordial attention from President Taft and his son at the White House. (Courtesy of Jessie Wainwright.)

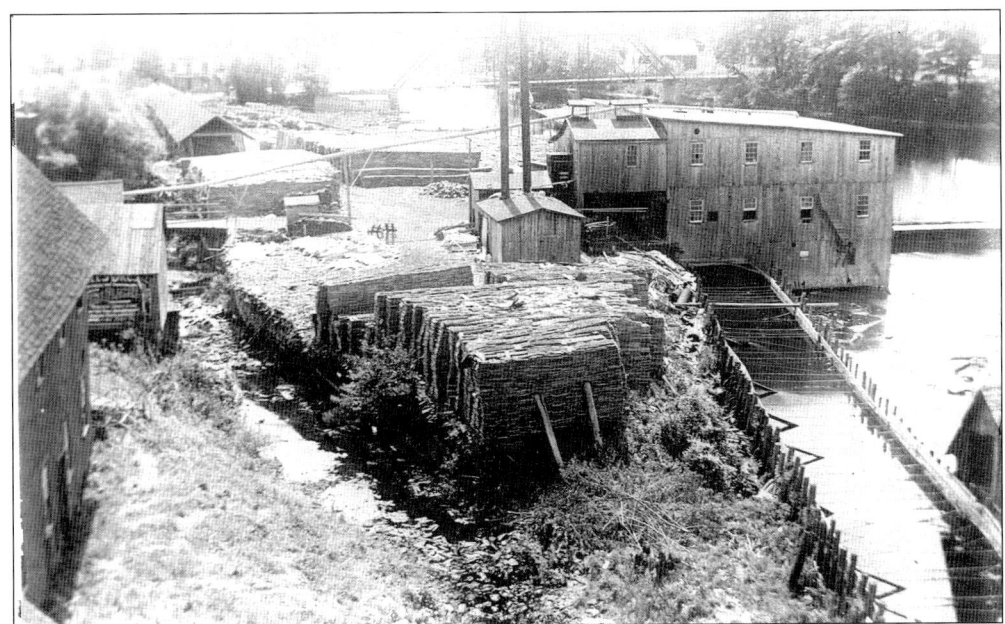

RENSSELAER FALLS CHEESE BOX FACTORY. In its early years, the Falls had many factories. The Box Factory, known especially for manufacturing cheese boxes, is pictured here. Around the early 1900s, ten milk-handling plants could be found in this farming region. Several became cheese factories, thus the need for cheese boxes. Three of these plants thrived until the 1930s, when they closed due to the milk strike. The box factory met its demise in 1949.

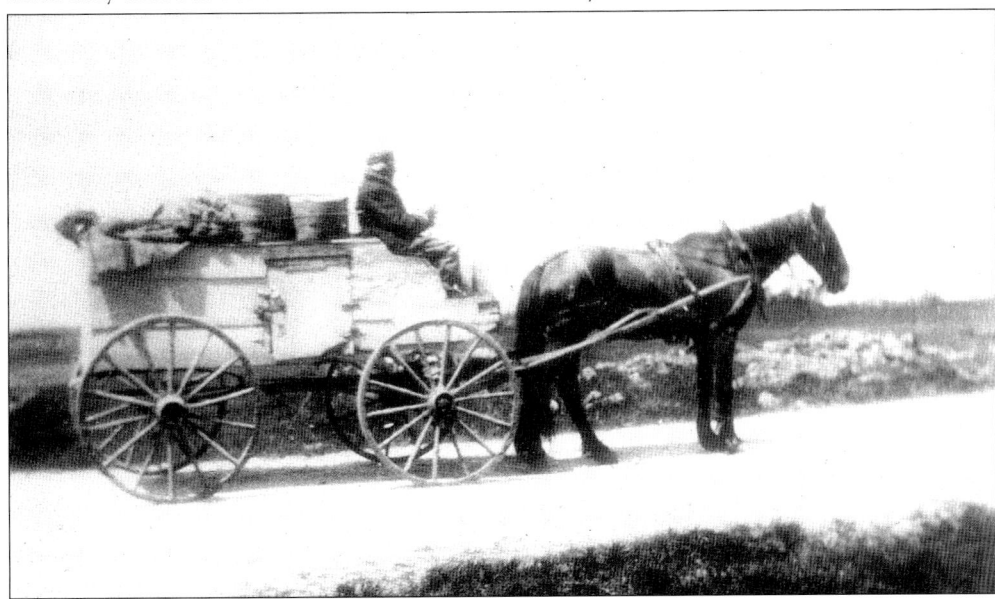

JULIUS IS COMING. How excited the children of the Falls must have been when Julius Wohlfarth appeared in their dooryard. Julius was a peddler who traveled the country roads and streets of Rensselaer Falls selling his wares. He brought everyday supplies such as flour, sugar, and salt as well as small kitchen or farming utensils. In 1913, five pounds of nails cost 17¢. Two spools of thread were 10¢, and a pound of tea was 35¢. One could buy a doorknob or a paintbrush for 20¢. (Courtesy of Jessie Wainwright.)

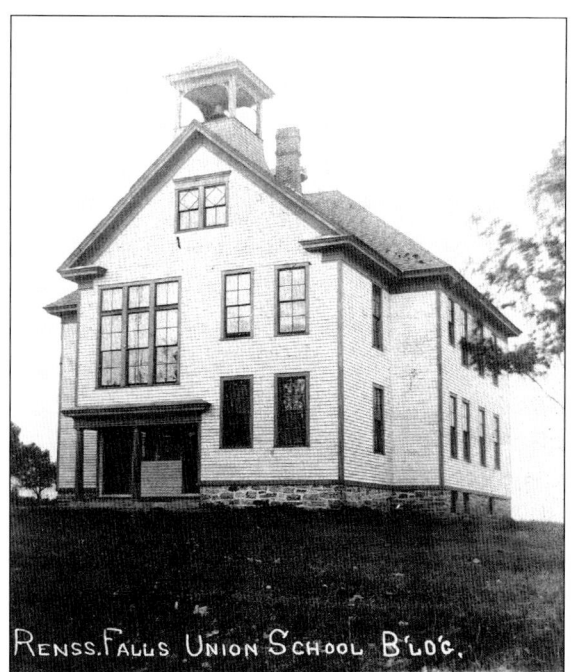

EARLY RENSSELAER FALLS SCHOOLS. The first school in Rensselaer Falls was built in 1842 on land donated by Thomas Tate. This two-story school, completed in 1882, had 150 students in attendance that first year. The school burned February 3, 1903. The new school, completed in 1904 and constructed with fire escapes, was a school in which the whole village took pride. Due to consolidation with Canton Schools, the last class graduated in 1945.

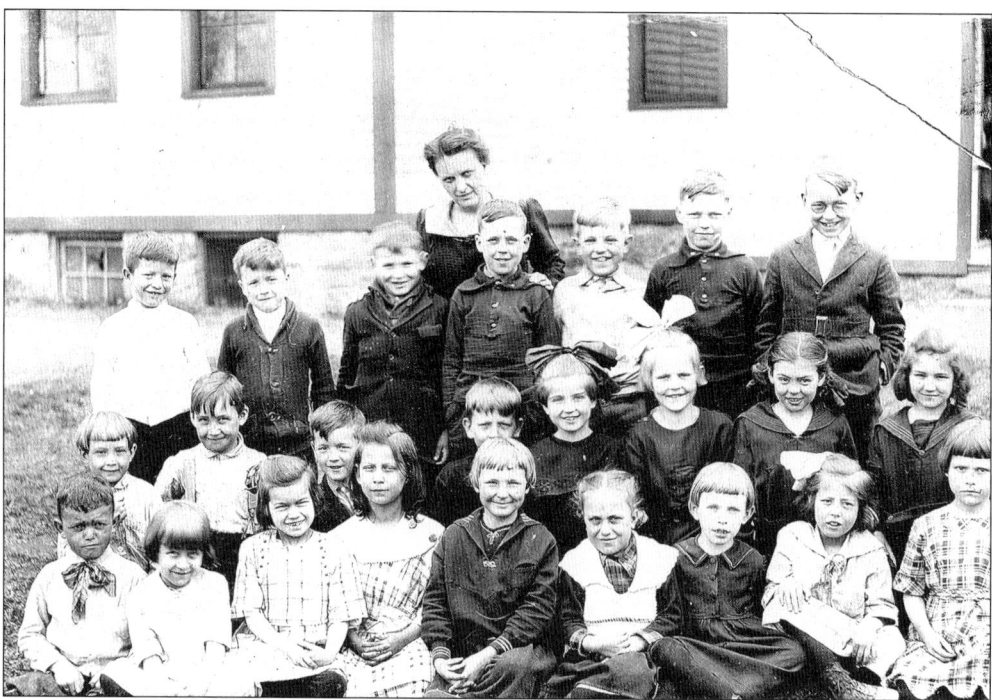

FIRST GRADERS AT THE FALLS SCHOOL, 1919. The Rensselaer Falls School could accommodate 200 pupils. These first graders posed with their teacher outside the school. Herb Wainwright, long time mayor and village businessman, is the second from the left in the middle row. (Courtesy of Jessie Wainwright)

Ten
Recreation and Historic Interest

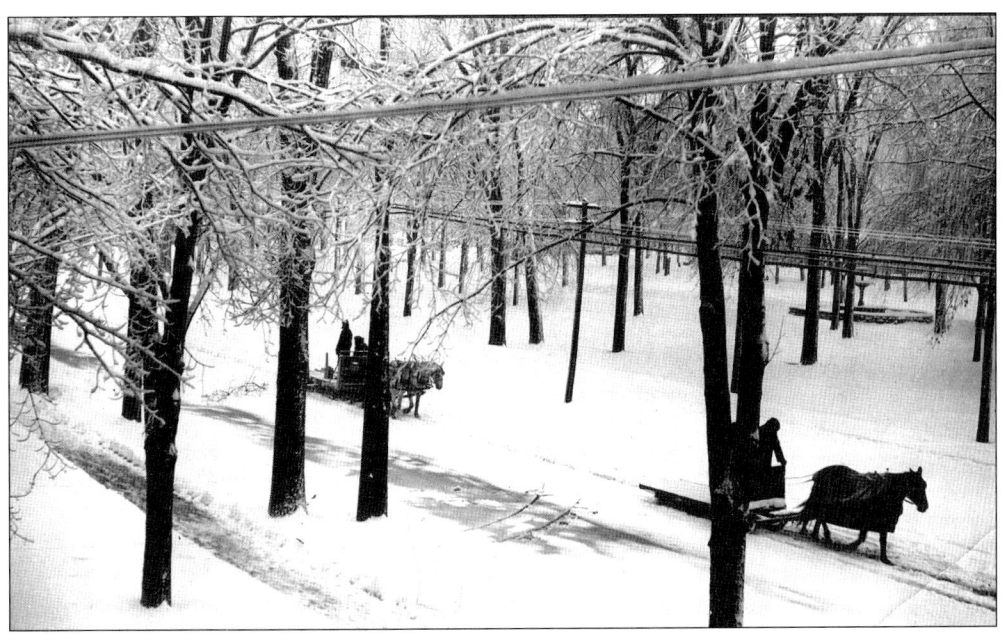

Horse-drawn Sleds, East Main Street at the Park. When a horse wears a blanket while working, pulling a sled, you know it is cold. Taken from a Main Street (north side) upstairs window, you can see the deserted park and the men on the sleds huddled into their coats with their backs to the westward wind that came howling down the street.

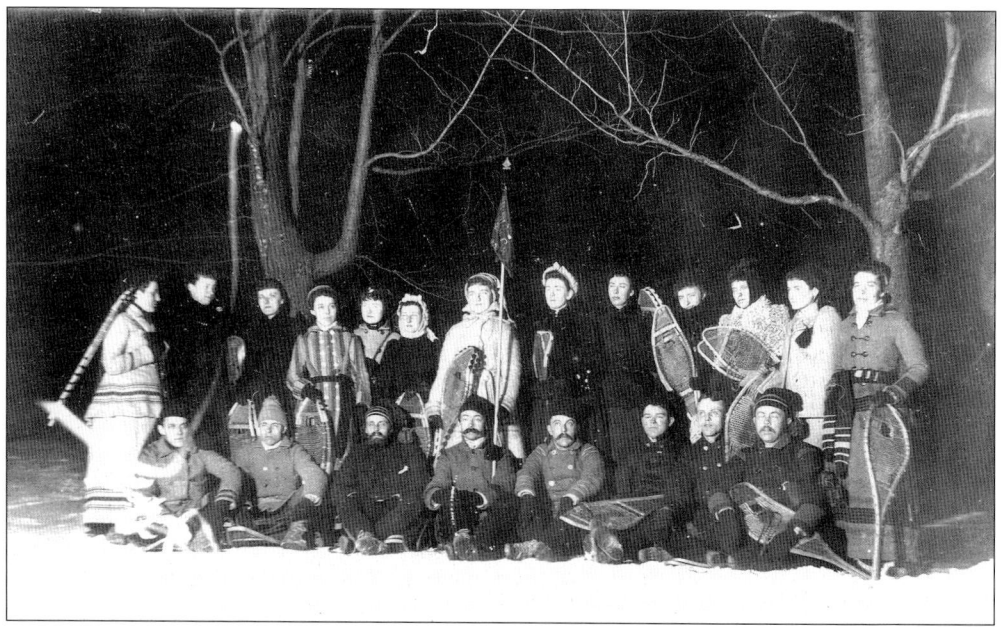

SNOWSHOE CLUB, MARCH 2, 1892. Dr. Henry "Hank" Priest, St. Lawrence University professor and dean, organized Canton's Snowshoe Club in the early 1890s. Together with the Snowshoe Clubs of Ogdensburg, Brockville, and Prescott, the Canton Club was a very active social as well as athletic club. In their colorful blanket costumes, members welcomed winter storms that often dumped horrific mountains of snow upon the countryside.

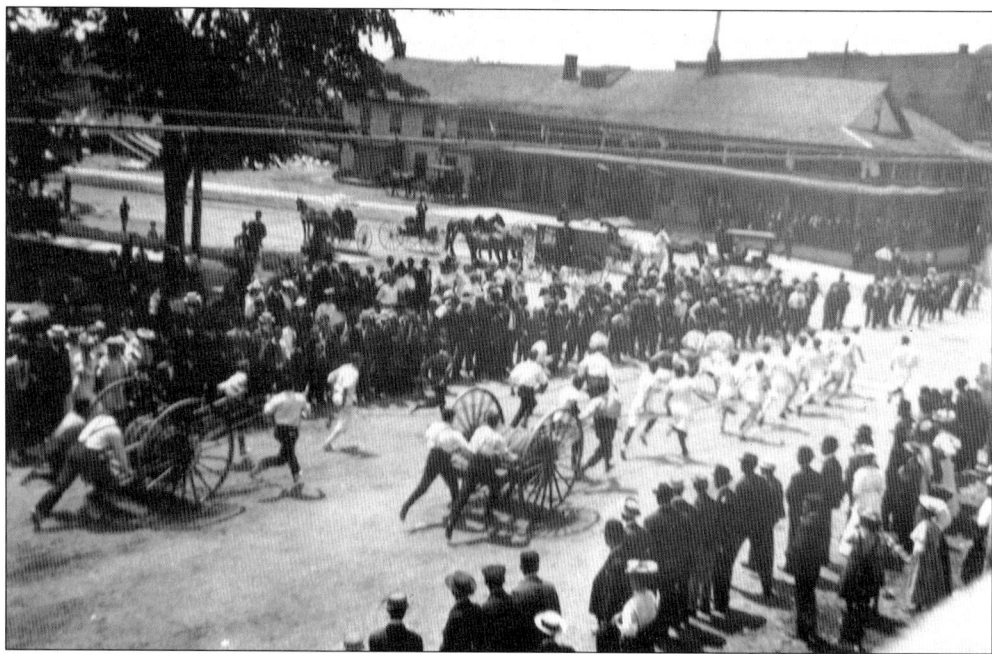

HOSE (NOT HORSE) RACES. From fire department minutes dated October 16, 1890, reference was made to "steps being taken to get a running team for the Hose Companies for the races at Brockville, Ontario" for a firemen's convention or tournament. In this hose race on Main Street at the Big Four Corners, the Canton team outfitted in running togs led the way.

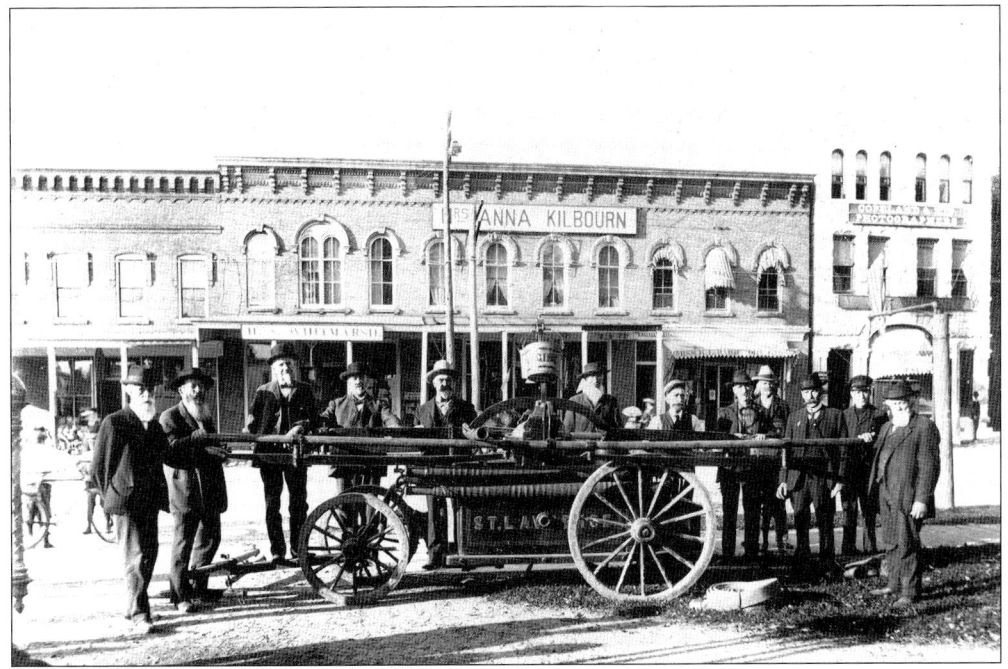

HAND-DRAWN PUMPER, PRIOR TO 1881. This hand-drawn pumper was used to battle the fires that devastated Canton in 1869 and the great fire of 1870. The Silas Wright pumper, pictured below, replaced it in 1881.

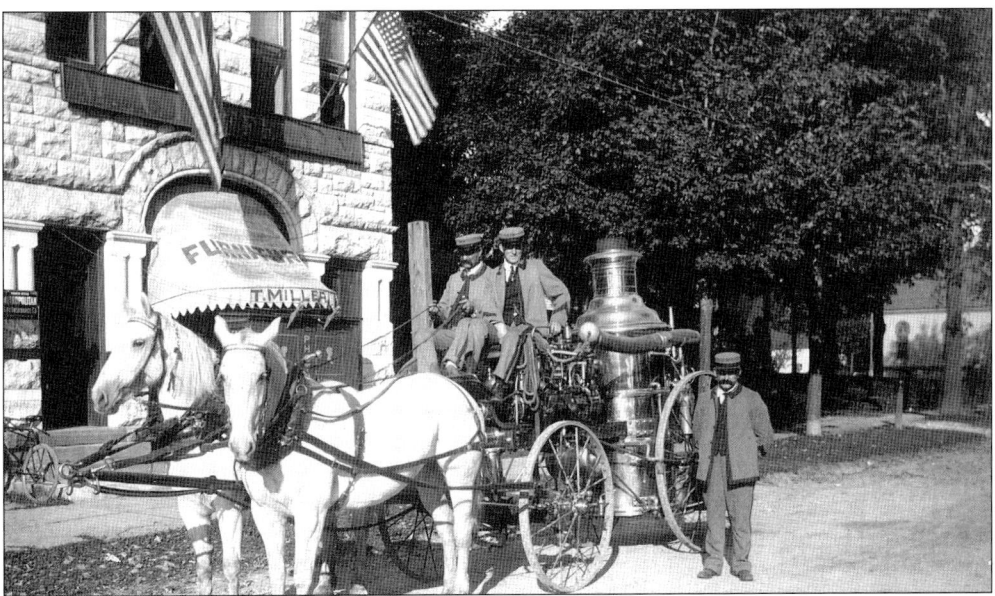

THE SILAS WRIGHT PUMPER, BETWEEN 1881 AND 1923. Canton's first horse-drawn fire engine was the Silas Wright steam pumper. It replaced the hand-drawn pumper in 1881 and was replaced in 1923 by The Stewart, Canton's first motorized pumper-truck. Pictured in front of the Drury Block, Thomas Miller's furniture store is on the first floor and the photograph gallery of Harry Copeland and Benjamin Kip is on the second floor. Dr. Alfred Drury built the building in 1897, using Canton marble from a quarry on the Miner Street Road.

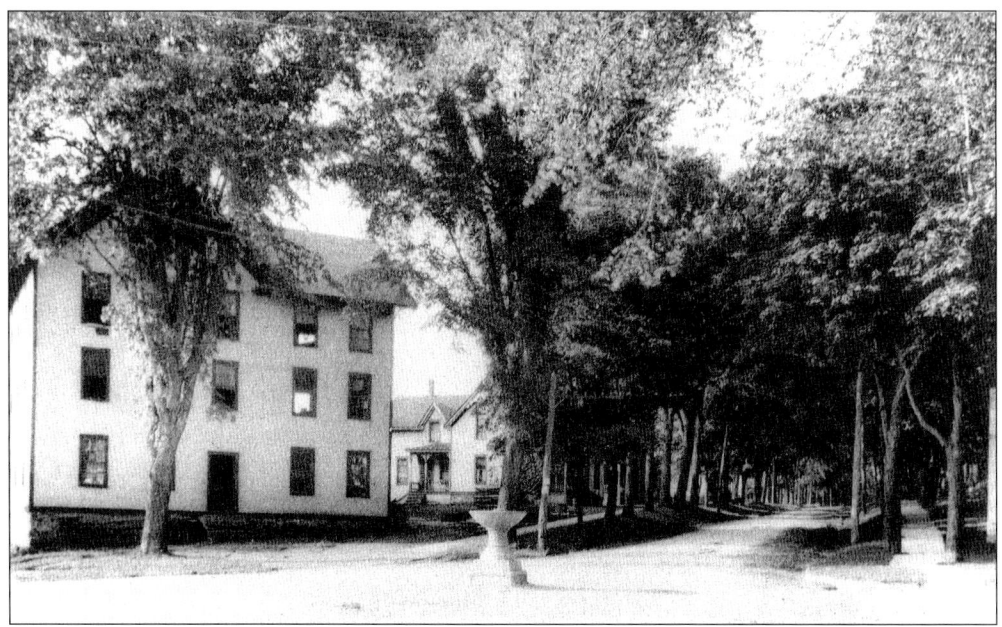

HORSE-WATERING FOUNTAIN. This horse-watering fountain was located at the junction of State, Chapel, and Water Streets, with the Rushton canoe factory on the left. Another was located between the American House and the opposite side of Park Street and the third was located at West Main and Gouverneur Streets.

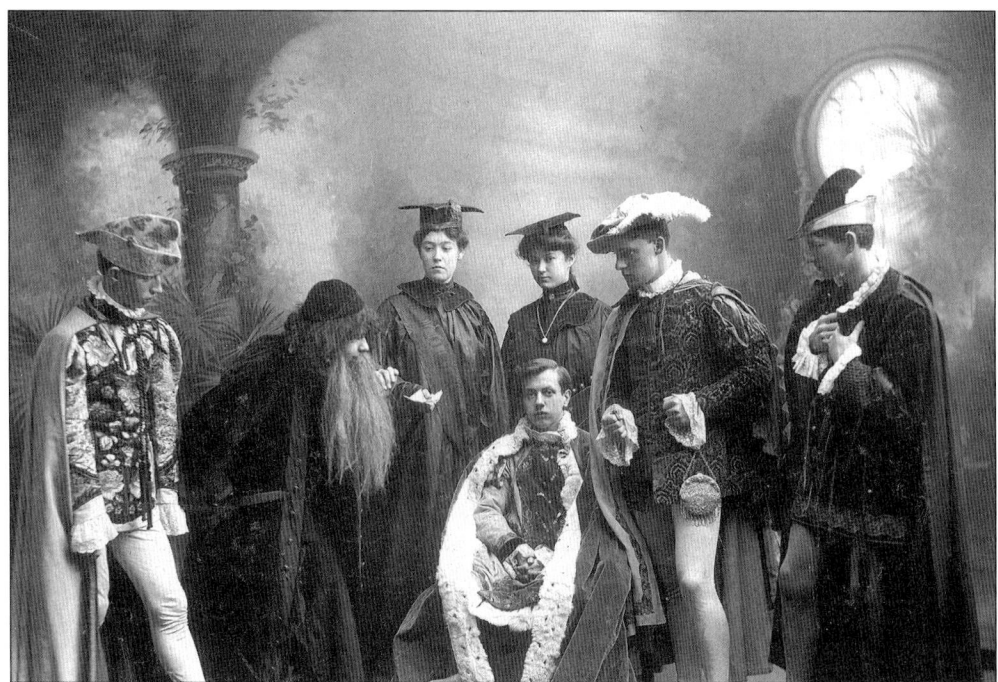

MERCHANT OF VENICE, OPERA HOUSE. Canton High School students produced *The Merchant of Venice* in 1903. Performers included, from left to right, Clarence Hayden, William Sims, Clara Payson, Bessie Farmer, Milford Brown, George Vanderlinder, and George Terry.

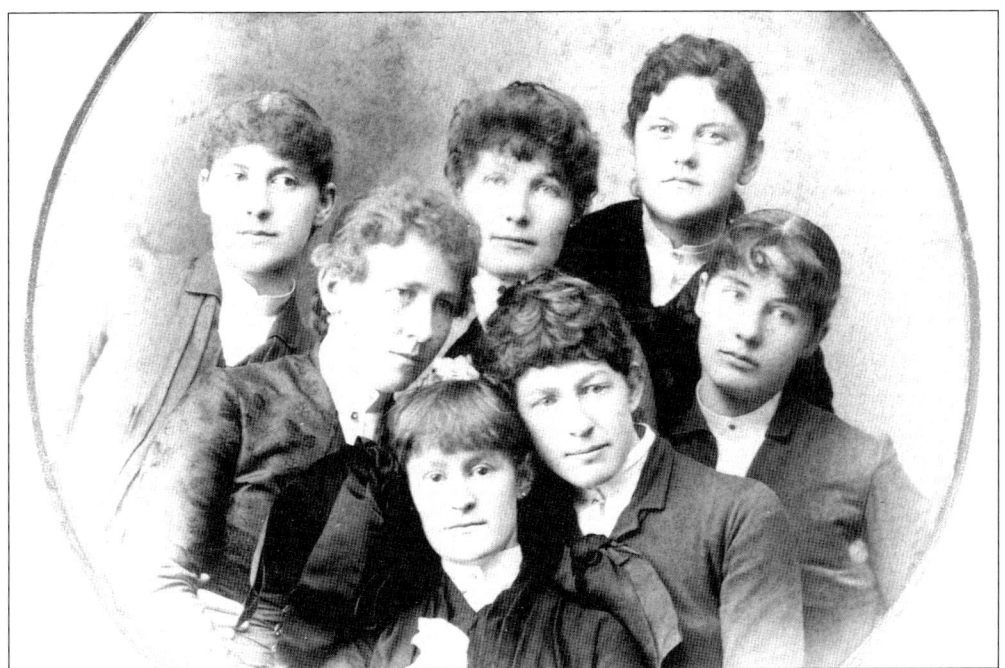

THE DICKIE CLUB, CANTON, C. 1880. From left to right are (first row) Marion Sawyer, Adele Haley Scribner, and Clara Pettibone; (second row) Alice Pettibone Helmle, Sue Heaton (middle), Nell Sykes McKindley, and Fannie Matthews Whitmyer.

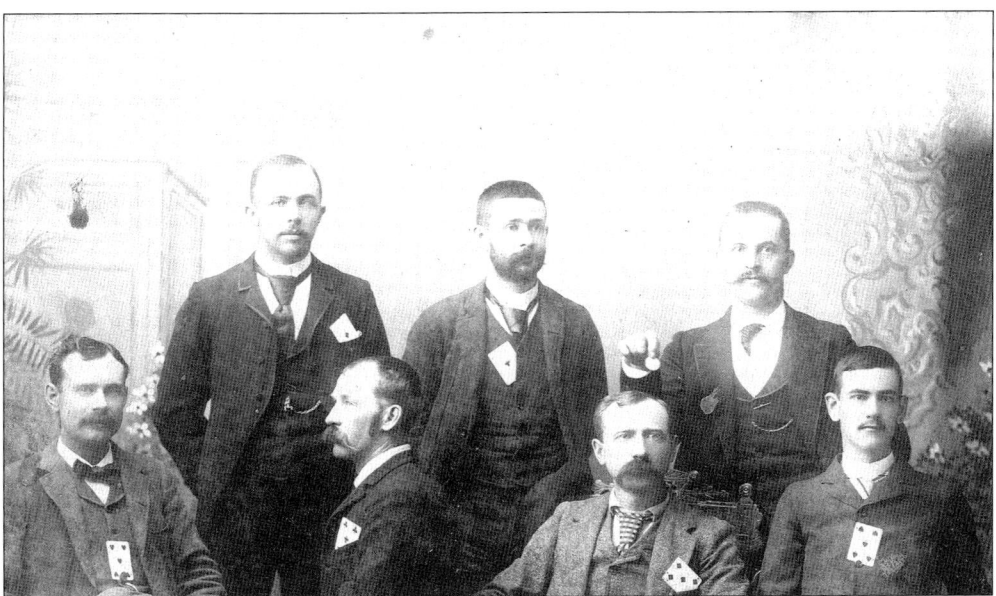

CANTON WHIST CLUB, C. 1894. From left to right, in the second row, is William Kip, perhaps J. Stanley Ellsworth, and Charles Jackson. The only man identified in the first row is Delos Jones in sideview. The rule book of the 1887–1888 Card Club with women and men members stipulated how long gatherings would last, and details regarding refreshments. Prizes were awarded to the winners of the most games ($1.00 value) as well as to the winners of the *least* number of games (10¢ value) per week and per season.

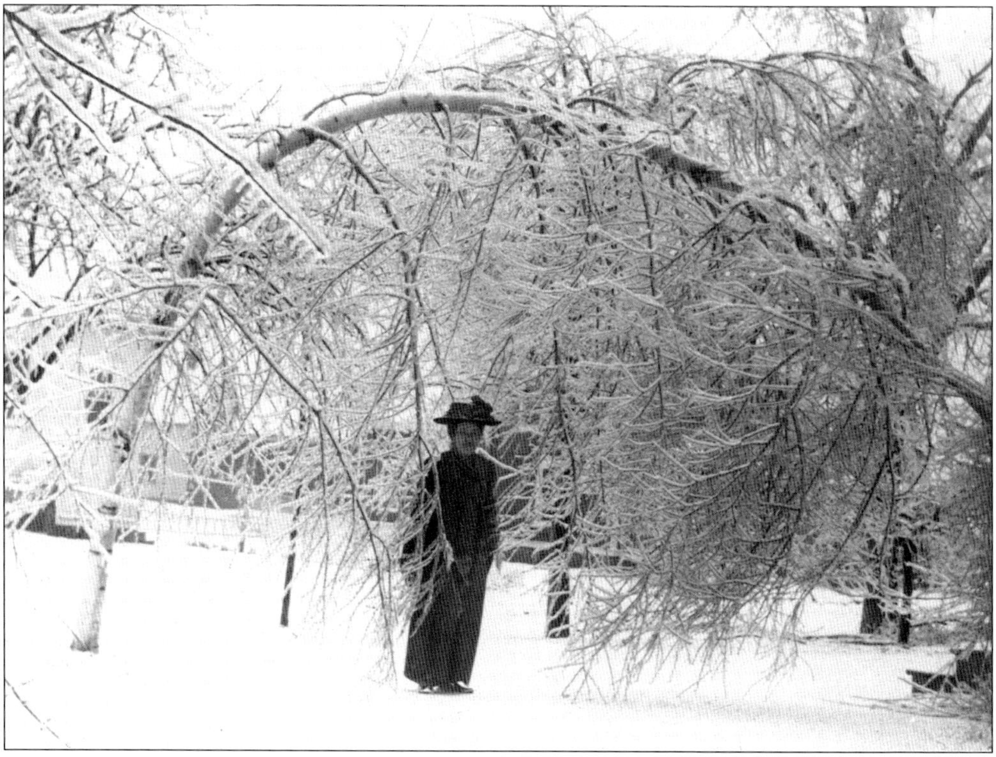

ICE AND SNOW, THE EARLY YEARS. These pictures provide evidence that Canton residents have long endured the hardships of North Country winter weather with a positive attitude (as shown by the cloaked woman under the ice arch, above), and by banding together during difficult times (as demonstrated by the men removing limbs from utility wires, below).

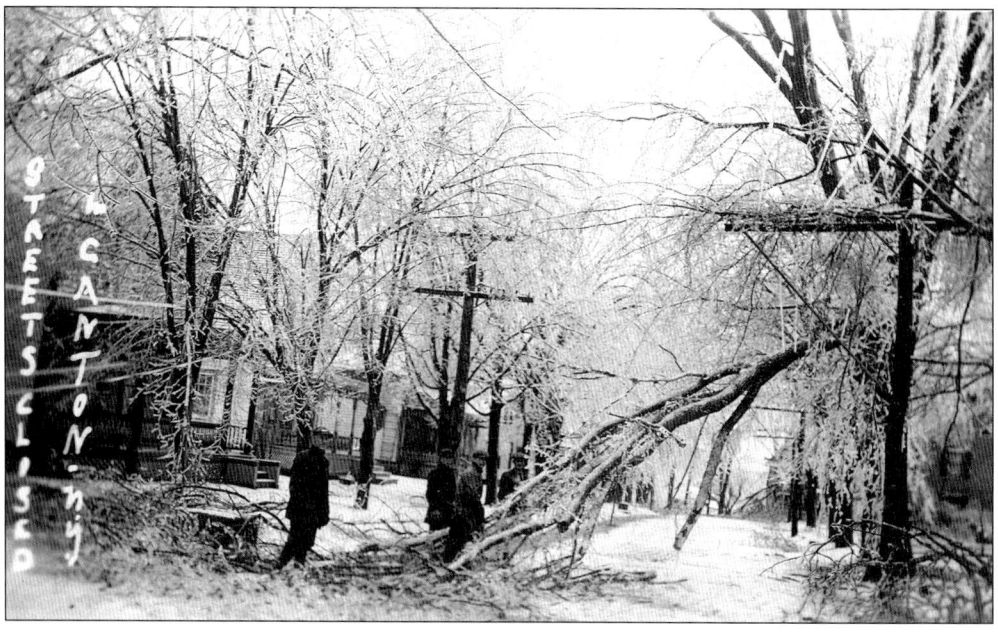

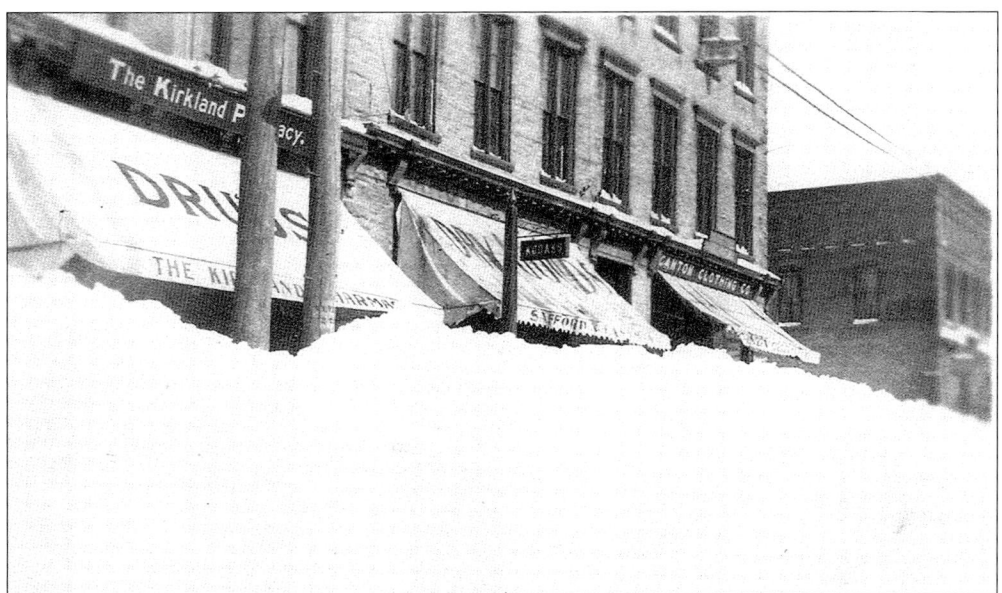

DIGGING OUT ON MAIN STREET. As evidenced in these two Main Street photographs, Canton residents and business owners prevailed through sheer determination to maintain the upper hand when Mother Nature dealt serious winter weather.

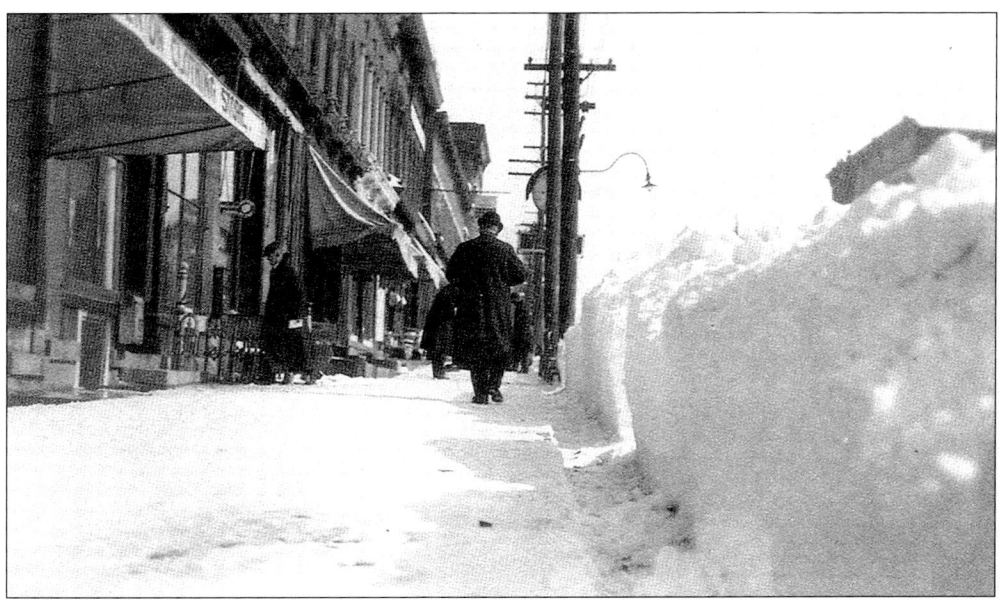

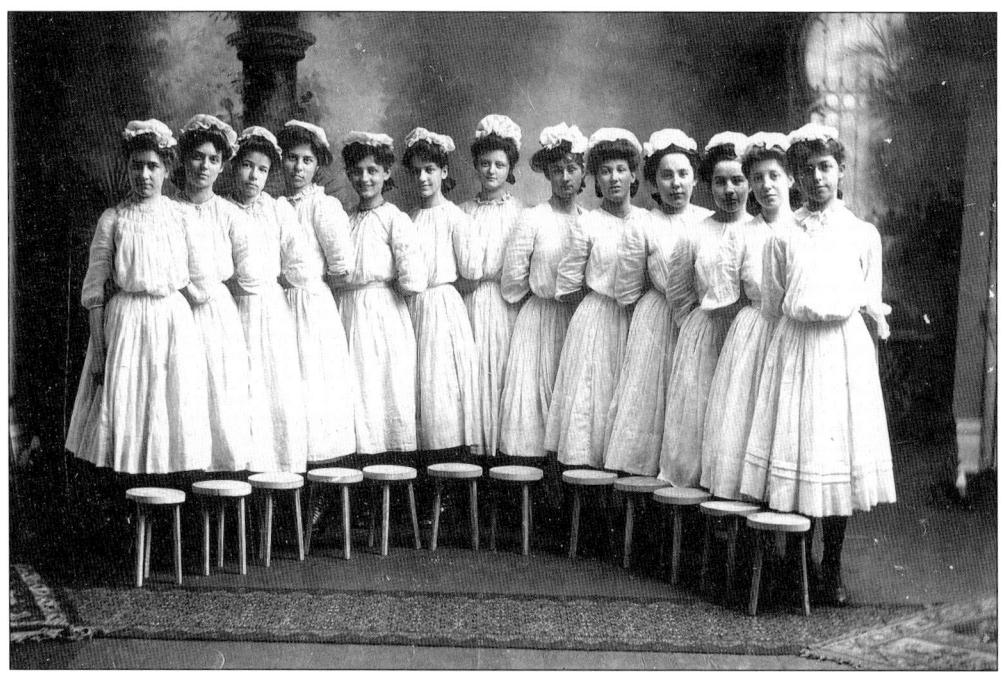

THE DAIRY MAIDS, C. 1904. In their white dresses and starched caps, these "pretty maids all in a row" pose with their milking stools (three legged, of course). The only person identified in this photograph is Mary Kelly Patterson, fourth from the right.

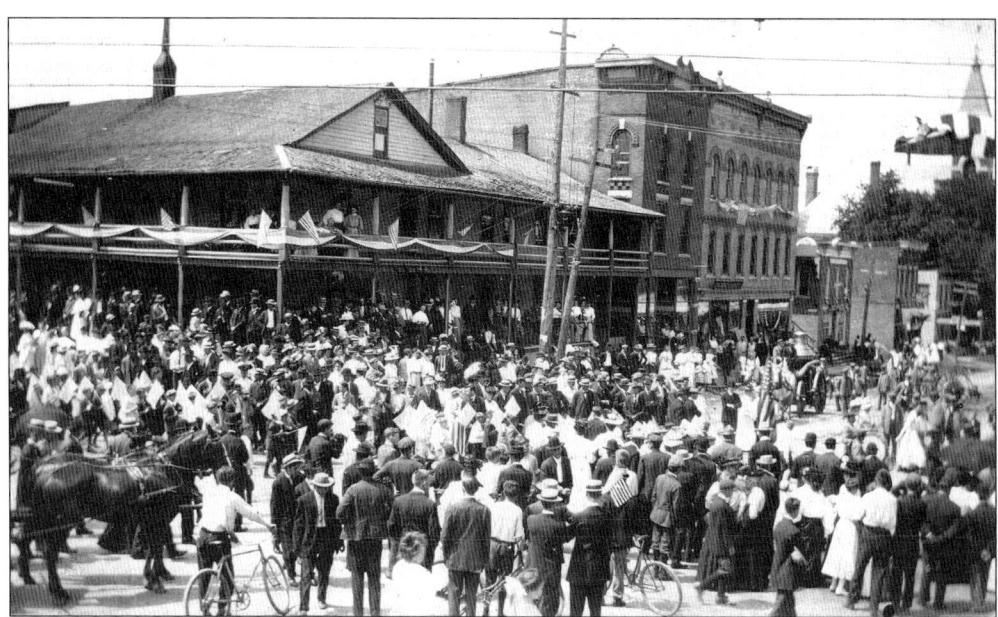

GAR CONVENTION. In 1906, the Grand Army of the Republic held its convention in Canton. An organization of Civil War Union veterans, the GAR was formed in Decatur, Illinois. The organization promoted comradeship among veterans, worked to increase pensions, assisted war widows and orphans, and maintained homes for old soldiers. Membership peaked at more than 409,000 in 1890. The last member died in 1955, and the GAR was discontinued in 1956.

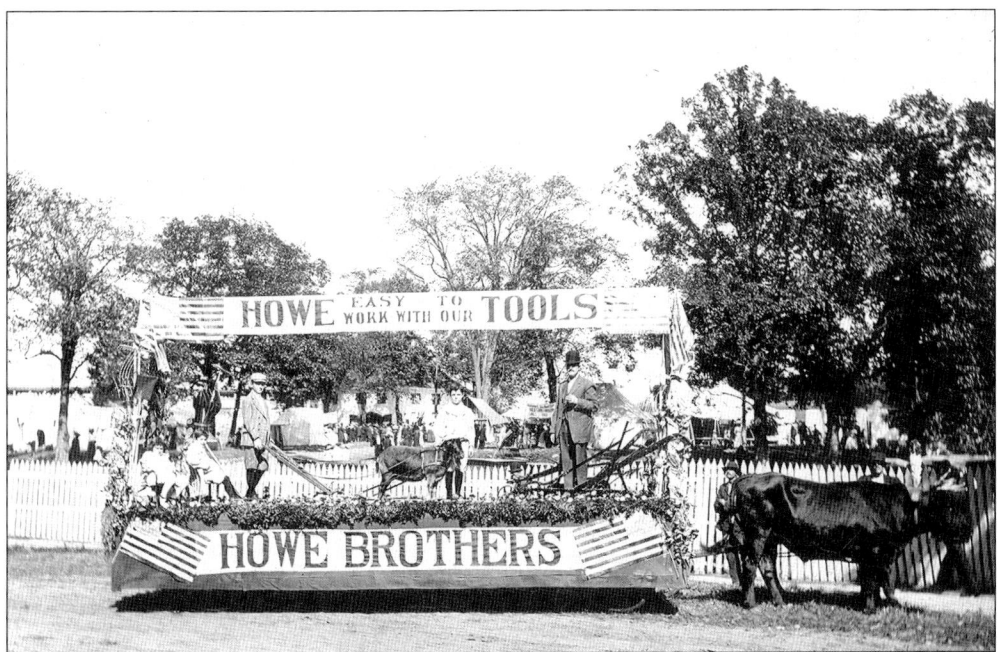

HOWE BROTHERS FLOAT, ST. LAWRENCE COUNTY FAIR, 1908. On the float, from left to right, are Leon Howe, Milford Howe (five years old), E. Barton Howe, Donald Howe, and Charles P. Howe (father). The billy goat was used on the Treadwell washing machine, and the ox was from Colton.

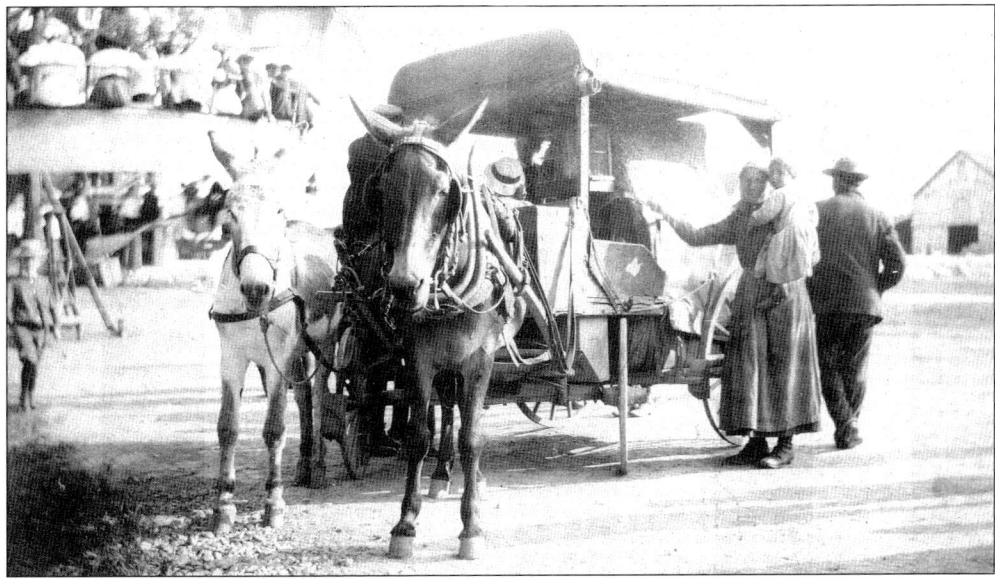

CARNIVAL AROUND THE PARK, 1905. In 1827, Silas Wright and Joseph Barnes donated land to the village which became the Village Park. Since that time it has been a focal point of village, town, and county activities. It has hosted fairs, musical presentations, honorary dedications, War Veterans' events, holiday celebrations, farm markets, the Dairy Princess celebrations, and countless other community activities.

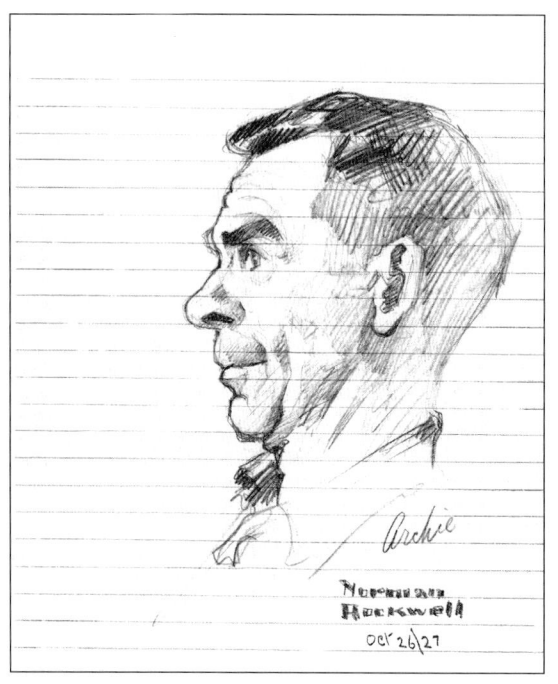

STILLWATER GUIDE. Archie Griffin, seen here in caricature, was one of the last old-time Adirondack guides, and served as warden of the North Branch camp for 35 years. He guided a number of noted personalities, including Teddy Roosevelt and Norman Rockwell. The artist sketched this caricature while hunting at the Stillwater camp, sometime in the early 1900s. Archie's grandson owns the original drawing, and a copy hangs on the Main Camp wall. (Courtesy of Kebbyn and Melanie Griffin.)

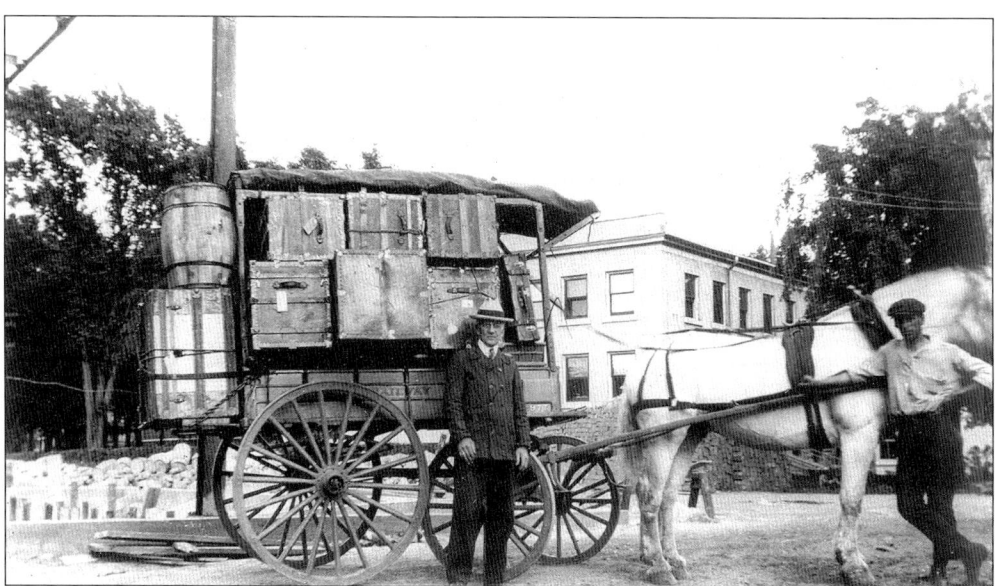

EXPRESS AGENT. William D. Whitman stands in front of his loaded wagon with an unidentified man on the right. Providing taxi services from 1917 to 1929, Whitman delivered luggage and trunks of North Country travelers and arriving students from the train station to Canton hotels, campuses, and houses.

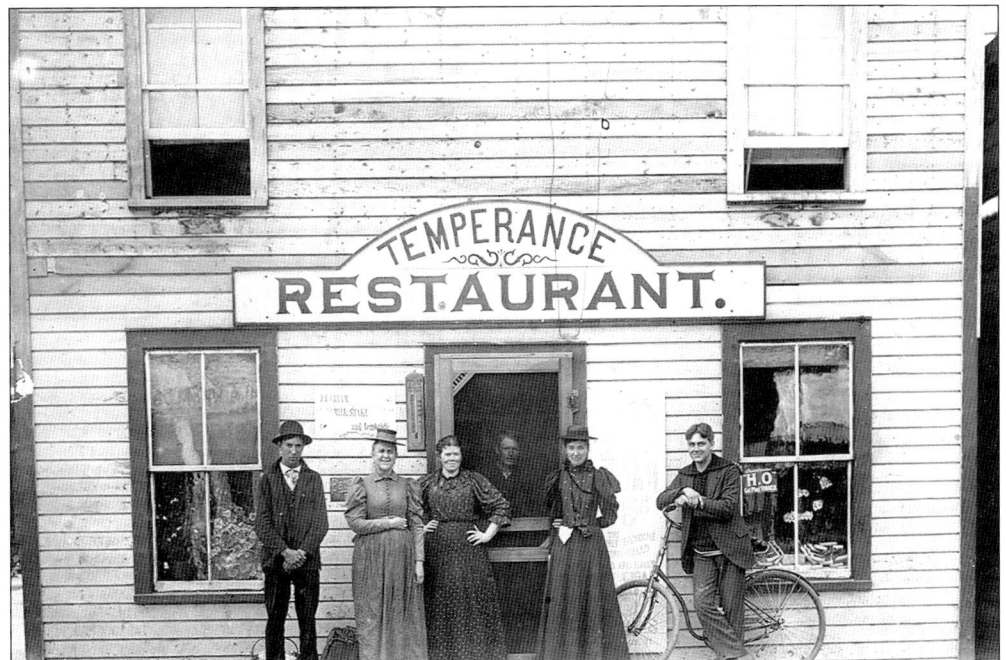

TEMPERANCE MEETINGHOUSE. The headquarters for Canton's women's temperance movement stood at 21 Main Street, between what is now the Oliver law firm and Dr. Adam Jaffee, optometrist. Each township had a temperance chapter. The Canton group was very active in the early years and donated the drinking fountain in the park.

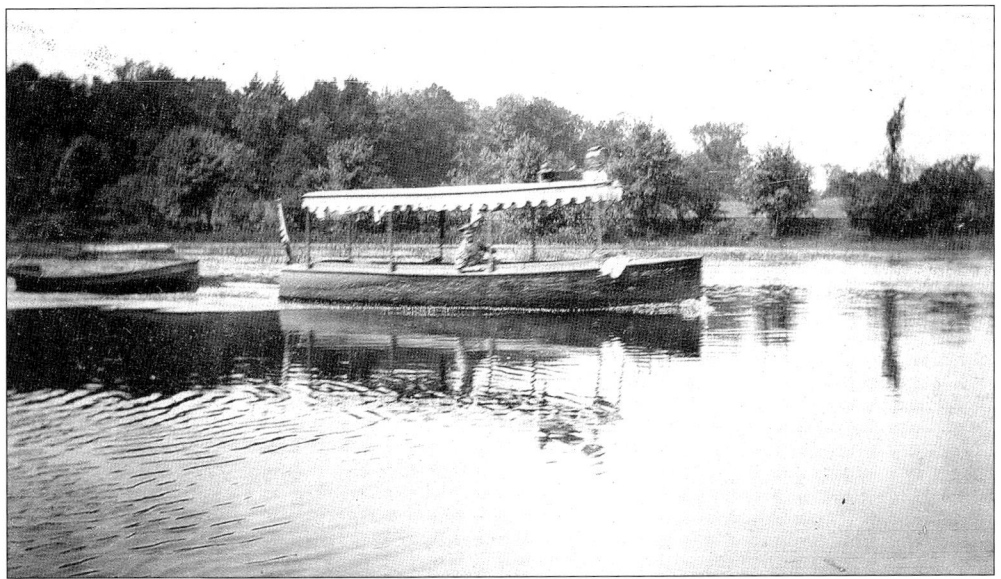

THE "U-AUTO-GO," FROM 1905 TO 1930. Winnie Taylor's boat livery transported people from the shores of the Little River near the Park Street bridge to Cold Springs and Bassets Woods (upriver from Taylor Park) where numerous summer camps were located. Other three-horsepower inboard motor boats ("putt puts") of the time were named: "The U-No," "The We-No," the "O My," and the "Little Joe," hence the rhyme "Oh My, Little Joe, We-No, U-No, U-Auto-Go, in the Merry Widow."

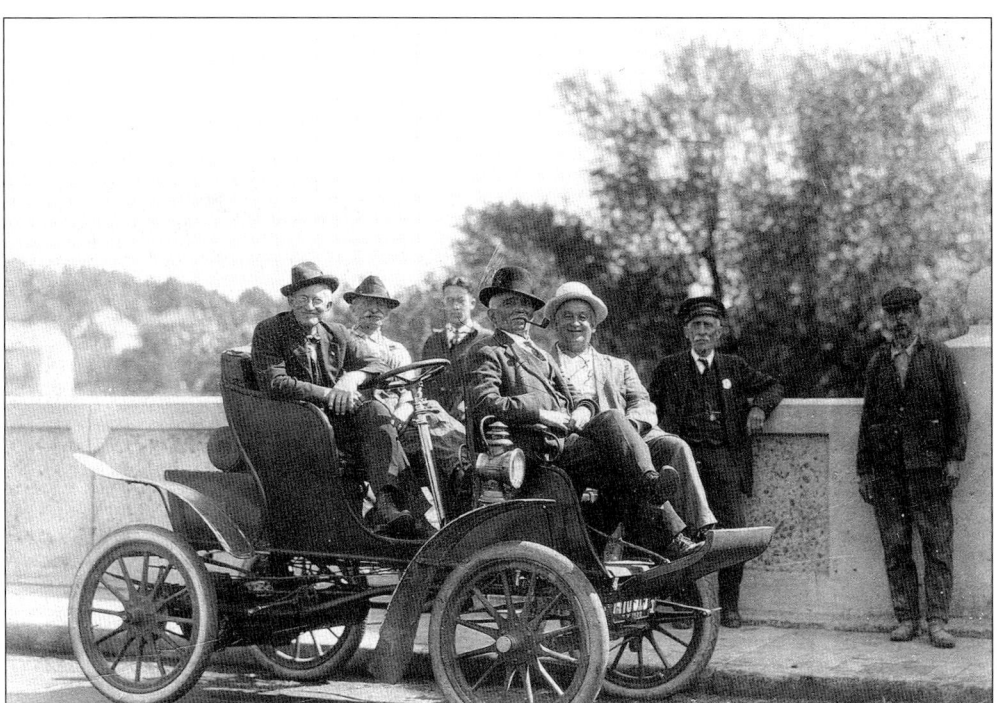

MEN IN MOTOR CAR. In 1922, men with their toys behaved no differently than men with their toys behave today. Posed in Chris Cook's Cadillac on the Main Street Bridge, from left to right, are Charles ("Chris") Cook, Mike Peters, Alvin Bernier, Mert Farmer (sheriff), Milly Lawrence, Winfred Leonard (police), and Ernie Goodbean.

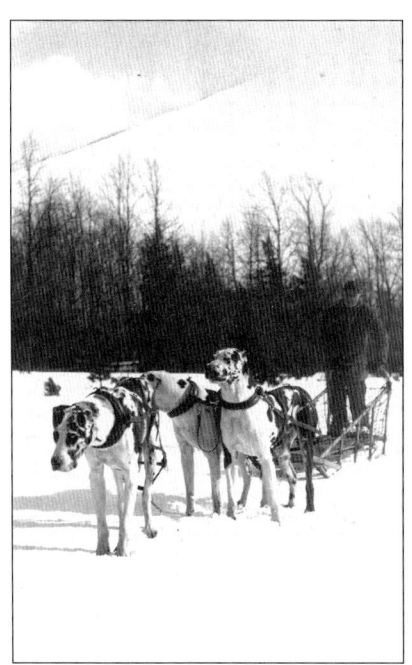

DOG SLED RACE. The master of this Great Dane dog sled team is Russell B. ("Biscuit") Lawrence Sr. Enamored with the Alaskan Iditarod while stationed there in the Army, Biscuit became interested in the Lake Placid dog sled races when he returned to the North Country. In the 1930s, he trained his Great Danes on "the five-mile square" and kept the shorthaired dogs inside as pets. His family recalls quite a number of blue-ribbon wins. (Courtesy of Judy Lawrence Gray.)

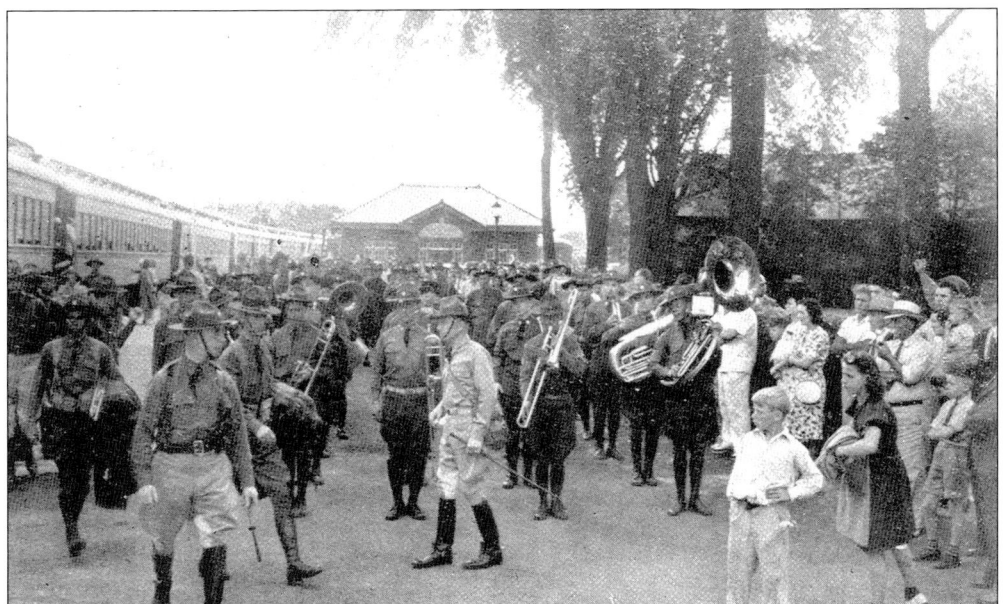

WAR MANEUVERS. Headquartered in Canton for training in 1940, troops arrived on trains and camped out on various farms throughout the township. Here, an army band and Canton residents greet troops as they detrain at the station.

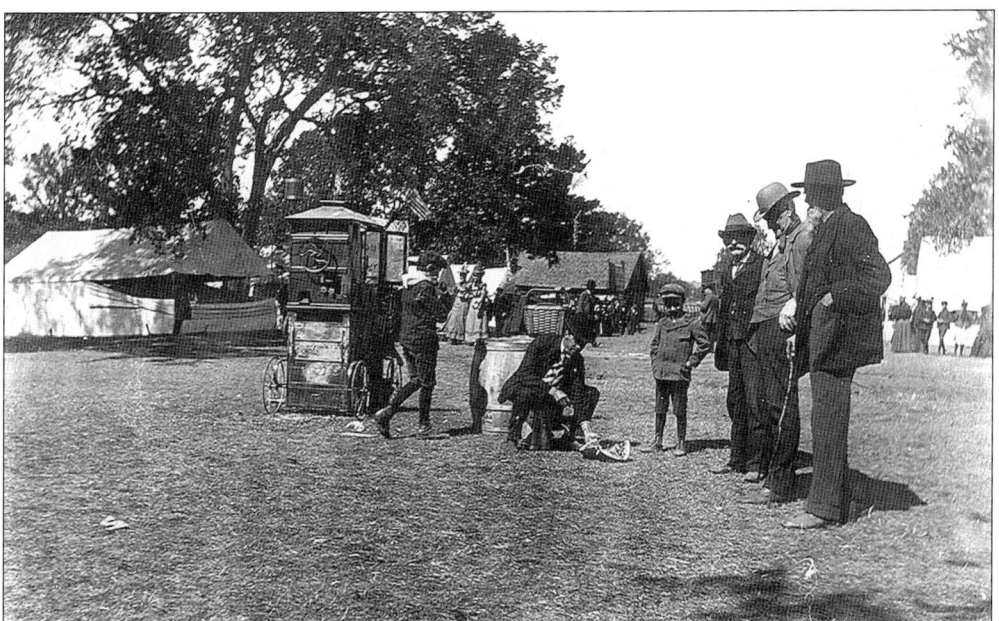

ST. LAWRENCE COUNTY FAIR GROUNDS, CANTON. Organized in 1852 at Canton, and held the week in which September 15 fell, the fair competed with rain and the first frost. Exhibits included dairy and animal halls, the floral hall, and the mechanics hall. Other highlights included the 5¢ merry-go-round ride, taffy candy, rifle shooting games, the "try your strength" machine, and the customary midway with its "girlie" and "freak" shows. The horse races were the highlight of the fair with Vaudeville acts performed every afternoon between races. Baseball games and hot air balloon ascensions provided additional festivities.

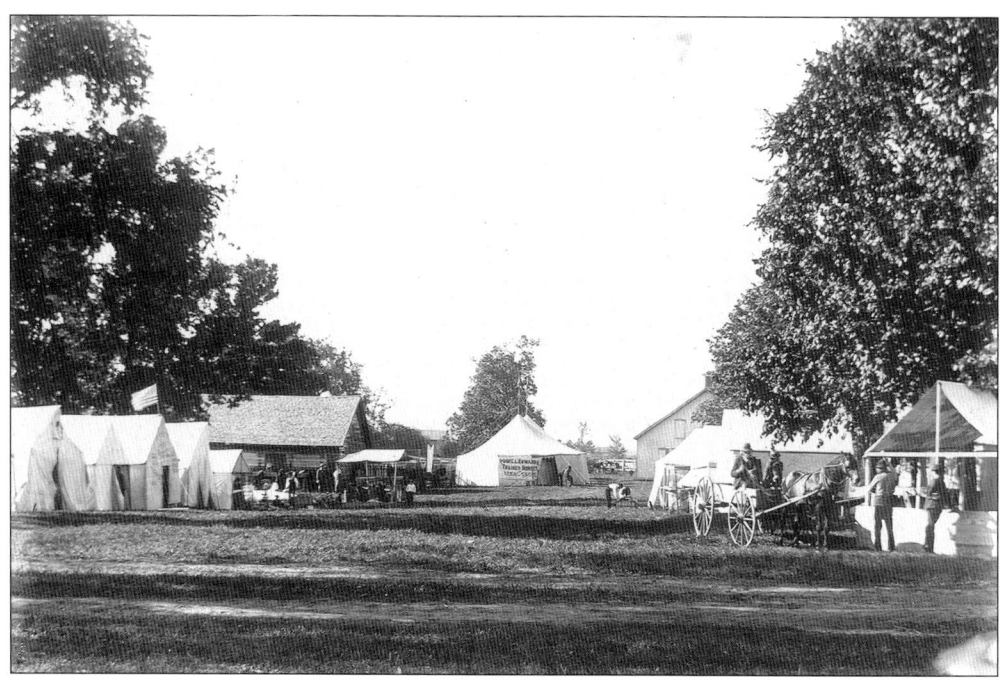

St. Lawrence County Fair Grounds, Canton. The center tent advertises "Prof. C. L. Edwards Trained Horses and Aerial Show." Now that's a combination worth seeing!

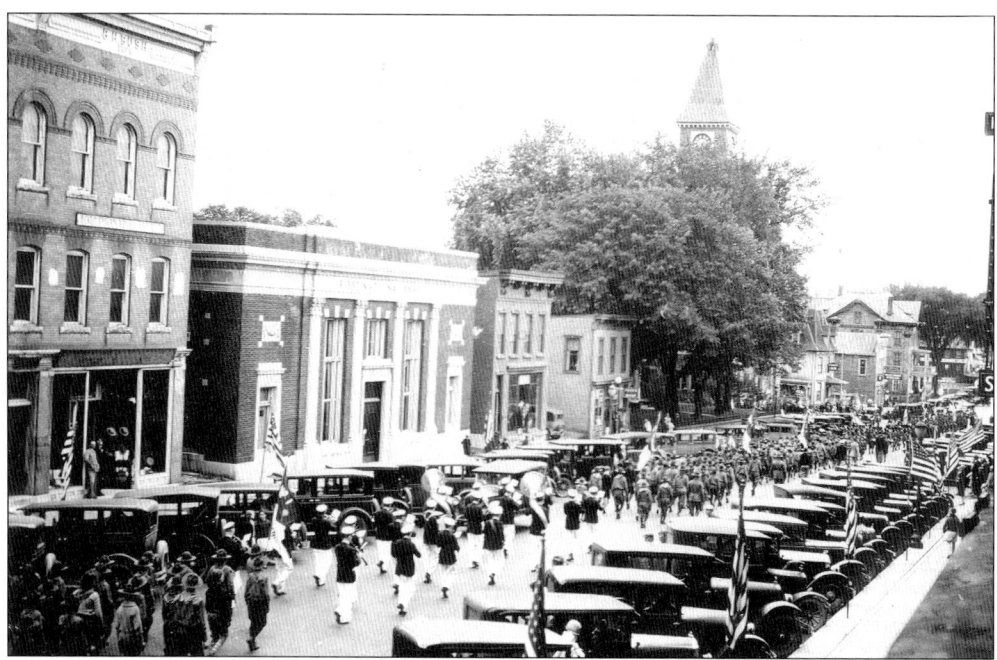

Parade on Main Street. Just look at the inspiring military representation in this parade. This photograph indicates that plentiful, un-metered parking was available on Main Street in "the good old days."

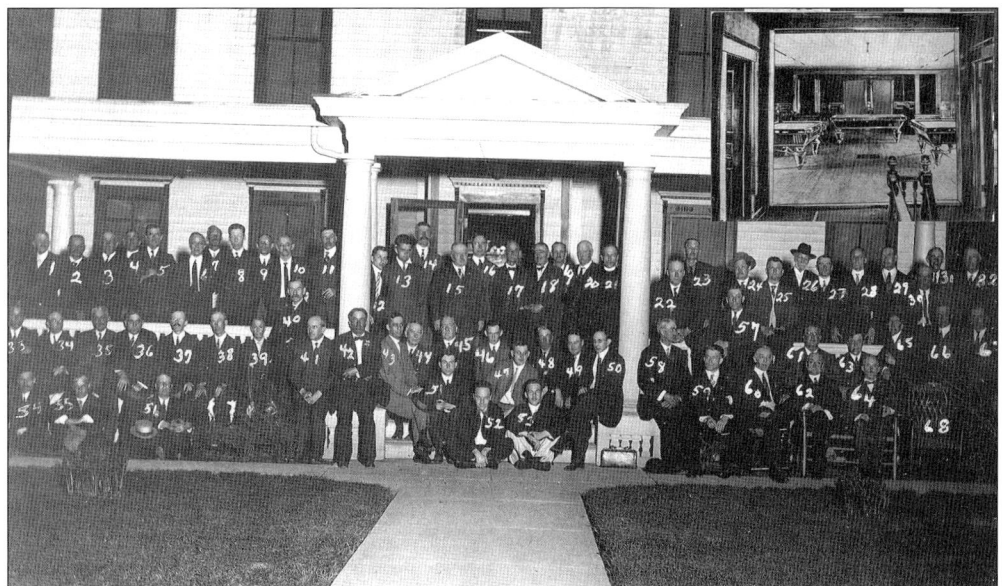

THE CANTON CLUB MEMBERS. The Canton Club originally occupied the entire second floor of the Donihee and Baker Building on the south side of Main Street. One side was the billiard and pool room, the other side was reserved for card games and reading. No games of any sort were played on Sunday. The club eventually moved to the Taylor home on Court Street where it remained the Canton Club until it was renovated and became the first Elegant Frog and later the Glass Onion in 1999.

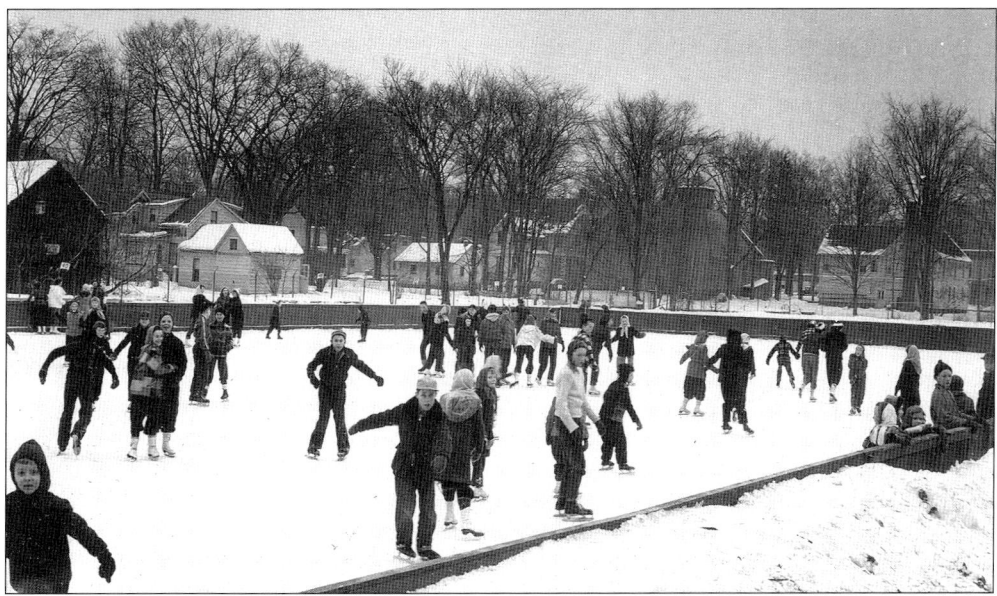

SKATING ON PRIEST FIELD. Grammar School students often spent their recess on this skating rink, which was part of the Grammar School athletic field. Dr. Henry Priest, St. Lawrence University professor and dean, and his wife, Flora Eaton Priest, donated Priest Field as a lasting gift to the children of the village. One of this book's authors, Judy Liscum, is on the rink (front middle) wearing her kerchief with Bobby Ruddy to her right, facing forward, and Jack Townsend behind Ruddy, also facing forward.

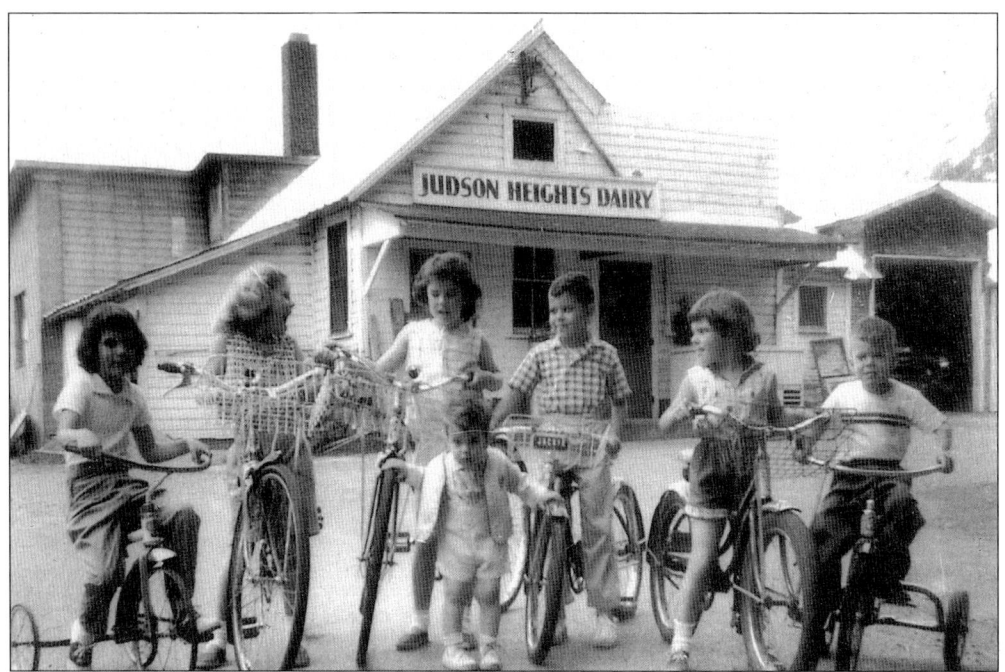

JUDSON HEIGHTS DAIRY, MID- TO LATE 1950S. The Judson Heights Dairy was located behind the Flanagan home on Judson Street. Proudly standing with their bikes are Flanagan siblings and cousins, from left to right, Lynn Flanagan, Judy Smith, Barb Smith, Jack Flanagan, Theresa Smith, and Paul Flanagan. The little boy in front is Bruce Flanagan.

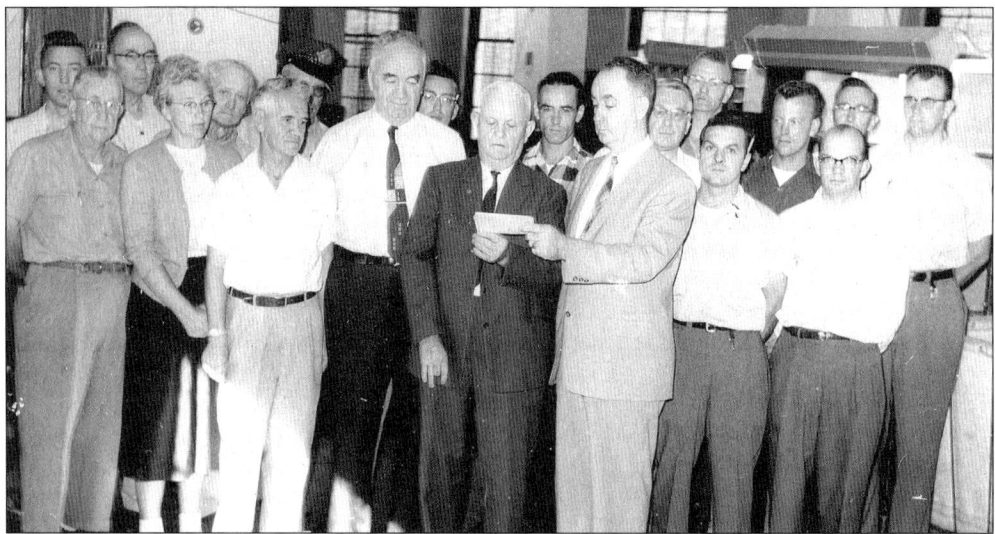

CANTON POST OFFICE, AUGUST 29, 1958. Pictured from left to right are (first row) Leon Gallinger, Margaret Rose, Philip Lavigne, Howard Nash, Raymond McKenna, John Cox, Nicholas Spadacinni, and Frances Christensen; (second row) Royal Snyder, Carl Ayers, Millard McCraken, Hugh Desmond, Joe Burnham, Neil Sheridan, Horace Ayers, Clarence Conant, Lawrence Elliott and John Lynch. Absent from the photograph are Richard Lobdell, Mike Maroney, Eldred Woods, and Charles Alexander.

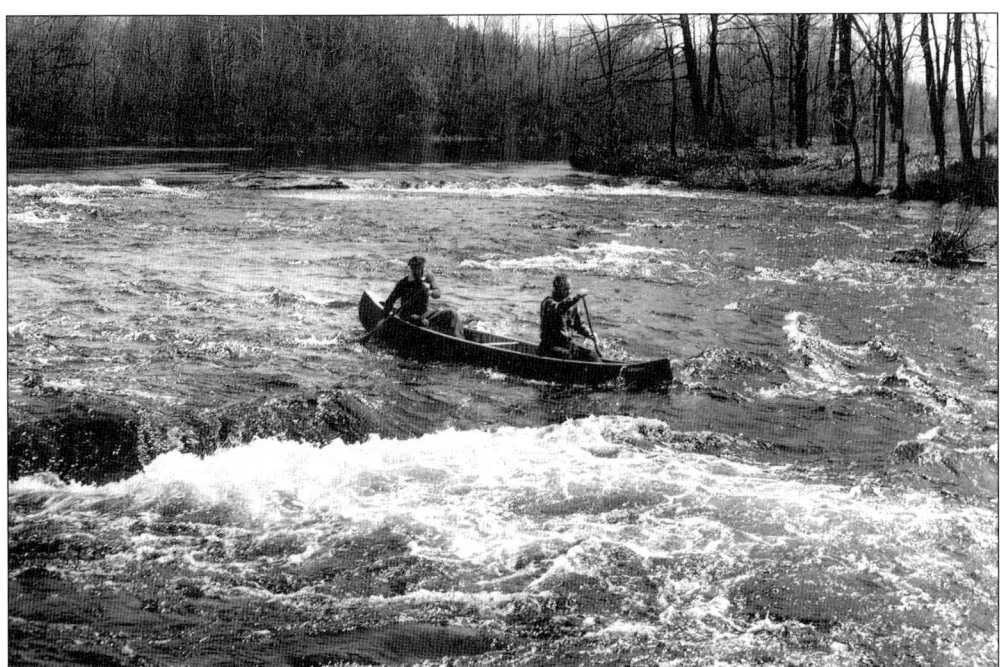

RUSHTON CANOE RACES. In 1962 with Edward Blanklman as President, and at the suggestion of Phil McMasters, the Canton Grasse River Historical Association held the first Rushton Memorial Canoe Race honoring J. Henry Rushton. In the first race, Dwight Church (age 70) and his son, David, paddled to the finish in one hour, eighteen minutes, and twenty-three seconds. Also in the 1962 race, pictured here is Frank White and Phil McMasters, paddling through Leigh Falls.

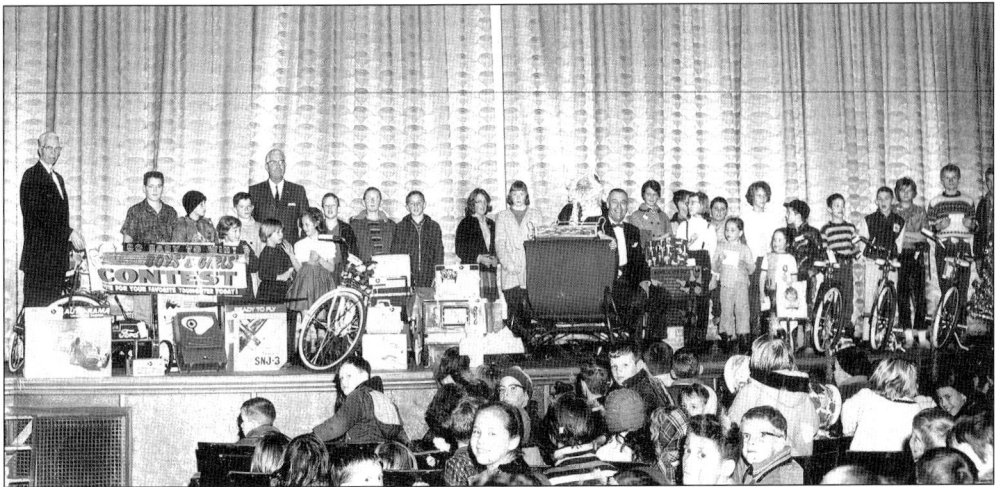

LIONS CHRISTMAS EVENT, AMERICAN THEATER, C. 1960. The bike donation, sponsored by the Lions Club, made Christmas a joyous occasion for numerous Canton children. Although identification is difficult, the boy in the audience with glasses and no hat may be Bruce Peckham, and the girl with the great grin is Becky Huntley. Among those identified on stage are T. Terry, Kevin Kelley, Lori Atkins, Carl Clark (or Royal Cleland), Pat Hughes, Cheryl Tiel, K Greenwood, Susie Taylor, Roberta Shirkey, J. Stevenson, Kathy Hamilton, David Peckham, Jon Gunnison, Gail Rogers, R. Stiles, and Marty Reasoner. Mayor Tom Patterson is in the sleigh and, of course, Santa plays Santa.

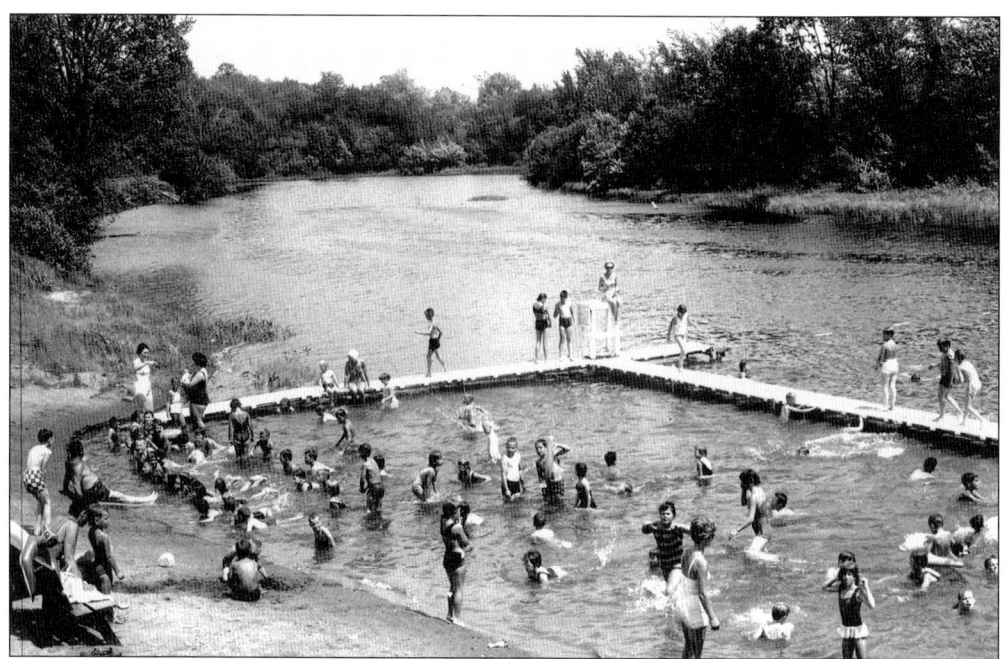

SWIMMING AT TAYLOR PARK IN THE 1950S TO 1960S. With the aid of his hockey stick, Johnny Oliver is giving swimming lessons on the beach at the left side of the enclosed swimming area. Missing from the modern pool experience is that distinctive feel of "mud ooze" between your toes while swimming in the river.

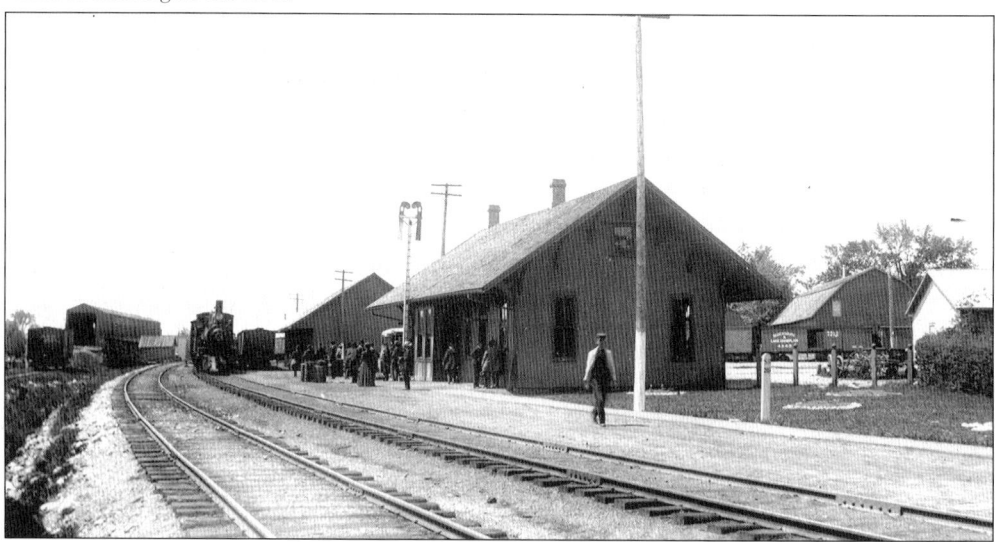

TRAIN STATION. The original train station was a wooden frame construction, which was later modernized. About 40 yards west of the station was a large freight house with a long platform parallel to the railroad. The platform was of a height and position to easily enable transfer of freight from train to storage. Weekday passenger trains numbered three northbound and three southbound, including one arriving at midnight. This one was often delayed in the winter months by weather. Each passenger train included a smoking car and morning and evening trains included a sleeping car. Freight and passenger train business deteriorated with the arrival of the automobile, trucks, and hard-surfaced roads.